Making Modern Meals

CALIFORNIA STUDIES IN FOOD AND CULTURE

Darra Goldstein, Editor

1. *Dangerous Tastes: The Story of Spices*, by Andrew Dalby
2. *Eating Right in the Renaissance*, by Ken Albala
3. *Food Politics: How the Food Industry Influences Nutrition and Health*, by Marion Nestle
4. *Camembert: A National Myth*, by Pierre Boisard
5. *Safe Food: The Politics of Food Safety*, by Marion Nestle
6. *Eating Apes*, by Dale Peterson
7. *Revolution at the Table: The Transformation of the American Diet*, by Harvey Levenstein
8. *Paradox of Plenty: A Social History of Eating in Modern America*, by Harvey Levenstein
9. *Encarnación's Kitchen: Mexican Recipes from Nineteenth-Century California: Selections from Encarnación Pinedo's* El cocinero español, by Encarnación Pinedo, edited and translated by Dan Strehl, with an essay by Victor Valle
10. *Zinfandel: A History of a Grape and Its Wine*, by Charles L. Sullivan, with a foreword by Paul Draper
11. *Tsukiji: The Fish Market at the Center of the World*, by Theodore C. Bestor
12. *Born Again Bodies: Flesh and Spirit in American Christianity*, by R. Marie Griffith
13. *Our Overweight Children: What Parents, Schools, and Communities Can Do to Control the Fatness Epidemic*, by Sharron Dalton
14. *The Art of Cooking: The First Modern Cookery Book*, by the Eminent Maestro Martino of Como, edited and with an introduction by Luigi Ballerini, translated and annotated by Jeremy Parzen, and with fifty modernized recipes by Stefania Barzini
15. *The Queen of Fats: Why Omega-3s Were Removed from the Western Diet and What We Can Do to Replace Them*, by Susan Allport

16. *Meals to Come: A History of the Future of Food*, by Warren Belasco
17. *The Spice Route: A History*, by John Keay
18. *Medieval Cuisine of the Islamic World: A Concise History with 174 Recipes*, by Lilia Zaouali, translated by M. B. DeBevoise, with a foreword by Charles Perry
19. *Arranging the Meal: A History of Table Service in France*, by Jean-Louis Flandrin, translated by Julie E. Johnson, with Sylvie and Antonio Roder; with a foreword to the English-language edition by Beatrice Fink
20. *The Taste of Place: A Cultural Journey into Terroir*, by Amy B. Trubek
21. *Food: The History of Taste*, edited by Paul Freedman
22. *M. F. K. Fisher among the Pots and Pans: Celebrating Her Kitchens*, by Joan Reardon, with a foreword by Amanda Hesser
23. *Cooking: The Quintessential Art*, by Hervé This and Pierre Gagnaire, translated by M. B. DeBevoise
24. *Perfection Salad: Women and Cooking at the Turn of the Century*, by Laura Shapiro
25. *Of Sugar and Snow: A History of Ice Cream Making*, by Jeri Quinzio
26. *Encyclopedia of Pasta*, by Oretta Zanini De Vita, translated by Maureen B. Fant, with a foreword by Carol Field
27. *Tastes and Temptations: Food and Art in Renaissance Italy*, by John Varriano
28. *Free for All: Fixing School Food in America*, by Janet Poppendieck
29. *Breaking Bread: Recipes and Stories from Immigrant Kitchens*, by Lynne Christy Anderson, with a foreword by Corby Kummer
30. *Culinary Ephemera: An Illustrated History*, by William Woys Weaver
31. *Eating Mud Crabs in Kandahar: Stories of Food during Wartime by the World's Leading Correspondents*, edited by Matt McAllester
32. *Weighing In: Obesity, Food Justice, and the Limits of Capitalism*, by Julie Guthman

33. *Why Calories Count: From Science to Politics*, by Marion Nestle and Malden Nesheim
34. *Curried Cultures: Globalization, Food, and South Asia*, edited by Krishnendu Ray and Tulasi Srinivas
35. *The Cookbook Library: Four Centuries of the Cooks, Writers, and Recipes That Made the Modern Cookbook*, by Anne Willan, with Mark Cherniavsky and Kyri Claflin
36. *Coffee Life in Japan*, by Merry White
37. *American Tuna: The Rise and Fall of an Improbable Food*, by Andrew F. Smith
38. *A Feast of Weeds: A Literary Guide to Foraging and Cooking Wild Edible Plants*, by Luigi Ballerini, translated by Gianpiero W. Doebler, with recipes by Ada De Santis and illustrations by Giuliano Della Casa
39. *The Philosophy of Food*, by David M. Kaplan
40. *Beyond Hummus and Falafel: Social and Political Aspects of Palestinian Food in Israel*, by Liora Gvion, translated by David Wesley and Elana Wesley
41. *The Life of Cheese: Crafting Food and Value in America*, by Heather Paxson
42. *Popes, Peasants, and Shepherds: Recipes and Lore from Rome and Lazio*, by Oretta Zanini De Vita, translated by Maureen B. Fant, foreword by Ernesto Di Renzo
43. *Cuisine and Empire: Cooking in World History*, by Rachel Laudan
44. *Inside the California Food Revolution: Thirty Years That Changed Our Culinary Consciousness*, by Joyce Goldstein, with Dore Brown
45. *Cumin, Camels, and Caravans: A Spice Odyssey*, by Gary Paul Nabhan
46. *Balancing on a Planet: The Future of Food and Agriculture*, by David A. Cleveland
47. *The Darjeeling Distinction: Labor and Justice on Fair-Trade Tea Plantations in India*, by Sarah Besky

48. *How the Other Half Ate: A History of Working-Class Meals at the Turn of the Century*, by Katherine Leonard Turner
49. *The Untold History of Ramen: How Political Crisis in Japan Spawned a Global Food Craze*, by George Solt
50. *Word of Mouth: What We Talk About When We Talk About Food*, by Priscilla Parkhurst Ferguson
51. *Inventing Baby Food: Taste, Health, and the Industrialization of the American Diet*, by Amy Bentley
52. *Secrets from the Greek Kitchen: Cooking, Skill, and Everyday Life on an Aegean Island*, by David E. Sutton
53. *Breadlines Knee-Deep in Wheat: Food Assistance in the Great Depression*, by Janet Poppendieck
54. *Tasting French Terroir: The History of an Idea*, by Thomas Parker
55. *Becoming Salmon: Aquaculture and the Domestication of a Fish*, by Marianne Elisabeth Lien
56. *Divided Spirits: Tequila, Mezcal, and the Politics of Production*, by Sarah Bowen
57. *The Weight of Obesity: Hunger and Global Health in Postwar Guatemala*, by Emily Yates-Doerr
58. *Dangerous Digestion: The Politics of American Dietary Advice*, by E. Melanie duPuis
59. *A Taste of Power: Food and American Identities*, by Katharina Vester
60. *More Than Just Food: Food Justice and Community Change*, by Garrett M. Broad
61. *Hoptopia: A World of Agriculture and Beer in Oregon's Willamette Valley*, by Peter A. Kopp
62. *A Geography of Digestion: Biotechnology and the Kellogg Cereal Enterprise*, by Nicholas Bauch
63. *Bitter and Sweet: Food, Meaning, and Modernity in Rural China*, by Ellen Oxfeld
64. *A History of Cookbooks: From Kitchen to Page over Seven Centuries*, by Henry Notaker

65. *Reinventing the Wheel: Milk, Microbes, and the Fight for Real Cheese*, by Bronwen Percival and Francis Percival
66. *Making Modern Meals: How Americans Cook Today*, by Amy B. Trubek
67. *Food and Power: A Culinary Ethnography of Israel*, by Nir Avieli

Making Modern Meals

How Americans Cook Today

AMY B. TRUBEK

UNIVERSITY OF CALIFORNIA PRESS

University of California Press, one of the most distinguished university presses in the United States, enriches lives around the world by advancing scholarship in the humanities, social sciences, and natural sciences. Its activities are supported by the UC Press Foundation and by philanthropic contributions from individuals and institutions. For more information, visit www.ucpress.edu.

University of California Press
Oakland, California

Library of Congress Cataloging-in-Publication Data

Names: Trubek, Amy B., author.
Title: Making modern meals : how Americans cook today / Amy B. Trubek.
Description: Oakland, California : University of California Press, [2017] | Series: California studies in food and culture ; 66 | Includes bibliographical references and index. | Identifiers: LCCN *2017012516* (print) | LCCN *2017014918* (ebook) | ISBN 9780520963979 () | ISBN 9780520289222 (cloth : alk. paper) | ISBN 9780520289239 (pbk. : alk. paper)
Subjects: LCSH: Cooking—United States—History.
Classification: LCC TX645 (ebook) | LCC TX645 .T78 2017 (print) | DDC 641.5973—dc23
LC record available at *https://lccn.loc.gov/2017012516*

Manufactured in the United States of America

24 23 22 21 20 19 18 17
10 9 8 7 6 5 4 3 2 1

To my mother, Louise
And to the memory of Rosa and Adelia
Cooks, one and all

CONTENTS

ILLUSTRATIONS

INTRODUCTION

From Cook to Cooks

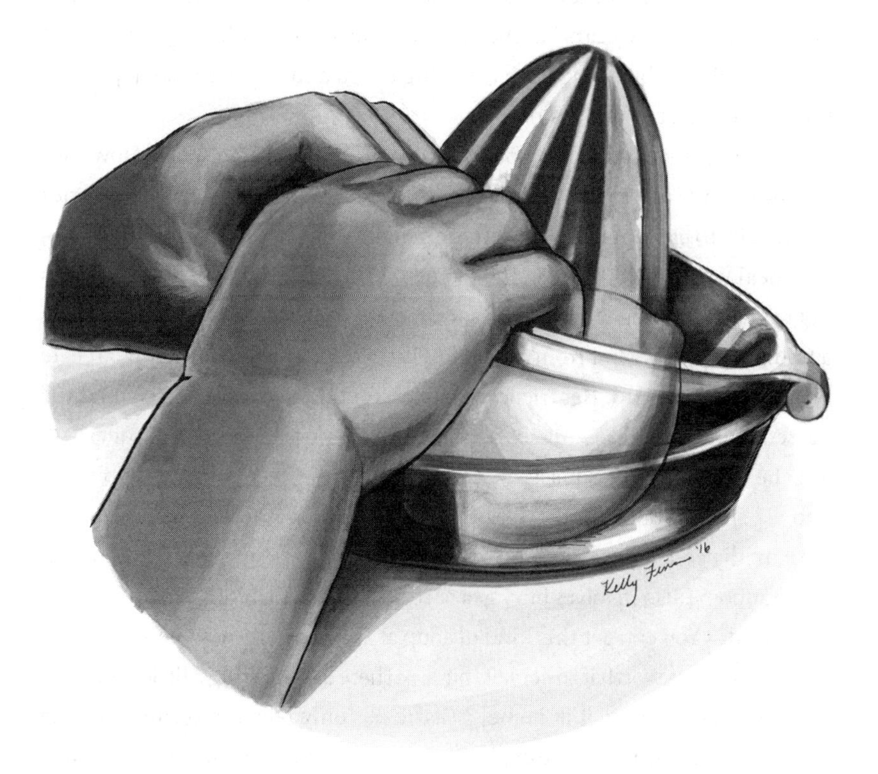

Claire, a middle-aged professional, is cooking dinner on a Friday night. She lives in an apartment near downtown Boston that has a large, recently renovated kitchen with loads of wood cabinets and long granite countertops. She is preparing, as she puts it, "just soup and salad." This is a soup she makes often—butternut squash and apple—and the salad—a mix of arugula, spinach, and sliced endive—is also a mealtime regular. The recipe for the soup is written on an index card that has "From the Kitchen of" printed at the top and a drawing of a bright yellow teapot in the left-hand corner. To find it, she pulls out a manila recipe folder full of recipe cards, recipes cut from newspaper articles, and more torn from magazines; this collection, she says, has been "at least thirty years" in the making. She has all her ingredients set out on the kitchen table along with a cutting board and knife; the soup pot and sauté pan sit on top of the stove.

At first glance, this does not appear to be a remarkable scene. However, certain details about the recipe, the choice of ingredients, and the stories Claire tells to explain her meal selection make this seemingly typical American meal worth a closer look. The recipe for the butternut-apple soup comes not from her mother—"I would no sooner cook with my mother than jump off a bridge," she says—but from a friend, who first ate the soup at a popular café on Martha's Vineyard. Her friend was able to get the signature recipe, and she passed it on to Claire. To make the soup, she uses precut butternut squash: "I am cheating with the squash. . . . You see a lot of time-saving cut up fruits and vegetables, but I think a lot of nutritional value is lost." She pauses and then finally concludes, "It's better than nothing." Ensuring that the soup gets made at home also involves buying a carton of vegetable broth, since, as Claire points out, "You can get this kind of soup at Whole Foods now, so sometimes it does not seem worth it to cook it, but . . . there's something a little more satisfying about [making it at home]." Claire has only recently started cooking regularly at home again. She explains that she "didn't cook for years, literally years. I suppose I ate a few things that came out of my kitchen, . . . but I had an expense account, and I was on the road and eating in restaurants." At another point, she lived with someone who did all the cooking, so although she ate more at home during that period, she didn't cook on a regular basis.

All is not what it seems. Claire's reflections on this single dinner reveal that making a meal is no obvious endeavor, either in the moment or when including the broader context. Considering it, the question arises: What exactly is cooking? This might seem easy to answer. To cook is to "prepare (food, a dish, a meal) by combining and heating the ingredients in various ways."[1] And the noun "cooking" is "the practice or skill of preparing food by combining, mixing, and heating ingredients."[2] If we look more deeply, however, it becomes apparent that it isn't a simple question. Walt Whitman declaims in *The Song of Myself*, "I am large, I contain multitudes," and perhaps the same is true of cooking. Everything Claire says inspires further queries. When considering her life as a cook, many questions emerge. Who do we think should teach us to prepare a meal, and why does Claire reject her mother's culinary knowledge but embrace that of an anonymous restaurant cook? What makes an ingredient a whole or healthy food? Is a practice the same as a skill? Where does cooking happen? When did restaurants become so central to cooking, providing us with meals and also inspiring us when we cook at home? Finally, how often does Claire have to cook to be considered a skillful cook? To cook food is to participate in a universal human act; there is always cooking happening sometime, somewhere. But the variations, the configurations, and the machinations are endless. Answers to these questions emerged though observing contemporary American cooks and investigating cooks of earlier eras. Cooking—in deeds and words—has changed.

In large, complex, and diverse societies, questions such as who does the cooking, what gets cooked, and where such practices happen must be seen as multifaceted and multiplex. Yet fairly narrow assumptions tend to dominate, the most notable of which being that women cook in home kitchens for their families. Cooking appears bound and constrained: domestic cooking is contained narrowly, nested in received categories and imperatives of the place of women in the private sphere, linked as much to biology as to culture. However, this ideal may now be disassociated from reality. Women's obligations in relation to home cooking have shifted. Thus, it is crucial to explore the many manners of making modern meals that involve home cooks (both women and men) without relying too heavily on what we think or imagine is the case at hand. Instead, there need to be more forensic examinations that integrate what is known—presumptions and trends—with specific tellings and realities. This requires observing and documenting the actual lived experiences of home cooks.

To begin, we should acknowledge that over the arc of the past century, cooking has remained an everyday choice (a continuity), but it is no longer an everyday chore (a change). American home cooks are at the heart of this inquiry, but there are other types of cooks to consider too. Today, there is a wide array of food work being done by many people in many different types of kitchens. When it comes to making *modern* meals, American women no longer need to fulfill their duties and obligations in terms of nourishment by cooking three meals a day for themselves and for others. Rather, this is but one option among many. The expanding number of opportunities to obtain food cooked outside the home and the increased possibility of relying on others to cook is both a result of and a response to a long-term shift in the link between food, domestic life, and gender: although the model of the woman as the primary cook and baker of the household and of the home as the primary site for kitchen work remains associated with *ideals and values* of domesticity, it no longer dominates in *actual lived practice*. A woman's "domestic sphere" might contain more chargers for electronics than tools for decorating cakes; as food scholar Kyla Wazana Tompkins pithily points it, when discussing her research on the semiotic economy of household food labor, "So public, private—whatever, right?"[3] During the past century, women have been able to transcend the limits of the private sphere by fighting to liberate themselves from obligations such as making meals. However, these are small battles being waged inside homes rather than outside in the streets. This has meant that the granular elements of this fight—the switch to frozen vegetables, the phone call to the local Chinese restaurant to order takeout, the decision for the husband to do the weekday cooking and the

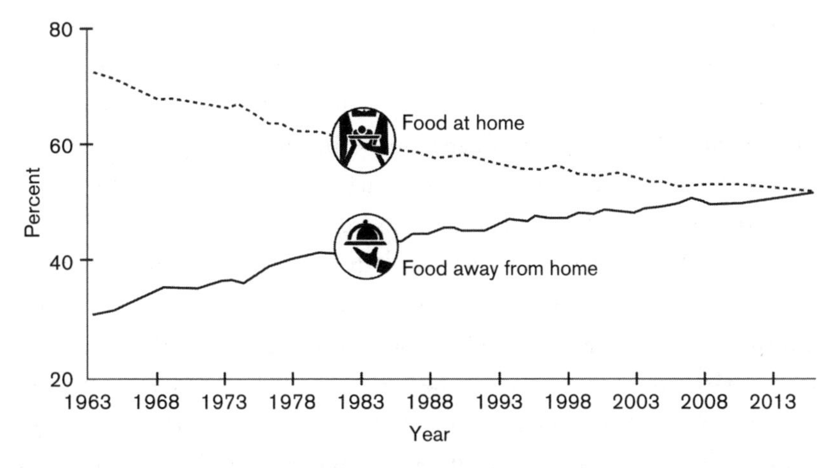

Figure 1. Shares of total food expenditures, food at home versus food away from home. *Source:* United States Department of Agriculture Economic Research Service, "Data Products: Table 8—Food Expenditures by Families and Individuals as a Share of Disposable Personal Money Income."

wife to do the grocery shopping—these small, constant choices build to days, weeks, months, and years of choices that have gone unnoticed for too long.

All these small skirmishes signify important changes for American women and families and also for American cuisine and culture. Consider the following very different descriptions (spanning a century) of what is seemingly the same practice: that of transforming raw ingredients into cooked food. In the 1860s, the high goddesses of domestic duty, sisters Catherine E. Beecher and Harriet Beecher Stowe, the authors of *The American Woman's Home, or The Principles of Domestic Science,* bemoaned, "The modern girls, as they have been brought up, cannot perform the labor of their own families as in those simpler, old-fashioned days; and what is worse, they have not practical skill with which to instruct servants, who come to us, as a class, raw and untrained."[4] Two realities of making meals during the nineteenth century are revealed here: one, the obligations of domestic tasks were increasingly under negotiation, and two, if a housewife had the economic means, she could pay someone else to perform those tasks. In the early twentieth century, the renowned chef Auguste Escoffier opined about cooking, saying, "Man is more thorough in his work, and thoroughness is at the root of all good, as of everything else. A man is more particular over the various little details which are necessary to make up a really perfect dish. . . . A woman, on the other hand, will manage with what she has handy."[5] Escoffier goes on to say, "This is very nice and obliging of her, no doubt, but it eventually spoils her cooking, and the dish is not a success."[6] During the transition to the twentieth century, cooking became more differentiated. The cook's abilities are not determined by biology (both men and women *can* cook); rather, they are shaped by gender (there is a cultural belief that men are artists and women are dutiful). The cook's identity becomes more variable, and so do the locations where he or she cooks. The hearth is not always in the home; cooking takes place in new environments. George Orwell provided a vivid account from his own experience working in a Parisian hotel during the 1920s: "The kitchen was like nothing I have ever seen or imagined—a stifling, low-ceilinged inferno of a cellar, red lit from the fires, and deafening with oaths and the clanging of pots and pans. . . . It was so hot that all the metal-work except for the stoves had to be covered with cloth. In the middle were furnaces, where twelve cooks skipped to and fro, their faces dripping sweat in spite of their white caps."[7] By the 1940s, the opportunity for a person to get a meal outside of the home, often cooked by a man, was well integrated into American life, especially when in an urban area or traveling by rail or car. And then, in the 1950s, almost a century after the Beecher sisters' lament, Peg Bracken published her manifesto, *The I Hate to Cook Book*: "Some women, it is said, like to cook. This book is not for them. This book is for those of us who hate to, who have learned through hard experience that some activities become no less powerful through repetition: childbearing, paying taxes, cooking."[8] Although making meals remained an essential everyday task, who cooked those meals, where they were cooked, and why they were cooked was no longer essentialized to any particular category of person or any particular place.

The complexity of cooking, thus, lies in its very fluidity; an accurate investigation requires engaging with it as a constantly morphing hybrid that involves both domestic duty and paid labor. In our modern culinary system, the many available choices allow individuals to constantly move between domestic and public domains. Many micro-moments—variously acts of compliance, complicity, exhaustion, and resistance—have created the perceptions and practices involved in making modern meals. Over the course of the twentieth century, there was an overall decline in the time spent making a typical meal. Meanwhile, paid cooking labor shifted out of the home kitchen and into commercial kitchens (there has been a decline in the employment of domestic servants and a concomitant increase in service workers). At the same time, procuring (and consuming) food cooked outside the home became a more common everyday option for all manner of people in varying circumstances—poor and rich, living in the countryside and residing in cities and towns.[9]

What happens to cooking when the location, the context, and the identity of the cook escape from certain confines, flowing over the usual channels and defying our assumptions? Anthropologists have long been interested in the complex and contradictory relationships between the actions of individuals or groups and the cultural categories of experience. Claire makes her soup and salad and serves it for dinner. Yet the meaning of her choices and the significance of the particular soup, the ingredients, and the recipe are not simply the result of a biological drive for sustenance or a defined division of labor. There are cultural processes at work shaping varied actions and their shared classifications. These categories are neither rigid nor necessarily permanent, but they define us as cooks and shape American cooking in the present. So although we might think that cooking can be easily defined, classified, and thereby understood, we might be wrong.

Classification and categorization are powerful analytic tools, but such modes of understanding can become ossified, ending up as relics of an earlier era or reliable but ultimately facile tropes. Anthropologist David Sutton, points out that the scholarship on women and domestic life has tended toward "lumping" rather than "splitting" domestic tasks, perhaps at the cost of understanding the nuances of various everyday practices, especially cooking. He argues that when feminist anthropologists brought women more to the front and center of anthropological inquiry, they often did so at the expense of analyzing daily domestic tasks, which they identified as generally the same across cultures and thus not necessarily useful for providing insight about social relations. Thus, there was an assumption that "it was only when women stepped into the so-called 'public sphere' that they became involved in socially valued activities" and that only these socially public activities would reveal the complexity of social relations in any given culture.[10] Sutton argues that cooking needs to be considered as a unique activity and also as a practice that is particularly important to any understanding of social relations. To make sense of cooking as above and beyond "mere" domestic tasks, Sutton concludes, it "needs to be studied as an activity *in the making*" (emphasis mine).[11] Although Sutton acknowledges that many people perceive cooking to be at times a chore, he argues that the practice cannot be contained solely by this category. Thus, although cooking a meal could seem unworthy of much attention and be dismissed as a daily nuisance, to do so is to miss out on grander cultural and culinary transformations. Cooking has slipped out of this classification and expanded beyond the categorical assumptions Americans have traditionally used to explain it.

In this case, the slippage involves both identity and action, for neither are fully contained in the domestic sphere, defined as a physical space where families are cooked for and fed each day. Values and practices, the stuff of everyday life, change, as revealed in varied patterns (e.g., commercial kitchen work now feeds families as much as small-scale domestic cookery) and events (e.g., the now everyday and commonsense actions of purchasing a meal or components of a meal). In this sense, modern American cooking occurs within a set of social relations and responds to social environments. Modern culinary practice both reflects and shapes structural shifts in the organization of everyday life, such as the increased movement of people from rural to urban areas, the changing organization of work and leisure time, the industrialization of food production from farm to table, and the increased use of technology in all forms of kitchen work. In this context, the quotidian decisions about what to cook, how to cook, who to cook for, or whether to cook at all are powerfully influenced by how individuals intersect with larger social, political, and economic institutions. For example, to borrow a nutritional term, women still predominate as food "gatekeepers" in the domestic sphere, but not all women are food "producers," at least not all of the time.

Today, our relationship to cooking is less internal, less determined by our gender, and much more external, influenced by our engagement not just with those we know and trust but also with those understood as trustworthy due to their expertise. The knowledge we get does not come exclusively from other (female) home cooks (remember the recipe boxes of our mothers and grandmothers?) but from people with special understandings. Health experts extol, chefs cajole, and food activists protest. Culinary conversations are no longer primarily the domain of women swapping their favorite recipes and tips of the trade, part and parcel of the care work long considered axiomatic to their identity. Instead, much of the conversation now revolves around explanations: the right way to maintain a healthy diet; the best way to purchase safe and fair food; the correct way to make a dish.

The experts have turned their attention to the act of cooking itself—their knowledge now intersects with our practices. The liberation of women from cooking as a daily chore has not unchained them from the *consequences* of their freedom. There is now a culinary discourse dominated by worry, concern, and well-meaning instruction. The experts (nutritionists, doctors, food advocates, celebrity chefs) are wringing their hands and sighing not only because American cooking practices have changed but also because, apparently, the new ways we do (or do not do) this work are fraught. Some experts worry that a serious decline in everyday cooking is underway and claim that the resulting loss of cooking skill and knowledge explains broader social concerns, such as lack of family cohesion. Another perceived problem of modern life is that fewer families are sharing meals and mealtimes, and this is blamed on the notion that there has been a nationwide decline in domestic cooking practices. Other experts in public health fields advocate for improvements in everyday cooking as a means of counteracting the obesity epidemic. These worries have been translated into numerous media articles, news stories, and op-ed pieces, creating a discourse of crisis. Recently, there was a spate of interviews and commentaries after Michael Pollan claimed in his book *Cooked: A Natural History of Transformation* (2013) that "the decline of home cooking closely tracks the rise in obesity and all the chronic diseases linked to diet," which he followed immediately with this commentary: "The rise of fast food and the decline in home cooking have also undermined the institution of the shared meal, by encouraging us to eat different things and to eat them on the run and often alone."[12] In the juxtaposition of these two statements, cooking simultaneously becomes the center of all problems *and* all solutions.

Such a singular claim of cause and effect is undoubtedly rhetorically powerful. Yet does it accurately reflect reality? Cooking happens. Every day. However, American *domestic* cooking is more episodic, is less clearly linked to gender, and differs from meal to meal. Meanwhile, the food being cooked is much more variable when it comes to ingredients, techniques, and methods than it was in the past. Does the emergence of new *styles* of domestic cooking reflect or signal decline? Or does the kaleidoscope of contexts for present-day cooking practices make it more difficult to create a connection between practice and meaning, to analytically "capture" such a complex and diverse lived reality?[13]

Americans are still cooks, but the tether between women, domesticity, and cooking has been cut. This is not say there remain no ties that bind; we may not cook all our meals, but we always have to find nourishment. Decisions are made every day in families (still primarily by women) about upcoming meals. However, these decisions now *sometimes*, but not *always*, involve household members engaging in the productive labor of cooking. The United States Department of Agriculture Economic Research Service (USAERS) reported an increase in the proportion of total food sales that come from food and beverage operations: Americans now spend 53.5 percent of their total food budget on foods eaten at home and a historical high of 46.5 percent on foods eaten outside of the home.[14] These transactions were taking place at eating and drinking establishments; full-service restaurants, hotels, and motels; retail stores and direct selling; recreational places; schools and colleges; and other locales. In 2005, it was estimated that the average American ate eighty meals at restaurants and purchased fifty-seven restaurant meals to take home and twenty-seven meals to take to work.[15] In the same year, it was reported that Americans ate a cooked meal at home five times a week and that four out of ten dinners were prepared in thirty minutes or less.[16]

Equally crucial to the story is the relationship *between* our choices—the ratio of our values. This is clearly delineated in a graphic produced by the USAERS as part of a 2016 report on household food expenditure and American reliance on convenience foods that shows the types of foods that are available and the overall proportion of sales in each category.[17] If we compile multiple national polls and surveys, Americans spend, on average, 23 percent of their household food expenditures on "complex and basic ingredients." A person (or some machine) then transforms those raw ingredients by cooking them.

Figure 2. "Class in cooking," 1904. Schomburg Center for Research in Black Culture, Jean Blackwell Hutson Research and Reference Division, New York Public Library Digital Collections.

Small gestures, like Claire searching for her recipe, and grand claims, like the current national average of our food purchases for meals at home and away, when integrated, reveal intersubjective and intersectional elements of everyday action that create our "lifeworld" (or *Lebenswelt*).[18] The culinary world we inhabit is built up of the decisions that create ratios such as spending sixty or twenty minutes making dinner, buying Hamburger Helper or ordering Chinese take-out, and growing tomatoes or purchasing the canned tomato paste. Our decisions are also made *in response* to our culinary world, in which the boundaries between the domestic and commercial spheres of making meals are increasingly porous.[19]

INVESTIGATING COMPLEXITY

The fluidity of contemporary cooking means that simple causality—between cooking and domesticity, between cooking and identity, between cooking and everyday labor, between cooking and individual health and well-being—is difficult to identify. Looking beyond the domestic kitchen to make sense of how we cook requires a consideration of the new categories that shape cooking: as practice, as an ideal, and as an imperative. Perhaps cooking's increased complexity is best served by acknowledging its breadth while simultaneously accounting for all the ways we seek to contain it. Or as Roland Barthes, a scholar who wrote eloquently on both the structure and meaning of modern life, put it, "[the] essential object is the taxonomy or distributive model which every human creation, . . . inevitably establishes, since there can be no culture without classification."[20] And there are many ways to categorize and classify. When we survey our expenditures on food and our choices for procuring food, we now classify all aspects of meal preparation into a number of categories, depending on place, person, desire, and context. We experience cooking across a number of categories as well; a woman might feel like a drudge in the kitchen some days but like a domestic diva other days. And then there are days someone else, in the house or at the restaurant, might cook instead. Acknowledging such fluidity and complexity can help explain our culinary selves as we are instead of condemning ourselves for what we are not.

In this schematic, the required knowledge is not universal but rather very specific to time and place. The ingredients vary. The tools and techniques shift. The tastes change. The expectations of the cook are not consistent. But each day, somehow, somewhere, individuals make a series of decisions so that meals get served and eaten. Somehow, somewhere, someone takes some set of ingredients and transforms them into an edible dish. Meanwhile, just as every new member of a generation must learn the language of his or her family or culture, so each one must learn how to cook, or figure out how to have someone else cook instead.

Spanning the course of a century and the continent, this book paints the broad strokes of our transformed culinary landscape. In this sense, the argument and evidence fall into the lumper rather than the splitter school of empirical research. Charles Darwin, in the early days of his formulation of the theory of evolution, commented on the tendency of botanists and others to either "lump" plants and animals into larger systematic categories or "split" them into smaller variegated classifications.[21] There are pitfalls to either approach. Lumpers can miss small telling details or the nuanced variations between times, places, and identities. Splitters can have trouble seeing beyond their horizon; they circle around specifics and struggle to connect the dots. My aim with this book is to reorient our gaze toward categories that might more accurately reflect our present condition. Once we've accomplished this, there is more to do if students of cuisine and culture want to move beyond (in the spirit of Darwin) family to genus and species.

In order to capture both grand claims and small gestures, I used varied research methods, including ethnographic interviewing and videography, surveys, participant observation, and analysis of contemporary and historical documents, datasets, and cookbooks. The geographic site for the investigations of home cooks and their lived experiences took place in parts of the Northeast (rural, semi-urban, and urban locales). This decision, based on feasibility, means that variations in meal preparation that might track closely to regional traditions were not able to be fully considered. This research cut a wide swath across race and class, and so the participants reflected the overall demographics of this region; they were primarily white but also black and Asian and included individuals of low-, middle-, and high-income status. The classifications that emerged through this research reflect realities of cooking that are culturally shared (if not by every individual in the same manner), guiding a contemporary understanding of our choices when trying to put dinner on the table. However, as a society ever more characterized by economic and racial inequality, more detailed analysis of the lived experiences of our contemporary cooking categories beyond geographic locales, perhaps focusing on other demographic variables (e.g., shared race and shared socioeconomic status) or identities (e.g., marital status, sexual orientation, political and religious beliefs), is a necessary next step.[22] Hopefully, this investigation will provide a relevant and revelatory framework for further inquiries, more public attention, and more dialogue about cooking, culture, and modern everyday life.

It would be convenient (and potentially flattering) to say that the research for this book was from the beginning designed to account for all the iterations of modern meal preparation. But this was not the case. There was no grand design but rather a series of intuitive leaps followed by more organized investigations. The research (and the researchers) followed cooks as they cooked.

The research to make sense of people's cooking knowledge and practice began with a project to carry out ethnographic interviews and videotapes of people making dinner in their homes. The goal was to examine cooking as an everyday skill and as knowledge while taking into consideration ideas about individual health. I worked with a group of graduate students over a five-year period on this project. First, three students and I fanned out to a number of locations and households, attempting to choose participants that reflected the overall demographics of the Northeast.[23] The decision to videotape people in situ and in action turned out to be remarkably useful because it allowed us to witness culinary practice in a way that other methods (e.g., talking, reading, counting) would not have permitted us to do as thoroughly or completely.[24] (For a detailed explanation of the research methods, see the appendix.)

We focused on dinner. We talked about breakfast and lunch, but these meals (except, perhaps, on the weekends) tend to be much less elaborate and more often rely on a certain version of cooking—assembling—rather than the broadest possible version, which requires some planning, an array of ingredients, the application of techniques, and the use of heat to transform foods from raw to cooked. This allowed us to capture our participants' largest set of perceptions and practices in relation to making a meal. Breakfast and lunch are also more frequently purchased outside the home, a reflection of the structural changes in modern life that have liberated us from some tasks but introduced others, such as commuting and longer workdays.[25]

Every participant (for the first study, there were twenty-five in total, thirteen of whom were videotaped twice) was a unique cook, which was due partly to our research design but also to the diverse possibilities of cooking practices. Filming people as they cook is a wonderful way to enter their everyday lives and acknowledge human diversity in the best tradition of ethnographic research. These were "real life" observations; mistakes happened with the recipes and equipment, certain ingredients were forgotten or misplaced, and children interfered. One of the unintended consequences, though, of having a permanent record of these meals was the ability to repeatedly witness them being made. Over the years, we continued to view the meals—both together and separately—always identifying new insights, commonalities, and distinctions. The videos allowed us to observe the behaviors of our participants long after the meals were made and listen to the things they said, which at times informed and at times contradicted their actions. We analyzed and reanalyzed the words and images numerous times, identifying a number of emergent themes that became the foundation for this larger inquiry into modern cooking.

Other people began to view the videotapes too; three more graduate students and several academic colleagues watched and responded. We discussed our individual reactions to the many and varied cooks, creating a larger community of observations through our dialogues. There were trained chefs concerned about one participant's awkward and hesitant knife skills and another's seemingly disorganized kitchen setup. There was a future registered dietitian who spent some time analyzing the nutrient composition of various meals. There were future nutrition and food scientists who were at times dismayed by the subjects' cleaning habits. With every viewing came new realizations—about American cooks, cooking in modern kitchens, and the values and ideas we all bring to this necessary part of our lives. Each video became a multilayered window into the many ways people cook, allowing for observations and realizations that went much deeper than if our research had relied solely on simple written records and interviews, which would have required us to recall events rather than witness them over and over again. As the surveys, interviews, and videotapes accumulated, and we began to look closely at our participants' practices and listen carefully to what they said, we were surprised by what we were documenting. By the time we concluded the multiple phases of research, thirty home cooks had participated, generating thirty interviews and over fifty hours of ethnographic video footage of home meals being prepared. We realized that there was a much larger project that needed to be done to look more expansively at contemporary American cooks and cooking practices. Contrary to our original assumption that we would find an overall decline in culinary knowledge and skill, we concluded that Americans have a decent basic level of cooking ability and understanding but simply do not use it all the time. We began the study as a response to the emerging cultural angst about culinary decline but then shifted our interpretation, and so our inquiry expanded. Although we were not working in a fieldwork setting in the most traditional sense, we adopted the iterative strategy of anthropological research. We realized that decline was not our main finding and so looked elsewhere to understand American cooks and cooking.

Once we acknowledged the wide horizon of places and people involved in making meals, a new difficulty arose. Witnessing so many diverse practices challenged typical research strategies such as interviewing people, looking for written records, and identifying some sort of bounded group (e.g., only home cooks, only one location, only a certain age group). But staying within a narrow frame, even for the sake of elegant research design or to complete a research project in a timely fashion, would perforce neglect taking account of what most needed to be understood. If the knowing and the doing that explain our actions deserved to be made sense of in all their messiness, then new research methods and design were required.

The landscape of cooking is varied, and people's relationships to that landscape are rich and diverse. Thus, in order to document the dynamic reality of Americans making meals, we decided to use a wider aperture. Mapping an entire landscape rather than a more defined region expands what we understand about the relationship of identity to cooking skill and knowledge. Also, actions rather than assumptions serve as the primary compass to orient our analysis because it is in small acts and daily decisions that the larger edifice of meaning is built.

The initial framing of the research used an idea based on the prevailing cultural common sense that cooking skill and knowledge are in decline. But when we began to listen carefully to what people said and look closely at their practices, another situation emerged. We found that our informants actually had culinary skills and knowledge but either did not access them all the time or ran into difficulties with issues outside of heating the pan and sautéing the chicken: How to shop? What to cook? When to shop and cook? Why make one choice over another? They talked about cooking in ways that were much more complex than we anticipated. For everyone in the study, cooking was often a chore, but it was also much, much more. Depending on the person, the place, and the context, cooking might be a creative act, a craft, a way to a healthy body and society, something other people did, or a pleasure. People's practices and perceptions moved between these categories on any given day. Understanding the reality of these categories, how and when they emerged historically, and why such classifications resonate culturally ultimately became the goal of our research. The emphasis on the central function of embodied knowledge overlaps with contemporary social theory; however, not all perceptions were determined by social status and social capital. The lived experiences of our participants revealed much more intentionality and internal conflict and many more contingencies of action and struggles that intersected with numerous constraints that were not only economic and social but also psychological and biological.

A close examination of actual cooking labor that accepts a fluidity shaped by the varying pressures and aspirations of the cooks reveals that cooking remains a rich and dynamic human activity. If the story of modern American cooks is not sufficiently contained in a narrative of decline or an argument about social status, what other voices can create the complex topography? Our engagement with cooks at home also led us to investigate the historical trends of the type and number of people paid to cook; every domestic act was seen to have an equal public reaction. This involved looking at historical statistics, focusing on categorizations of labor occupations in the United States since 1860. I decided to expand the research agenda to also include archival and textual research on two iconic cookbooks of the twentieth century, *The Joy of Cooking* and *Mastering the Art of French Cooking;* the authors of these cookbooks have become trustworthy companions for countless home cooks over the years. These now iconic works, along with pamphlets, books, and other primary sources concerning how

Americans cook (and bake) and ways to learn to do such work reflect transformations in everyday decisions around cooking. At the same time, changes in their form and content reveal a new landscape of choices in regard to all aspects of making a meal, from shopping for ingredients to sitting down to eat.

Also, if everyday cooking was taking place as much outside of the home as inside of it, why not also observe cooking practices in commercial venues? Since purchasing baked goods, especially bread, is now a cultural commonplace, looking at baking as a form of commercial craftwork became part of the overall investigation. This led to more ethnographic inquiry, involving interviews and participant observations of two home bakers. I also did participant observation in three artisan bakeries, located in Vermont and California. The question of cooking as an occupation also emerged as an important issue, and so I reviewed historical and contemporary materials on domestic servants, commercial cooks, artisan bakers, and other culinary trades. Slowly, a fuller account of the modern culinary landscape was constructed—a complex portrait of what we know and what we do when it comes to cooking.

Over the past three years, we returned to talking to home cooks as part of an multidisciplinary project that looked at how and why individuals become "empowered to act" to meet their everyday need to obtain sustenance, since Americans can choose not to cook and still be fed. We ran classes based on a pedagogy promoting such agency, held multiple focus groups to build the definition of agency, carried out participant observation and semistructured interviews of people taking a cooking course in two locales, and developed a scale to help measure agency in cooking and food preparation.[26] The voices, concerns, and perceptions of these cooks also informed the final portrait of the American culinary landscape.

LEARNING TO COOK

Observing cooking, therefore, required us to come up with innovative methodologies, because an accurate investigation involved pondering Americans and their meal preparation in light of both the grand trends and the tiny moments. The small gestures we captured—a young man forgetting to close the freezer door and moving on to measure water for rice, a woman walking out into her garden to collect herbs while onions were sautéing on the stove, a recent immigrant's admiration for a celebrity chef—told us not just about that person but also about their culinary lifeworld. As such, no single strand of this multifaceted research is singular; rather they are all part of a large tapestry replete with small and large threads. At its base, cooking requires knowledge and is an everyday practice. And although we all may intuitively understand that the ability to cook is not innate, much like a myriad of other human practices (e.g., playing music, hunting animals, building houses), surprisingly little sustained scholarship has looked closely at cooking skill: the acts, knacks, and tips that make a person a cook.

First, we all figure out how to eat dinner, but the process of making it—the transformation of ingredients to dishes—is now episodic rather than intrinsic to daily life. With the "essential" requirement removed, domestic cooking can best be understood as operating within a "taskscape." Second, after we observed and talked to home cooks, we concluded that no cook, at home or away, male or female, rich or poor, works alone. Important realizations—possibly obvious but nonetheless significant—emerged from these insights: Acting on what you know to engage in everyday meal preparation is a learned practice, and much like riding a bicycle or playing an instrument, you can stop and start again. But you cannot start if you were never taught in the first place. Above all, in order to cook, we must *learn;* ability is always linked to social environments, experience, and access to knowledge.

Take this example from our research: Isabel, a young girl, the oldest of four children, is in the kitchen with her parents as they make an evening meal. She really wants to help, perhaps because she knows that we are videotaping the preparation of this particular meal, but perhaps also because she wants to learn. Of all the children, she is the most engaged in the process. Her parents are talking about their everyday cooking practices while they move around the kitchen, preparing dinner. Isabel keeps interrupting, "Daddy, Daddy, can I help?" After several minutes, her father acquiesces. He gets her to stand on a chair and instructs, "You can juice the lemon." He sets on the counter the following items: a lemon, a juicer made of metal, and a cutting board. In the pantheon of possible tools to extract juice from a citrus fruit, this juicer is fairly simple. The bottom half is a simple metal bowl; on the top half, a rounded, molded piece of metal with numerous ridges protrudes from the center, which is connected to a flat area and pierced so that the juice can drip into the bowl. The two halves are attached with a hinge. Isabel picks up the whole lemon, lifts the top part of the juicer, puts the lemon in the bottom bowl, and presses down on the lemon with the top half. Nothing happens. The lemon stays exactly the same, and there is definitely no juice. Quickly realizing there is something wrong with her method, she calls out to her father: "Daddy, can you cut this open?" Isabel then carefully places the lemon on the cutting board. She notices that the sell-by sticker is still on the fruit and peels it off. Her father comes over and explains the process: "When you're juicing something, cut it in half. You take it and smash it as hard as you can." Isabel takes half of the lemon and slams it onto the ridged metal. "No, no, put it on there, sorry. And then you turn it back and forth while you are pushing down. You can do it." And then she does. The juice is extracted from the lemon.

Whatever our cultural assumptions about who cooks, when, and why and whether these notions reflect our realities or our ideals, there remains a constant: we still *learn* how to cook. Making a meal involves knowing how to put it together, somehow. This young girl is instructed by her father. Her context involves a large family and a small kitchen space. The anthropologist Tim Ingold has long argued for an integration of knowledge and practice, one that brings together "the whole person, indissolubly body and mind, in a richly structured environment."[27] These are environments shaped by social interactions and informed by social expectations. The skilled practice of cooking rarely occurs in isolation. Even when a cook prepares food for herself, she uses a specific repertoire of skills that comes from somewhere and is informed by other cooks. And with the transmission of knowledge, "skills are not transmitted from generation to generation but are regrown in each, incorporated into the *modus operandi* of the developing human organism through training and experience in the performance of particular tasks."[28] This book looks very closely at cooking as an embodied activity and at the process of meal preparation as a locus of multiple meanings and values. To paraphrase David Sutton, this approach reveals that "each time a moussaka is made, a category is put at risk *in practice*" (emphasis mine); there are constant negotiations, transformations, and realizations of much more than the dish.[29] As each and every dish is made, multiple stories can be told, and varied meanings can be interpreted.

FORM AND CONTENT

In this book, individual people's actions—the cooking talk and cooking practices—introduce the small gestures, the knowledge, and the skill found in *their* hands, inspiring and then authenticating our culinary classifications. These details lead to a deeper consideration of the categories that frame our culinary labors.

Chapter 1, "Cooking Is a Chore," looks at continuities and changes in managing the daily *obligation* to prepare dinner (and sometime breakfast and lunch). A number of ethnographic interviews are interspersed with a close examination of the importance of the seminal American cookbook, *The Joy of*

Cooking, as continuities and changes in the seven editions of what is the most popular cookbook in the nation's history can be seen as a bellwether for the state of domestic cooking. Chapter 2, "Cooking Is an Occupation," focuses on labor statistics and primary source documents to demonstrate the continuous involvement of paid laborers to do cooking work over the course of the past century. Different perspectives on the affective dimensions of home cooking are explored using vignettes from domestic cooks and their employers. Chapter 3, "Cooking Is an Art," examines the intersection of an aesthetic standard and creative desires for both home cooks and professional cooks and chefs. The power of expertise, the ability to improvise as a means of elevating cooking that goes "above" or "beyond" the everyday, and the variable identities around cooking that emerge in the modern period are also considered. Pulling apart these strands opens up a larger discussion about how cooking intersects with philosophies of aesthetics, values toward creativity, and social expectations about artful cooking. Chapter 4, "Cooking Is a Craft," considers craft as form of virtuosity, exploring the crucial aspect of learning through intention and repetition. The focus is on what emerges from the mastery of certain culinary skills, but in the contemporary American context, craftwork is also identified as a type of *intervention* into a universe of food products and practices based on industrial methods for making dishes and meals. Chapter 5, "Cooking Is for Health," focuses on the cultural preoccupation with serving healthy meals. In the American context, the definition of a healthy meal is quite elastic; this is seen in the shifting perceptions of Americans when it comes to how their food has been processed and sourced and why processed foods are now categorized as more harmful than helpful. The conclusion considers a number of possible futures for the knowledge and practices related to making American meals. Here, one final category, cooking as a pleasure, is discussed in light of another broad ideal: the quest to cook and eat together as a form of both individual sensory pleasure *and* shared social pleasure.

In the prologue to his eloquent book *The Craftsman*, Richard Sennett muses on the neglected power of technique in the modern age, arguing that we cannot fall into a psychic despair at the seemingly endless list of possible catastrophes facing the human species. Instead, he writes that he has "become hopeful about the human animal at work," explaining that "we can achieve a more human life if only we better understand the making of things."[30] Thinking about making meals as a necessary and instrumental element of the human experience, casting cooking as elemental human labor writ large, expands our analytic horizons. The labor of cooking, a labor born of both necessity and desire, needs to be central to our understanding of American cuisine, American domestic life, and American values and ideals. To generalize, often shrilly, that no one cooks at home and then to concentrate on how this "lost" labor both produces and reflects larger social concerns is to miss out on so much human ingenuity and possibility.

In fact, contemporary cooking serves as a perfect practice to do a "thick description" about our everyday lives, for as Sennett argues, "thinking and feeling are contained within the process of making.[31] The facts—that we eat food prepared outside of the home as much as food prepared inside the home; that women are no longer solely responsible for transforming food from raw ingredients into cooked meals; that our reasons and rationales for cooking can change from meal to meal, week to week, and year to year; that we cook with ingredients that come from the ground, from boxes, from warehouses, or from farmers markets—reveal our thoughts, our feelings, and our labors.

We cook *because* it is a chore, and we cook *as if* it were a chore. But we also cook because we *want to be* creative, we want to be culinary artists, and we cook to *create artful food*. Certain connections and obligations between the laborer and the fruits of such labor have changed over the past century. But change does not necessarily mean decline. I am hopeful about cooking, and my hopefulness comes from broad explorations and then careful close readings of cooking talk and cooking practices. In doing so, I have come to see that our gestures reveal what we know and what we do. A humble ingredient like a carrot can be made into sticks and coins, cake, and flower garnishes. Making dinner can involve a package of rice pilaf, a free-range organic chicken breast, and a bottle of teriyaki sauce. Eating lunch can involve going to a cafeteria at the hospital and making a choice between chicken soup made by a cook in the commissary kitchen and Domino's pizza in cardboard boxes. All this just on any given day.[32]

CHAPTER ONE

Cooking Is a Chore

Laura, a woman in her mid-fifties, lives on a farm in rural New England. Originally from Rhode Island, she moved in her thirties from an urban area to live on a small family-run dairy farm. She is a knowledgeable cook, primarily self-trained, and frequently relies on her intuition. Her kitchen is a large open room, although the "work area" is just in one corner. There is a freestanding refrigerator along a wall that also has a large built-in set of cabinets, open shelves, and a counter; on the shelves sits a large collection of cookbooks. To the right of the stove stands a counter that is cluttered with reused glass jars (filled with maple syrup, honey, etc.), bread, bowls, and other items, including a KitchenAid mixer. Over the counter hangs a set of three wire baskets that are full of a variety of dried spices. Behind the work area is a round table.

Although Laura's active cooking space is fairly small, the old farmhouse kitchen permits an ambling approach to cooking. She does not have all her ingredients set out and ready to go before she starts preparing her meal; rather, she constantly moves around the room as she cooks. Her active cooking takes place at the stove and the small counter immediately to the right of the stove. She picks up the ingredients as she reads through the recipes. While making bread dough, she moves from the counter to the cabinet to get measuring cups and spoons, goes back to the counter to cut butter into a glass measuring cup, and then puts it in the microwave—which is placed on top of the refrigerator—to melt. Meanwhile, she gets another glass measuring cup from the cabinet, takes the milk out of the refrigerator, pours the milk into the measuring cup, bending down to accurately read the measurement, and then puts the milk into the microwave along with the butter, explaining: "If you put them in together from the start, the butter does not melt well."

Laura prepares two dishes that she has made many times before: dinner rolls and a black bean soup. She checks both of the recipes often, but she also has many "tips" or "adaptations" that she has developed over the years, such as those to melt the butter and warm the milk, as described above. She is not a planner, but she is a good reactor. At another point in the meal preparation, she goes hunting for the right spices to put in the soup. Her hanging baskets are full of spices—some in clear glass bottles, some in small brown bags, and others in clear plastic bags. She looks for the dry mustard called for in the recipe by rustling through the spices in all three baskets. No luck. She goes over to the far cabinet—success. But when she opens up the jar, she sees that the mustard has caked and cannot be used. Off she goes to the refrigerator for wet mustard. She says, "This is not ideal, but the soup needs the mustardy taste." She moves back over to the hanging basket and rummages around looking for cumin, but she comes up empty-handed. So she substitutes cardamom, saying, "This is the closest." Laura's cooking is like an improvised dance.

Her engagement with cooking has waxed and waned over the years, influenced by the many obligations of raising a family and running a farm. Necessary and mundane, food *always* requires attention. As she puts it, "The biggest challenge [of cooking] is losing track of what I'm doing. There is so much going on in the house all the time." When she explains her relationship to cooking, she often talks about her mother. In explorations of the lived experiences of home cooks, the stories of people's mothers inevitably emerge, as they did while Claire was making butternut squash soup and as they do now as Laura cooks. Often, such memories of home cooking turn to stories of the mother's feelings about the *necessity* of making meals.[1] These associations are automatic; when cooking is categorized as a type of care work, the quality of the food is directly connected to the maker of the meal. These are complex connections, however, involving the person who shopped and chopped and stirred but also this person's affective role in the family (however "family" might be defined). It appears that for most women, these are ties that bind. In her study of social inequality and commensality, sociologist Alice Julier notes that "associations between caring and food are long-standing, particularly in terms of gendered labor on behalf of families."[2] This point is echoed in anthropologist Megan Carney's work with women from Mexico and Central America. These women, who were vulnerable due to both their undocumented status and their poverty, placed great emphasis on their effort to make meals for their families, which was seen as a form of "caring labor."[3]

Laura does not remember her mother as either a good or enthusiastic cook; as she puts it, "I am afraid she cooked." In particular, her mother did not really think about whether or not the food tasted good or was pleasing to her family. Laura remembers that the vegetables were always overcooked:

> She would do things like take fresh green beans, they always had a garden. . . . She would bring the green beans in and scrub them and tail them and cut them up and put them in a pan of cold water and set it on the back of the stove. And then she would make something like a pot roast. After she got the meat going, she would turn the beans on and boil them in copious amounts of water until they were like canned green beans. She would serve [certain meals]; if it was Saturday night, it was beans and franks. And it was always—well, they didn't have much money—but it was always the absolutely cheapest ingredients and sometimes it was really awful.

In contrast, while Laura is cooking the black bean soup, she points out that she is using olive oil and mentions that her in-laws introduced her to using it in cooking. Then she elaborates: "I never would have found [it] in my mother's house."

Laura did learn from her mother that one way to manage the chore of cooking was to have a method:

> On Sundays, we generally had a roast, usually a pot roast, so Monday was sliced leftover pot roast with gravy, heated up in the gravy, with boiled potatoes. Tuesday night was usually American chop suey or spaghetti. It was a pasta dish, except we didn't call it pasta, we called it macaroni. Wednesday night varied a little bit. I'm trying to think what we had on Thursday. . . . Oh, Wednesday was usually tuna and noodles.

With the passage of time, Laura realizes that her mother's rigid approach to meals must have helped her cope with a daily task that she did not enjoy, but Laura still seems to wish her mother had been a better and happier cook.

Social obligation has long defined domestic cooking for the Americans who have dominated as home cooks: women. Learning what it takes to make a meal has historically been women's work and so, to a certain extent, it remains. Women have cooked because their families, the dominant domestic unit, needed to be fed. Cooking is often defined as a chore, a necessary daily task, but also as one's obligation to others; it is part and parcel of social networks and thus creates webs of expectation. Cooking can thus be classified as a chore when the series of skilled tasks also involves constant expectations and obligations. In many ways, this category—cooking as a chore—serves as a given, like a street name for a road traveled often, so often that it is easier to describe by features rather than by name. Cooking (and foodwork in general) intersects with both obligations and expectations to such an extent that separating the tasks from the associated values is no easy feat. In this sense, the category of "chore" highlights the necessity of the task of meal preparation as well as women's ambivalence toward it. Laura's reflections on cooking capture such an everyday push and pull between cooking as preparing a meal and cooking as the *obligation* of preparing a meal for oneself and for others.

Carol, who is in her late twenties, is a single professional living in urban Boston. Her kitchen does not resemble Laura's cavernous room; it is a small galley space where every item is neatly stored in cabinets and all surfaces are kept clean. She admits that she is a planner in all aspects of her life and certainly in her approach to preparing a meal. She likes to host dinner parties on the weekends and clearly enjoys the entire process, from creating the menu to shopping and cooking to hosting the event: "If I'm having a dinner party on Saturday, I plan my Saturday so that I can clean the house, clean the kitchen, get all my stuff ready, go food shopping, make sure that I have everything. . . . I kind of have a timeline." Carol is documented preparing for a dinner party; she wants to share her love of hospitality. Carol proudly displays the printed menu for the evening's dinner, and then goes on to display what she calls her tricks of the trade. One is a baked brie appetizer: "The secret to this is you don't buy the baked brie they sell to warm up, you just buy a wedge, slice some apples and put that in halfway through: heat it for twenty minutes, put in the apples, and pour on maple syrup." She serves this to her guests and then continues to prepare the main dish. Another of her secrets is spending money on ingredients: "This is a $40 bottle of olive oil, which makes a huge difference." She prides herself on her engagement with cooking, which she characterizes as being important to her social life: "When I cook for others I take it very seriously. I put a lot more time and love into it." She enjoys all aspects of preparing a meal when it is a special event: "I love doing it, and I love the display. . . . I spend a lot of time prepping." She likes being known for being a good cook, but she aims even higher: "I think my next step is to be more creative in what I'm doing. It's one thing to be a good cook, but I want to be really creative." She actively engages in the process, figuring out a good recipe, testing it before she uses it at a dinner party, shopping at multiple stores (e.g., Shaw's, Trader Joe's, Whole Foods, Russo's) to get the best ingredients, and setting up her house. In fact, the excitement of the *process* of making a meal for more than sustenance—the adventure of cooking, in a sense—is her passion: "The part about cooking that I love is seeing something I've never done before come out. I guess I like the final product."

Carol acknowledges, however, that not all domestic cooking is about adventure. When she is by herself, the type of cooking she does is generally different: "I will throw a salad together, and I will do very simple things for myself." When she's just cooking for herself, she shops once a week and doesn't plan ahead. She also sees that her love of cooking for others relies on the fact that these meals are special events: "I think I wouldn't love it as much if I had to cook for my family every single night, but [I enjoy it] because it's more of a novelty." Her sense that cooking can, in some circumstances, be more of a chore than a pleasure comes from seeing her mother's relationship to cooking change over the years: "I just never saw my mom loving cooking. I never saw her just love to cook. There were always five of us running around. . . . The food was always awesome, but I don't think we truly appreciated what she gave us." At another point, Carol both identifies with her mother's burden and distances herself from it: "She cooked every night, and she was an awesome cook, but for her it was a chore. . . . I think it's a generational thing."

Ultimately, Carol's articulation of her own identity as a cook is intertwined with her social relationships. These are between her and other cooks but also between her and a group of eaters. She understands she is not obliged to these eaters, although as she attests, her mother was not so lucky. As the contrast between Carol's passion for cooking and her mother's sense of drudgery reveals, cooking skills and knowledge, especially when categorized as a chore, cannot easily be extricated from the Gordian knot of social expectations. Cooking can all too easily develop a negative connotation, or at least a sense of ambivalence. Women often talk about their mothers' cooking with a twinge of regret; although cooking *can* be an expression of nurturance, it certainly isn't always. Carol intuitively makes a distinction between her planned dinner party—an event enhanced by the labor of thoughtfully making a meal—and her mother's daily social responsibility to make a meal for her family. She sees the complexities of the ties that bind when making sense of her relationship to cooking.

Merriam-Webster's Collegiate Dictionary gives the following definitions for the word "chore": "1. the regular or daily light work of a household or farm; 2. a routine task or job; 3. a difficult or disagreeable task."[4] Defining cooking as a chore seems to make a lot of sense at first glance. It is certainly part of the regular work of a household; the fact that we must eat to live makes cooking a necessary daily activity and thus it could easily be considered routine; and this regularity and necessity can certainly make it disagreeable, if not difficult. What a dictionary definition does not make explicit, however, is that the symbolic meanings of all chores are not equal. Cooking is not the same as sweeping or taking out the trash because the end result is not household cleanliness or order. Making a meal merges certain types of household tasks, webs of social relationships, and needs for nourishment and nurturance. Categorizing cooking as a chore is tempting, and it is common in contemporary American discussions of the task, but perhaps Carol's point that cooking *can* be a chore but can also be much more needs to be examined in more detail, especially in terms of what cooking means to nurturing social relations.

The entanglements of food and care work are well documented. In her rich ethnographic work *A Tortilla Is Like Life: Food and Culture in the San Luis Valley of Colorado*, Carole Counihan intersperses long excerpts from women's food-centered life histories with analysis of the meaning and purpose of food in the lives of a group of women all residing in a small Colorado town. Many of these excerpts weave together discussions of the importance of social relations to cooking and sharing meals, revealing that "women have usually valued cooking, . . . but [it] has represented challenges to their agency."[5] The women of this town, along with Laura and Carol, were well aware of a tension between, as Counihan puts it, expressing "creativity and nurturance" versus carrying out "inescapable domestic duties."[6] Perhaps when people invoke the "chore" of cooking, it is a proxy for a series of other expectations and responsibilities that extend far beyond preparing meals, such as feeling maternal guilt or promoting healthy behaviors.

This labor, whatever the affective meaning of the actions, is widely understood to be women's work, as linked to biology as it is to culture. Whether they live in small tribes of hunter-gatherers or apartments in vast urban areas, women have been primarily responsible for feeding families, however those are culturally defined. In the Arctic, Inuit women were solely responsible for transforming raw seal, caribou, and other animal meat hunted by Inuit men into palatable meals. In rural Mexico, women have long been responsible for making tortillas, the caloric and symbolic center of Mexican cuisine. The daily responsibility for food production has remained strongly associated with gender in all manner of modern societies: urban and industrial, western and eastern, northern and southern, rural, agrarian, and hunter-gatherer. A 1973 survey by anthropologists George Murdock and Catarina Provost of 185 cultures documents the near-universal cultural connection between women and cooking, reporting that "women were predominantly or almost exclusively responsible for cooking in 97.8% of societies."[7] In fact, Richard Wrangham argues that the gender division of labor understood as crucial to the evolution of modern humans long relied on women being in charge of cooking food for entire families.[8]

The acts involved in preparing meals are clearly nested in a number of social obligations; they are more difficult to transcend and harder to divorce from gender than other daily chores such as taking out the garbage or shoveling snow. Such obligations, however, are also not always consistently integrated into the many changes in circumstance that often occur over the course of any person's life. A young girl of eight may feel no responsibility for making meals, but by the time she is twenty-one, this may be crucial to figure out. At fifty, after thirty years of being obligated to make meals, that same woman, like Peg Bracken, may have had enough of cooking or at least be much less ambitious about it. All over the world, cooking remains very strongly associated with women's work, although there can be significant meanderings in any woman's life from a straight path of cooking all meals. So, gender identity always matters when it comes to making meals, but *how* and *when* it matters—which depends on location, life course, and lifestyle—is also revealing and meaningful.

Among Americans, although circumstances vary (from earlier eras through today and from childhood to old age), the transfer of culinary knowledge continues to be cast in light of women's obligations. The essays found in *Through the Kitchen Window*, edited by Arlene Avakian, were written by women exploring their food memories. The importance of relationships to eating and cooking are reiterated time and again. The tensions articulated by

Carol and Laura are echoed in these women's stories: they are aware that good cooking skills can lead to domestic pleasure; however, their ambivalence at being required to master such skills is always lurking. These memoirs were written by women of all ages and ethnicities—one describes her grandmother's dolmas, another remembers her grandmother's sweet pickles—but all revolve around a hearth overseen by a relative—a mother, a grandmother, an aunt. Memories of cooks in action abound. In one essay, E. Barrie Kavasch highlights the skill her grandmother brings to making biscuits and the comfort such mundane actions provided her during childhood:

> Birdlike, deeply veined, and lightly floured. . . . I can still see them firmly kneading—patting—rolling out biscuit dough on the old maple board. . . . One of my earliest childhood memories is of my grandmother's hands and of her soft voice drifting somewhere above them. . . . Cutting biscuits from the large white circle of dough was a daily activity at Old Ferguson Farm. This task was so ordinary and essential that we just did it—like morning and evening meditations, filled with love and sweet energies, and the strength of my grandmother's hands.[9]

The mastery of certain skills often figures in the essays. Many of them share the elegiac and laudatory tone of Kavasch's memory of her grandmother baking biscuits, but just as often, the memories are darker. The author of one essay emigrated from Pakistan. When her mother comes to visit, she is not satisfied with how her daughter prepares a classic family dish made with *karela*, or bitter melon. The cook and author tells her: "Amma, *karelas* in Lahore are different." "'I'll show you,'" her mother responds, "a small bony hand reaching for the vegetable knife. You can get the same results from this *karela*, only you must know what to do."[10] Daughters remember what they learned from their mothers, for better or worse.

A feeling of nostalgia often works in tandem with a sense of loss; a similar push and pull arises in these stories. Nestled within these women's narratives exists an ambivalence about the necessity of cooking. Caroline

Urvater aptly describes the impulse to be liberated from such obligations that are so embedded with complex emotions: "When my last child left home I put flowerpots on the burners on the stove. After twenty years of cooking I was through. My new motto was: any fool can cook, but it takes brains to find a good restaurant."[11] In refusing to turn on the flames, she humorously exposed a paradox of modern American life: the universal assumption that women will take responsibility for preparing all meals is not exactly universally *practiced*. Women can seek out many ways to get around the obligation, whether during the week or at a certain moment in the life course, or can try to rid themselves of the disagreeable task altogether.

Closer examination of women's relationship to cooking reveals regular confrontations and interference, not just today but also throughout history. Over the past decade, scholars have begun to "split" rather than "lump" domestic tasks and women's obligations, splitting (separating) the task of making meals from other chores. These more nuanced analyses have revealed more about our social relations and gender identities, tracing many opportunities to wield power or to reject norms in regards to food and nurturance. Today, American women can more actively choose their relationship to cooking, even if they continue to navigate broader cultural and social expectations.[12] Everyday cooking emerges as a situated practice rooted in cultural values and expectations yet at the same time less fixed in time and space than might be imagined.

IDEALS OF DOMESTICITY

Why, then, is a clearly fluid activity with multiple meanings so often categorized as a tedious social obligation?[13] Well, women remain the primary household cooks. Of course, this does not mean that men do not cook, but the majority of men who cook neither cook primarily for households (rather, they cook in commercial settings) nor are they the everyday cooks for these domestic groups (rather, they cook for special occasions). The job of transforming raw food into cooked meals, although not biologically linked to gender traits, remains, socially speaking, a women's task in the overall division of human household labor. They get the job done. From place to place and household to household, there are negotiations about everyday tasks, but these negotiations emerge in relation to categories of practice mediated by gender. As one of Carole Counihan's informants explains it: "My husband put it this way—he doesn't care about anything except to have the supper when he walks in the door. He don't [*sic*] care about laundry, a dirty house, unswept floors; the only thing he cares about is he has to have that dinner. So I knew what my focus had to be."[14]

In the daily allocation of household labor, social expectations also trump any individual capacity or engagement. The web of social connections that mediate cooking always emerges when people share personal stories about how they learned to cook; these stories never revolve around a narrative of rugged individualism, the narrator navigating some foreign territory without a map. Other people, particularly family members and notably mothers, play important roles. In some ways, even if the immediate goal might appear to be individual nourishment for survival, cooking is *always* a social task; nourishment, nurturance, and social identities are intertwined each and every day.

Cooking *could* be a matter of simply making the products of nature into a palatable concoction. However, social expectations mean adequate nourishment is about much more than caloric intake. What makes someone a "good" cook involves more than creating edible, or even tasty, food. Often, larger gender-specific role expectations also need to be fulfilled. The reflections of all the women discussed above, from the recent Pakistani immigrant to the middle-class single urbanite to the tired middle-aged farm wife, reveal a general discontentment with the symbolic load inherent in a female cook's everyday work. Such expectations of what makes a good cook, in this context, are not primarily aesthetic evaluations but rather social ones. In this casting, Carol's desire to make a fun meal instead of a necessary one might be an attempt to avoid her mother's lot in life, whereas the Pakistani mom's criticism of her daughter's improper use of the knife might be an attempt to bring her daughter closer.

Thus, American women may consider cooking a chore as much because of the social *ideals* each meal is supposed to fulfill as because of the *inconvenience* of chopping onions and making a good gravy after the roast has come out of the oven. The need to cook due to physiological *necessity* does not correlate simply with *nurturance;* rather, such connections are social matters. And in the United States, associations between making a meal and producing idealized domestic environments are crucial to understanding our culinary history. American home cooking, and the identity of home cooks, exists as part and parcel of the nation's "moral economy." In this characterization of the division of labor, women's work involves the creation of the American home, the responsibility of reproducing the cultural value and vision of a singular type of social unit: the nuclear family. Within these assumptions, nourishment and nurturance are one and the same.[15] The social obligation to fulfill such expectations—the sense that one must aspire to attain a home that is a "haven in a heartless world"—is made manifest within the daily round of household tasks, including the simmering soup on the stovetop and the neat and tidy family rooms. The morally inflected principles of conduct, in turn, are in part made and reinforced by the cooking of the soup and the cleaning of the counters. In the American cultural context, the association between women and making meals has long been intertwined with such moral claims. These ideals are often understood as burdensome, as we have seen above.

Making meals is experienced as a chore not only because it is a routine task but also because it is perceived as a *disagreeable* one. The roots of such burdens, as attested to in all of these women's memories of the relationships their mothers had to cooking, lie in disappointments that are externally created if internally experienced. The potential for a lack of alignment always exists between what happened and what was expected—between mother and daughter, between husband and wife, between grandmother and granddaughter. And there is a cultural cast to the disappointments; such failures and losses are part of a particularly American story that helps to fully explain the long arc of women's ambivalence toward cooking and their sense of these acts as burdensome.

As historian Nicole Tonkovich aptly states about American domestic life since the 1800s, "The seductiveness of a lovely and apparently effortlessly achieved domestic space and the discontent of those upon whom this illusion depends are not new phenomena."[16] The connection of the task of cooking to values of domesticity and nurturance can be linked to bourgeois standards of taste and tastefulness (which themselves can be traced back to European ideals), but there is an added complex moral dimension with a very Puritan inflection. By the early nineteenth century, books dispensing advice to women to help them become proper housekeepers were common. These books were popular with women, especially since by the mid-1800s, a higher percentage of Americans had incomes that allowed their families to move beyond subsistence, lived in urban areas, and were educated. Maintaining a house, feeding a family, and keeping that family happy and healthy were all part of a woman's job description, either as a wife and mother or as a single woman living with family members or others. Amelia Simmons's *American Cookery*, first published in 1796 and still in publication in the 1820s, educated Americans about European-style dishes using uniquely American ingredients (such as corn). Lydia Marie Child's *The American Frugal Housewife* (1835) was the first domestic manual-cum-cookbook written and published by and for an exclusively American audience. It was first of many books designed to instruct women not just how to do certain tasks but also how to do them right, with the goal of creating an ideal domestic environment for their families. During this period, the

American culinary discourse articulated the importance of a woman's *duty* to take care of the domestic sphere, and so by the end of the nineteenth century, interweaving values, practices, and identities had become standard fare. The chore of cooking became an obligation riddled with grand expectations.

Catherine Beecher and Harriet Beecher Stowe's *The American Woman's Home*, first published in 1869, is considered the most influential of the many books and treatises that have been published from the nineteenth century to today with explicit aims of educating and informing American women about their domestic duties. It became one of the best-selling books of the nineteenth century, and, as noted by Megan Elias, its success spurred the introduction of courses and the publication of manuals during the 1870s and 1880s: "A focus on helping women become good cooks by combining knowledge of tasks with a set of expectations as to the goals of such tasks became a new genre: the book covered many of the topics that home economics would later embrace, such as sanitation, interior design and health."[17] In many ways, the first page of the introduction to *The American Woman's Home* set the stage for generations of American women. The Beechers' argue that women need to accept the importance of their labors and then learn to do their daily tasks with skill and grace. The idea of "separate spheres" linked to noble social goals shaped the life experiences of American women. The Beecher sisters' agenda was complicated; first, they sought to clearly articulate women's roles; second, they wanted to vouch for their crucial role in the reproduction of American cultural life; and third, they bemoaned the fact that the work of these women did not share equal status with the increasingly differentiated work of paid labor outside of the home. But that was not all; they also felt the need to set increasingly high expectations for the household tasks they claimed were too easily belittled. They believed that "the honor and duties of the family state are not duly appreciated," and thus, "women are not trained for these duties as men are trained for their trades and professions, and that, as the consequence, family labor is poorly done, poorly paid, and regarded as menial and disgraceful."[18]

Manuals for "best domestic practices" are standard American fare, and these tomes have been an important genre for authors, publishers, and readers. One of the more fascinating aspects of the culinary narratives in nineteenth- and twentieth-century books is that the expectations *and* the disappointments of making family meals are very often linked. At the beginning of the chapter titled "Good Cooking" in the *American Woman's Home*, the Beechers warn: "You may make houses enchantingly beautiful, hang them with pictures, have them clean and airy and convenient; but if the stomach is fed with sour bread and burnt meats, it will raise such rebellions that the eyes will see not beauty anywhere."[19] As in Laura's and Carol's stories, the *necessity* of cooking is combined with the idea that making good meals fulfills expectations about providing for your family; much is at stake. The intersection of necessity and expectations creates social engagements that are not consistently meaningful or positive. For the Beecher sisters, as for generations of subsequent women struggling with the everyday task of cooking, the constant and messy act was best handled by "integrating [it] into a larger system of social, scientific, patriotic and evangelical meaning."[20] The Beechers' acceptance of the precept of "separate spheres" led them to seek household-level improvements of women's abilities. Making meals a more "important" endeavor certainly became central to culinary instructions; to be this type of a "good" cook was to embrace the nobility of the chore.

Thus, another recurrent theme of American culinary discourse is that women not only need to know how to cook but also need help learning how to be *good* cooks (in the moral sense of "good"); they need to understand that their duty goes far beyond providing sustenance. As Mrs. Mary J. Lincoln baldly puts it in the preface of her 1884 *Boston Cook Book: What to Do and What Not to Do in Cooking:*

> To one who from childhood has been trained in all details of housework, learning by observation or by actual books, the amount of ignorance shown by many women is surprising. That a person of ordinary intelligence presiding over her household can be satisfied with only a vague conception of the common domestic methods, or that any true woman can see anything degrading in any labor necessary for the highest physical condition of her family, would be incredible if the truth of it were not daily manifest.[21]

Lincoln clearly considers being capable of "good" domestic work a moral issue, both for the individual and for society. The challenge of meeting the appropriate standard of a tasteful home and a happy family was particularly acute when it came to preparing meals: "The statement will appear incredible to most people, and yet it is true, that many women do not know what the simplest things in our daily food are; cannot tell when water boils, or the difference between lamb and veal, lard and drippings. They cannot give the names of kitchen utensils; do not know anything about stoves, or how to pare a potato."[22] Lincoln consistently adds idealist aspirations and social obligations to her exhortations about cooking. For example, she uses this quotation from Milton as an epigraph:

> Not to know at large of things remote
> From use, obscure and subtle, but to know
> That which before us lies in daily life
> Is the prime wisdom.[23]

The implication is that the small everyday tasks of women's work can be understood as the pursuit of wisdom; in that regard, a woman must not be neglectful and must make sure to pursue these tasks in the right manner. In domestic treatises, especially those published up until the mid-twentieth century, the definition of cooking constantly shifts between a necessary evil and a noble task. It never ceases to be seen as a chore, but the meaning of cooking for the individual cook and the community of eaters becomes more explicitly delineated. At the same time, the tasks are rarely disassociated from the social expectations of the cook. As Charlotte Biltekoff observes of this historical period, a woman needs not only to cook but to cook well to be considered an upright and moral person: "Domestic scientists, the first of the modern dietary reformers, leveraged both the empirical and the ethical aspects of nutrition, applying its factual framework to the aims of moral uplift and social amelioration."[24] Apparently, according to the authors of these tomes outlining good and right living, teaching women involves addressing their ignorance as to making the necessary task of cooking into something both noble and good.

But how should women learn to cook and thus live up to the standards set for them? Not only is the act of making meals embedded in social relations, so is *learning* to make them. Female babies are not born imprinted (at least not yet!) with the knowledge needed to make the Sunday pot roast, enchiladas, or fried chicken. A means for transferring the knowledge deemed cultural suitable has to occur, because as Tim Ingold points out, "Skills are not transmitted from generation to generation but are regrown in each."[25] Being a cook helps a person perform duties required of a good person, but learning and performing this skill in what is considered to be a morally correct manner is not based on biological determinisms but rather on cultural values. Thus, for the nineteenth-century American domestic reformers and later for the twentieth-century home economists who promoted the moral goodness of bourgeois domestic life, the "problem" of women needing to learn to cook was pressing for two reasons: first, bad cooks created neglected families and poor citizens, and second, good cooks needed to be appreciated for their service to the preservation of the social fabric.

Domestic skills, however, were not considered formal "book learning," for these skilled tasks, which were increasingly considered crucial to the making of upright citizens, still remained chained to another reality, that of their mundane nature. During the nineteenth century, the lack of esteem given to women's domestic work and society's failure to see cooking as a skillful practice was often lamented, as here again articulated by the Beechers: "These duties of woman are as sacred and important as any ordained to man; and yet no such advantages for preparations have been accorded to her, nor is there any qualified body to certify the public that a woman is duly prepared to give proper instruction in her profession."[26] The tendency to relegate all the complex tasks and expectations involved in making a meal into the omnibus category of household chore became part of a larger set of social issues for American women reformers. If cooking skill was left unarticulated and considered primarily as an intuitive and experiential practice, then this daily labor was without social value, its meaning and significance hidden from view. As the activity of feeding a household became connected to women's roles as primary nurturers, the category of the "good cook" became something to fight for. Women needed to enhance the social value of cooking—they needed to show it to be more than mere tedium or necessity.

It can be argued that ambivalence toward making everyday meals has long run wide and deep in the case of American women because they are laboring with such a heavy symbolic load on their backs. Even though women can now vote, wear pants, and work outside the home, cooking as "the regular or daily light work of a household or farm" remains part of a woman's role as the center of family life. When it comes to this everyday chore, a woman's responsibility—creating sustenance and nurturance—is hard to ignore. Cooking needs to be elevated to more than "a routine task or job" to demonstrate the symbolic significance of a meal prepared by a woman for her family. However, the assumption that cooking is "a difficult or disagreeable task" tests the socially important gendered division of labor. Such classifications of cooking became part and parcel of the "problem" in various attempts to improve women's conditions and promote upright citizens.

HOW TO GUARANTEE AN UPRIGHT HOME? TEACHING ABOUT COOKING

Cooking manuals, classes teaching basic cooking (and other household skills), and cooking schools for amateurs and professionals became important means of embracing and elevating the chore of cooking for American women from the mid-nineteenth to mid-twentieth century. At the same time, no real, consistent, and universally shared "canon," no culturally shared system for attaining domestic culinary knowledge and skill, emerged. Perhaps due to the emphasis on the moral "goodness" of making meals, American women have never characterized care work of this manner as being without costs, but they have never cast it primarily as a type of technical know-how either, one where good meals involve a specific set of skills or more efficient practices. Apprenticeship (e.g., mother to daughter, teacher to student) remained the most consistent strategy of transferring this information. Learning to cook was always an *education*, but the transmission of knowledge from master to apprentice remained ad hoc, varied, and inconsistent. In the American context, culinary instruction has not been uniform, nor has it been uniformly successful.

For example, in Rebecca Sharpless's history of African American domestic workers, a young girl who worked as a domestic servant in the early twentieth century recalls a time when she was asked to prepare chestnuts but not given any specific instructions: "You know I had never fixed a chestnut before in my life. So I got me a hammer and hit this chestnut and boop. . . . I looked at that thing and I said where on earth did it go. Well, when I found it, I hit it harder; I thought Lord have mercy, how am I going to get these chestnuts fixed?"[27] She was expected to cook this dish, but her previous culinary education had not prepared her for doing so. In this case, the young girl did not go to her new employer to ask for help but rather reached out to a familiar social relation, her sister: "So I went to the telephone and I called her, I said, 'Frances, tell me how do you fix chestnuts?' She said put them in some water. I finally learned how."[28]

Over the course of the twentieth century, various strategies for "regrowing" cooking skill from generation to generation emerged, but there was no systematic, long-term integration developed that transcended gender roles and expectations. Among the reformers, the main mode of learning to cook remained osmosis, the unelaborated assumption that, as cooking happens primarily in the home, the standard-bearers of domesticity in any given home will facilitate such a process. Since the mid-nineteenth century, these efforts were primarily initiated by individual reformers and entrepreneurs. One of the country's first schools for culinary instruction was the Boston Cooking School. Founded in 1879 by the Women's Education Association, an organization run by important Boston women who were social reformers, the initial audience was young women who were expected to go on to manage their own households or become cooks in private homes.[29] Mary Lincoln was the school's first principal. She was so troubled by female ignorance of the important knowledge necessary to successfully run a household that she made it her mission to teach cooking through magazines, books, and classes. She helped develop the burgeoning attention to "cookery" (as it was called at the time) through courses, lectures, and the publication of the *New England Kitchen Magazine* and *Mrs. Lincoln's Boston Cook Book*. Fannie Farmer was also an advocate for culinary education. She took over the Boston Cooking School in 1891 and published the extremely popular *Boston Cooking-School Cook Book*, a relative of Lincoln's earlier work, in 1896. The cookbook, written with the tone of an expert lecturing novice cooks, sold 360,000 copies in its first twenty years.[30]

These efforts started to coalesce around the other long-term concern for champions of women's work: convincing women that mastering domestic tasks like cooking promoted the social and moral good. Lincoln and Farmer realized that learning to be a "good" cook, as defined by social aspirations, was not easy. The domestic science (later changed to home economics) movement sought to create an educational field around household tasks so that women could learn the skills deemed not just crucial but also appropriate. These standards, the underlying principles of home economics, were always more complicated then feeding hungry mouths.

How could women break free from their obligations to cook while simultaneously accepting the association between making meals and women's work? The early home economists aimed to liberate and elevate. As historian Megan Elias points out, "Home economists repeatedly identified 'drudgery' as their nemesis."[31] Early efforts to create an association championing everyday domestic tasks—which was to be known as the National Household Economics Association—failed, but a group of dedicated domestic scientists decided to persevere, organizing a series of conferences with the aim of "grant[ing] professional status and respectability to the discipline of housekeeping."[32] The first organized conference of home economists was held in 1899 in Lake Placid, New York. These meetings were held annually for a decade and were extremely influential to the movement. The women who attended them believed that cooking was not a chore or, perhaps more accurately, that it needed to be liberated from such a definition.

Marion Talbot, who taught at the University of Chicago, did not want the movement to be ridiculed or seen as inferior to the more exalted topics of the era, such as classics or philosophy: "Home economics must always be regarded in the light of its relation to the general social system, that men and women are alike concerned in understanding the processes, activities, obligations and opportunities which make the home and the family effective parts of the social fabric."[33] The reformers believed that good cooks made good citizens, and this idea of social obligation made sense given the larger goals of the domestic science and home economics movement. By the 1920s, the long-term institutionalization of culinary instruction succeeded within their larger systematic effort to elevate household work. The United States

Figure 3. Agricultural extension class on canning, Middlebury, Vermont, circa 1930. Box 2, folder 49, Agricultural Extension Service Photographs, Special Collections, University of Vermont Library.

Department of Agriculture developed and offered courses provided through its Agricultural Extension Service; these were designed for rural women and involved lessons with manuals of instruction for "proper" domestic life. The passage of the Smith-Lever Act in 1914 legitimized the work of the reformers and provided funds to support the development of home economics courses in elementary and secondary schools and to found departments of home economics in many colleges and universities. By the early twentieth century, there were home economics courses offered at over two hundred colleges and universities and twenty-eight programs that led to a bachelor's degree, and by the 1940s, home economics majors and even departments were commonplace, especially in land-grant universities.[34]

Making meals did not stop being part and parcel of women's everyday care work over the course of the twentieth century, but the means and modes of completing the task underwent transformations and became more externalized. By the 1950s, the tactic of creating value for women's work by teaching new generations the appropriate methods of becoming good cooks while simultaneously enacting moral principles began to be tested. For one, changes in the organization of the food system challenged the importance of the singular domestic household as the primary site of meal preparation. In her masterful *Something from the Oven*, Laura Shapiro argues that the American processed food industry, which took flight in the 1950s, created a new scenario for women, one of expanded choices, thereby allowing them to question their cooking obligations. New social conditions combined with technological innovations opened up new possible ways of categorizing cooking: "The table was set, the smiling family was gathered, the mother wore a pretty apron, and the food was frozen."[35] The result was a widening of the gap between *perception* and *practice* when it came to cooking in 1950s America. As preparing meals became increasingly less laborious with the introduction of new food products and cooking technologies, not only did cooking change but so did expectations; there were new means for meeting high culinary standards. Shapiro points out that the new products offered some space for women. They had more means to get the job done: "There was homemade custard; there was instant chocolate pudding; there was crème caramel," but she finishes this sentence with an important point: "[Women] had to know what kind of cook they wanted to be."[36] The technical skills and the definition of ingredients were shifting, and so "cooking" involved more agency than ever before. Women, though, still had many obligations to fulfill and decisions to make as to what to make for dinner every day.

HOME ECONOMICS AND DOMESTIC REALITIES

Barbara grew up in a small, working-class New England town during the 1960s and '70s. She is now a working woman, mother, and wife living in a university town not too far away. Her memories of learning to cook involve her female relatives: "I had two grandmothers who taught me how to cook. My mother was not interested in cooking. She [only] did it when she had to. One of my grandmothers lived with us, and the other one lived across the street, and so from as far back as I can remember I was encouraged to pull a chair up to the stove and start cooking."

Due to the influence of her grandmothers, she generally has a positive regard for making meals, although she sees her cooking methods as connected to but not replications of those of her mother and grandmothers. She explains that when she was growing up, no one ate dinner until her father came home from work. This is not the case for her family. She feeds the kids first, making foods they like (her son is a picky eater), and then she cooks a separate meal that she eats with her husband later in the evening. Barbara adopted this multiple-meal strategy partly because she (unlike her mother and grandmothers) works outside the home, which means that she must cook dinner after getting home at the end of the day, and partly because she does not plan her meals in advance. This allows her to quickly feed the children more basic meals and then spend more time on the meal she shares with her husband. Her cooking is always ad hoc and rushed, and her husband works long hours, so the full family meal is put on the back burner. As she says, "It's really a curse because I don't plan and I never shop with a list. . . . I just can't do it. So, that's a drag. I'll have in mind that I'm going to make something and then I don't have a key ingredient and then my whole plan is shot." She likes the physical process of cooking and does not mind making meals, but she cannot always meet her expectations; the result is that her children often eat chicken fingers and she and her husband often eat takeout.

The multiplicity of options of what to cook, when to cook, and how to cook and the multiple roles of the cooks (mother, wife, professional) changed the dynamics of making meals. Although Barbara's father may never have helped make dinner, Barbara's husband could. The problem of the "second shift"—the disproportionate amount of responsibility American working women take for domestic chores—is well documented.[37] However, when women discuss how decisions about the various tasks related to feeding their families (e.g., shopping, organizing, cooking, cleaning) are made, they frequently articulate the reason the men in the household do not do the cooking as their *choice*, often explaining that the men are deemed incapable of adequately upholding a perceived standard. When we film Barbara making dinner for her family, we ask whether her husband does much cooking. As she moves from the counter to the refrigerator and opens it up, reaches in, and pulls out a cucumber and red pepper, she says, "He definitely *can* cook. But he generally makes his food much spicier than I do, so I don't generally"—she drops her voice—"allow him to cook."

The complex tensions involved in accomplishing a daily task that intersects with strong affects and values have not diminished, even as women's expectations, obligations, and labors outside of the home have increased. For a 2008 study, a group of Canadian researchers interviewed families from three different ethnic groups about each family's relationship to foodwork (i.e., shopping, cooking, and cleaning). They wanted to understand why Canadian women spend twice as much time on these domestic tasks as their male spouses, even if both spouses are employed full-time outside the home.[38] They concluded that it was a case of gender expectations "gone underground." For example, in most families, foodwork is seen as simply part of the duties that come with being a mother. Asked whether her mother ever tired of doing most of the foodwork, one teen responded, "Usually we [say], but you're the Mum."[39]

Women's expectations for food and the importance of food to the health and well-being of each woman's social milieu are often seen as reasons

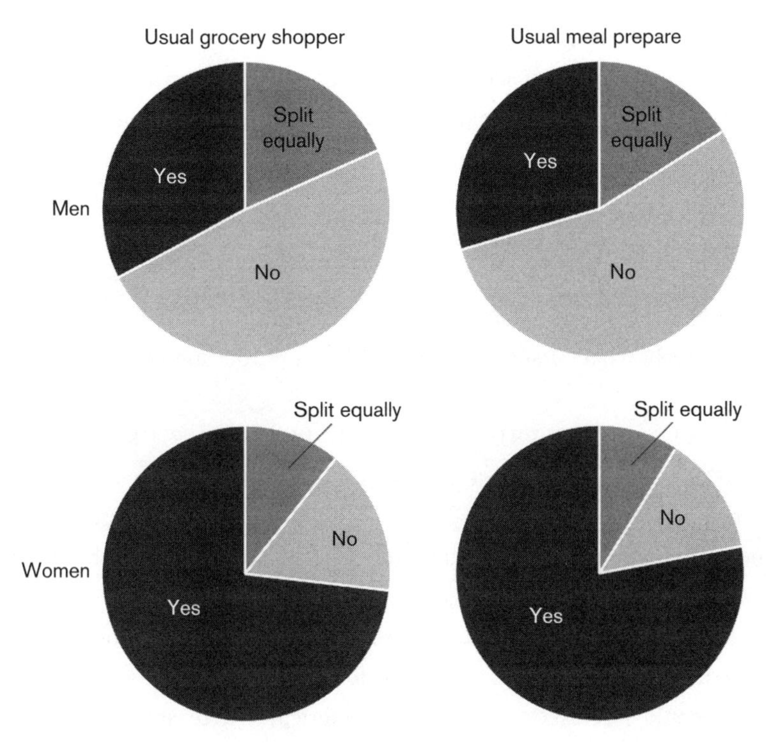

Figure 4. Perception of household work, women versus men. In 2008, women were more likely to report being the household grocery shopper and meal preparer; men were more likely to report either that they did not do the shopping or that the task was "split equally." *Source:* USDA Economic Research service using data from 2014 Bureau of Labor Statistics American Time Use Survey and ERS Eating Health Module, www.ers.usda.gov/amber-waves/2016/november/americans-spend-an-average-of-37-minutes-a-day-preparing-and-serving-food-and-cleaning-up.

women end up spending a larger percentage of their time in the kitchen: "Health is being employed, primarily by women, to justify women's over-involvement in foodwork" because providing food defined as "healthy" confirms a Western value as to what makes a "good mother."[40] Here again, the chore of cooking, theoretically a set of manual tasks, has become entangled with social obligations. However, these days, such obligations are not always explicit—"You *must* cook because you are a woman"—rather, they get articulated as a set of somehow objective *standards*. The families interviewed maintained that women do more of the foodwork because they have such high expectations. Thus, in the social unit of the family, "men, women and teens all agreed on women's exacting standards and desire for control as major reasons why women end up doing more foodwork."[41] If women would only reject the social values *ascribed* to cooking, then this chore would become, well, what? Easier to accomplish? Less burdensome?

MANUALS OF INSTRUCTION AND THE MOVE FROM DISAGREEABLE TASK TO JOYFUL ACT

The responsibilities for making meals remain women's work even if the expectations and methods for how to do it have shifted. Perhaps this is why cooking manuals, introduced starting in the 1860s as a means of setting the tone for American domestic life, have remained influential as a didactic tool of instruction. The methods and means for learning how to cook expanded after the mid-twentieth century, and Americans increasingly resided in urban and suburban locales. The first tasks for most cooks became deciding on a meal and then doing the shopping. Cooking was no longer a response to the bounty of a harvest or a means of figuring out yet another way to cook potatoes, corn, or cabbage. Carol relies not just on her mother but also on many other resources as she figures out what to cook: "I call my mom, I call my friends. I look in *The Joy of Cooking*—that's a very basic book that's like the 'Bible'—so I have some basic cookbooks that I use or [I] go online now, which is great." There is a repertoire of possible aids for learning how to cook; Carol uses many of them.

When Laura, who is in her mid-fifties, characterizes her relationship to cooking, she says: "There have been times when it's been a fun adventure, like when I got into *Larousse Gastronomique*. . . . [But] now it's more of a chore." She associates this chore view of cooking with her mother: "Sometimes, I just fall back and do the dreaded thing my mother did: . . . I don't want to think about cooking, so I just make the same thing every night without a cookbook for a month or two until my family screams."

Interestingly, Carol's mother's active cooking practice stopped with the end of her most intimate social obligations: "My mom is a perfect example [of someone for whom cooking is a chore]. She had had five kids, and when my father died and . . . she moved near my sister, she said, 'I'm done, I'm not cooking anymore.'" However, she still actively engages with the skill of cooking, continuing to encourage her children to keep learning about and exploring this domestic duty: "She still clips out recipes and sends them to us. She cooked every night, and she was an awesome cook, but for her it was a chore." Even with all the helpful hints and didactic instruction available, telling people why or how to cook does not necessarily translate into either the desire to cook or the action of cooking. Carol's mother's current relationship with cooking represents what has become *normal* practice today: episodic cooking activity but consistent engagement with culinary knowledge and possibility.

One explanation for women's ability to keep up to date on culinary advancements without ever picking up a knife or heating a pan lies in the myriad resources people can now access to learn about cooking. You no longer have to learn by doing; now you can learn by reading, listening, or watching. For over a century, the printed word figured prominently in helping women figure out what to make for dinner and why. First, there was the Beechers' *The American Woman's Home*, which was followed by Mary Lincoln's *Boston Cook Book* and Fannie Farmer's perennial favorite, the *Boston Cooking-School Cook Book*. Then there were the home economics courses that started to be offered by high schools, colleges, and universities, with required texts and curricula.

Yet the success of certain cookbooks—the books that became crucial to American cuisine and culture, the required household manuals that

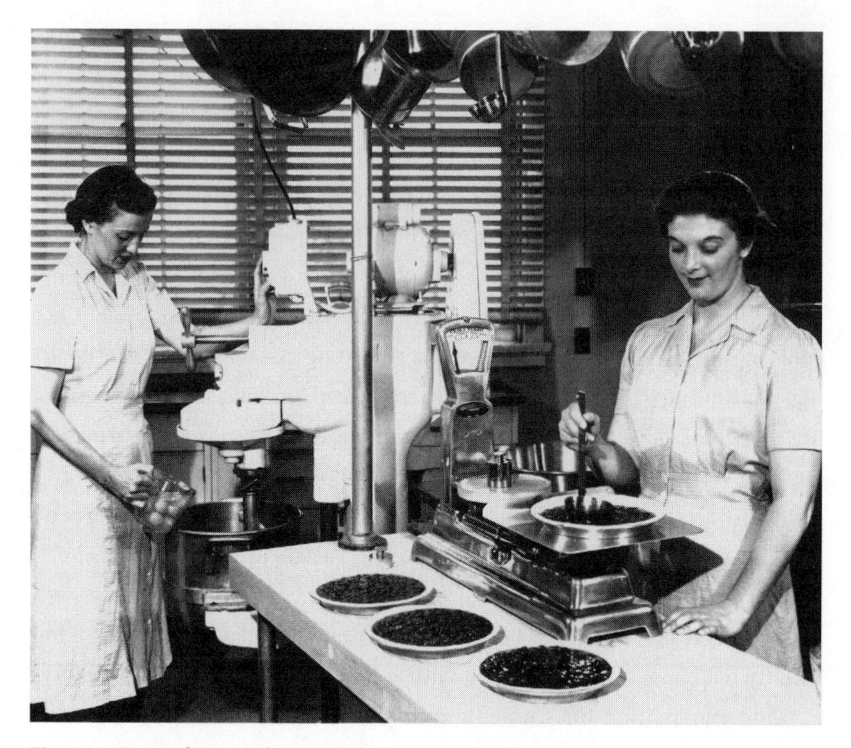

Figure 5. Women learning how to make berry pies, circa 1950. University of Vermont School of Home Economics Records, Publicity Photographs, Special Collections, University of Vermont Library.

transcended class, ethnicity, and race in their popularity—do reveal what messages are most compelling to those trying to make a meal every day, in word if not always in any final deed. And in the twentieth century, no cookbook sold more copies or was more influential than *The Joy of Cooking*. This book, first published in 1931, has been continuously in print for over eighty years, with millions of copies (by some accounts over 26 million) sold.[42] There have been seven editions, and each has responded to continuities and changes in American home cooking. Irma Rombauer, from an elite upper-middle-class family in Saint Louis, Missouri, has always been listed as the first author, although her daughter, Marion Rombauer Becker, and then her grandson, Ethan Becker, were added as coauthors for later editions.[43] Irma wrote the first edition of the book after falling on hard times after her husband died in 1930, in the middle of the Depression. Her initial goals were quite modest: she wanted to pull together recipes from family and friends for useful and approachable dishes for feeding families.[44] She had three thousand copies printed and set about selling them to anyone who showed an interest. As culinary historian Anne Mendelson points out, one of the great gifts of *The Joy of Cooking* is that it was "written with no thought of posterity," and thus "many levels of taste . . . cheerfully coexist."[45] Rombauer's main focus, from the first edition through all subsequent editions, was to improve how cookbooks provided culinary instruction. She realized that women were no longer primarily learning how to cook through "long hours spent daily in handling the tools of the trade and constant reinforcement from other people engaged in the same work on the same spot."[46] She wanted to build a better manual for cooking, and she succeeded. *The Joy of Cooking* was the first "text" many women consulted when they started to run a household.

The book was embraced by home cooks throughout the United States; in fact, *The Joy of Cooking* can be seen as the first truly *national* cookbook. The book's breezy tone, encyclopedic approach, and innovative recipe format appealed to new cooks all over the country. It bore similarities to earlier books published by the Beecher sisters and others but was also very different. Initially, the striking difference was its style. Two elements of stylistic divergence from earlier cookbooks were concrete and tangible: first, the ingredients were separated out from the methods more distinctly than in most earlier cookbooks, and second, the recipes were organized as variations on a theme. For example, in the soup chapter, there is a recipe for Soup Stock I, followed by a recipe for Soup Stock II. Then, there is the recipe for Left-Over Soup:

2 cups meat and bone	1 cup tomatoes
5 cups water	2 teaspoons barley
Left-over gravy	1/2 teaspoon sugar
1 cup vegetables (carrots turnips, celery)	Salt
	Paprika
1 onion	Celery salt

If clear soup is desired, omit the gravy and the barley. Follow the method for making Soup Stock II.[47]

This systematic approach of providing a recipe and then referring to other recipes was unique and helpful to American housewives trying to put dinner on the table.

There are other reasons for the initial success of the cookbook as well as for its longevity as the must-have book for millions of Americans, but above all, there was Rombauer's tone and tenor. Rombauer understood that many, if not most, women considered cooking a chore, a necessary evil of domestic life. She fully acknowledged this ambivalence while simultaneously encouraging that women rise above it and take on cooking as an adventure. As she states in the foreword to the 1946 edition, "This book is the result of a long practical experience, a lively curiosity and a real love for cookery. In it I have made an attempt to meet the needs of the average household, to make palatable dishes with simple means and to lift everyday cooking out of the commonplace."[48] It is almost as if Rombauer accepted that the regular and routine work of cooking was indeed the "regular work of a household" but resisted any associated judgments. However, she refused to accept that cooking was "a disagreeable task" or a form of drudgery. Julia Child even mentioned the book while reminiscing about her enjoyment of cooking in an article published in *McCall's Magazine* in 1975: "Just married, . . . I found

I loved my new role as family cook, although even with *Gourmet Magazine* and Mrs. Joy [shorthand for *The Joy of Cooking*] at my side, I never managed to get dinner on the table until nine or ten o'clock in the evening."[49]

Mendelson argues that even the book's title stakes a claim against the pervasive sentiment that cooking was both a chore and a noble obligation: "Marion and her mother knew very well that people did not find joy where they do not perceive freedom, control, leisure or esteem."[50] She points out that the book appeared during the Depression, a time when many middle-class women could no longer afford a cook or even a domestic to come in and cook at least some of the meals. Many women had to shift from seeing cooking as a task they supervised to cooking as a task they had to perform: "To put the matter in bald historical perspective, such things were not socially appropriate to cooking in the days when it was [only] done by servants or those too poor to hire them."[51] Rombauer's brilliance was thus to "assure people that their new responsibility really wasn't menial, that the social implications of cookery could now be enlarged to include 'joy,' a discreet rearrangement of necessity so as to make it not only a virtue but a delight."[52] Rombauer was perhaps also able to strike the vein of exalted obligation that had first been mined by the Beecher sisters seventy-five years earlier and to rework the definition of cooking as both a joy and an obligation for the context of her contemporaries.

At the same time, Rombauer understood the landscape of kitchen work in the twentieth century. She knew that many women needed help learning to cook: "Encouragement came from many sources—especially from the eloping bride who telegraphed her family: 'Am married—order announcements—send me a Rombauer cookbook at once'; . . . and from an unknown Cincinnati maid who stole her mistress' copy of *The Joy of Cooking*." Her ability to acknowledge her readers' skills and varied backgrounds while also providing inspiration to move beyond the everyday is clear in every chapter. The sauce chapter includes recipes for hollandaise sauce, easy hollandaise sauce, cheese sauce I (with mild cheese), cheese sauce II (with processed cheese), chestnut sauce, and barbecue sauce. Rombauer and her daughter Marion (who became her collaborator and continued to oversee subsequent editions after Irma's death in 1962) understood that American home cooks increasingly had greater *aspirations* than *skills*. As a young female college student explained in a fan letter to Rombauer, dated September 29, 1954, "The most unique thing about your book is the fact that it assumes the reader knows *nothing*—which in my case wasn't far from wrong!"[53]

By the 1975 edition, which was published after the advent of the women's movement, the decline of domestic servants, and the increased editorial involvement of Rombauer's daughter, the tone had shifted somewhat. The possible ways of using *The Joy of Cooking* had been cast wider, as Marion notes in the preface: "Choose from our offerings what suits your person, your life-style, your pleasure; and join us in the joy of cooking." But beyond advocating for the joy possible in finding a dish for dinner, she also acknowledges that the cook may not know how to cook it. She continues the emphasis on cooking technique when she describes how to use the index: "There is a back-door key, too—the Index. This will open up for you and lead you to such action terms as simmer, casserole, braise and sauté; such descriptive ones as printanière, bonne femme, rémoulade, allemande and meunière."[54] She adds that cooks should now also understand nutrition, and the edition includes a new section that aids the home cook in trying to navigate such knowledge.

Irma and Marion took their roles as teachers to fledgling American cooks very seriously. They wanted to help people learn how to cook and to celebrate everyday cooking. From the very first edition, Rombauer adopted a no-fuss approach for her recipes. They were short, to the point, and very flexible. In the soups chapter, she has a section called "Emergency Soups." The strategy is as follows: "Here are two recipes for delicious soup, delicately flavored and quickly made. They are neither thick nor thin. Both call for stock. If this is not available, use Savita, or beef cubes, in this case an acceptable substitute."[55] The author never *judged* or *cajoled;* rather, her tone made readers, who were often alone and befuddled in the kitchen, feel supported.

In 1933, when Bobbs-Merrill Publishing House first considered publishing *The Joy of Cooking*, the manuscript was sent to a number of outside experts, many of them home economists or nutritionists. Many of the reviewers commented on Rombauer's tone and tenor. One of them noted: "Another more or less unusual feature of the book is the 'casual culinary chat' that runs through it. . . . This gives an attractive, informal note to the book, and should be particularly helpful to an inexperienced cook."[56] Anne Ross, a reviewer who compared *The Joy of Cooking* to other popular selling cookbooks of the era—*The Boston Cookbook*, *The Settlement Cookbook*, and *The Mystery Chef's Own Cookbook*—said, "It is also, like *The Mystery Chef*, written in a friendly, informal style, addressed not only to professional or at least whole-souled cooks, but also to amateurs, hobbyists, business men and women who have little time for elaborate recipes, but wish to cook well and efficiently."[57] Although Rombauer was interested in passing on her culinary knowledge to others and identified herself as a teacher, she was not didactic or moralistic, which was a welcome relief to many. An early review in her hometown newspaper remarked: "A running accompaniment of amusing comment, always apropos, anecdotes, personal experiences, witticisms, characteristic of the author as her friends know her, keep you entertained as well as instructed."[58] It could be argued that Rombauer understood that what American cooks wanted above all was a knowledgeable *friend* in the kitchen, a friend who fully understood the many expectations that came with the decision of what to make for dinner.

Irma and Marion recognized and anticipated the new normal for American cooks that was just starting to emerge in the 1930s and was fully in place by the turn of the twenty-first century. Considering cooking a chore had become one choice among many. There is an increasingly variable sense of *duty* in our relationship to cooking that transforms every decision when making a meal. In *Culinary Art and Anthropology*, anthropologist Joy Adapon puts cooking at the center of an extended analysis of the aesthetics of Mexican cuisine. She looks closely at the importance of cooking to the communication of emotion and sentiment, not simply within a household but also within a community. Duty and drudgery are not the dominant tropes. In her interviews with both home and commercial cooks, she found that although some of them described preparing food as a chore, they more readily articulated the emotional and artful aspects of the embodied knowledge of cooking. Her informants—a mix of amateur, semiprofessional, and professional cooks—described their cooking as the ability "to draw upon a 'stock of knowledge' that is stored in their heads, hearts, hands, noses and mouths . . . rather than strictly following a recipe."[59] Adapon argues that Mexican women embrace a category of creativity when it comes to cooking, perhaps to help them find some agency within fairly constrained circumstances.

Cooking *can* be categorized as chore, but is it solely understood or practiced in that manner? The Rombauers' advocacy for the joy of cooking succeeded because, by the mid-twentieth century, American women's perception of cooking as a chore was not absolute. Rather, their attitudes and actions morphed and shifted with the moment-by-moment, day-by-day, and year-by-year obligations to cook. To posit that making a meal always feels like chore, a burden of a woman's domestic responsibilities, sidelines moments of creativity and days of engagement. Cooking always has the *potential* to be transformed into something more than an obligation, even if such a transformation does not always occur. The case can be made that when associating cooking and domestic chores, people know that the map (i.e., calling cooking a chore) is not the territory (i.e., all the possible meanings of cooking for all involved).

Laura's wish for herself as a cook is "to feel more creative. It's difficult to whip up creativity when I am doing it all the time. Some people just exude that, but I have to work at it." Carol has managed to hold on to the creativity in her culinary practice; she wants to avoid feeling like cooking is a chore. With her more involved daily responsibilities to others in her household, Laura does not have that level of flexibility. As Carol sees it, if you have cooking obligations toward others, then it is much harder to keep the chore out of the task: "I try not to get her [my mom] to put that [cooking as a chore] on me because for me it's not yet a chore because I don't have to cook for people. . . . I think it's a generational thing." However, the variability has not rendered the "chore" category completely obsolete.

In the midst of such fluidity, Carol still relies on others when figuring out how to cook. She outlines her strategy: "Well, I call my mom. 'Yeah mom, what is so and so?' And it's funny because if you're using an older recipe it might be called something different than it is now, and so she'll say, 'Oh, it's this.'"

The task at hand is not always obvious, especially if the skills involved are new or being tested in certain ways. On the one hand, the need to consult others—relatives, friends, trusted culinary experts—could be seen as particular to cooking, since this household chore retains a strong, possibly unbreakable link, to ideals of nurturance. On the other hand, perhaps cooking's ubiquity highlights a broader reality about human social experience.[60] Ingold argues that *all* tasks are socially embedded activities; without the requirement of making meals at home, how do bonds between mothers and daughters get made or when does family life happen? But such tasks may no longer be for only certain sorts of social obligations and aspirations. We all learn skills for the required tasks of everyday life; the skills we must learn versus the skills we choose to learn might reveal the transforming circumstances of our social relationships and our social identity. The young African American girl mentioned earlier in the chapter consults her sister when she can't figure out how to prepare chestnuts. Carol, when telling her story says, "I try not to get her [my mom] to put that [cooking as a chore] on me because for me it's not yet a chore." Both of these women need their relations to help them succeed at their cooking tasks, but the two women do not share the same feelings about performing them. The African American girl needs to please her new employer. Carol wants to display her independence and creativity. Cooking happens. And while a woman cooks, numerous identities are potentially enacted and confirmed. Sometimes, cooking is a chore. But not always, and not forever.

CHAPTER TWO

Cooking Is an Occupation

Working at a nonprofit job, I would routinely be getting out of work at seven or eight o'clock at night and just be too fried to cook. So, I would say [on] an average week I was eating out probably three nights a week. [At restaurants,] I look for the variety of what I either don't know how to prepare at home or [am] just kind of too lazy to prepare at home. I can tell things are really fresh, and . . . it's an activity. It's like, "Can we get takeout?" . . . [is just] like, "Wow, can we go to the zoo?" It's got this exciting [feel] to me, and it also always happens on a day when I don't want to cook.

Rebecca, twenty-eight years old

The drudgery of cooking no longer defines the practice. These days the tasks of meal preparation can be taken care of on an ad hoc basis, systematically, or not at all. Perhaps the privilege of being a modern American cook lies in the ease by which you can decide *not* to cook but still be fed. Whole ingredients are still transformed before they become the components of a desired dish—an entire chicken is processed into parts (including boneless skinless breasts), wheat berries are milled into all-purpose flour, cows are milked, and butter is churned—and then the chicken, butter, and flour get turned into a dish. But these days, someone else can do all that work because the labor of cooking happens as much outside the home as inside it. Rebecca, a young, single professional living in a small city, reflects such ease in her relationship to the obligation of cooking: Why bother? And as she points out, going out to eat doesn't just take care of the chore of preparing a meal, it can also be an adventure and a form of entertainment.

The evidence is clear; over the past seventy years, we have transitioned from spending the majority of our food dollars on meals prepared at home to spending most of our food budget outside of the home, relying on other people and places to make our meals. Home cooks can now take advantage of an expansive set of choices, giving them the opportunity to be "some days and sometimes" cooks rather than "everyday and all the time" cooks. This transition started almost a century ago and is seemingly permanent. Historians estimate that prior to the Industrial Revolution, almost all food preparation occurred at the household level, with only 3–5 percent of food costs (on average) spent on food eaten away from the home.[1] The United States Department of Agriculture began officially reporting national statistics on annual food expenditures in 1929. At that time, Americans spent 85 percent of their total food budget on food prepared and consumed at home and only 15 percent on food eaten outside the home.[2] With every decade, we have spent less and less on food purchases for home-cooked meals; in 2012, Americans spent over 50 percent of their total food budget on foods eaten outside the home. In 2010, we spent just 23 percent of our total food budget on "unique ingredients (basic or complex)," according to the United States Department of Agriculture's 2014 report "U.S. Households' Demand for Convenience Foods"; the rest of our food dollars were spent on foods that had already been prepared in some way.[3] The report defines basic ingredients (5 percent of the total food budget) as: "Raw or minimally processed foods used in producing a meal or snack that are generally composed of a single ingredient, such as milk, dried beans, rice, grains, fresh meat, fruits, vegetables, poultry, and seafood." The definition of complex ingredients slips between products that were untouched and those that had been touched by other hands (18 percent of the budget): "Processed foods used in producing a meal/snack that generally, though not always, are composed of multiple ingredients. Examples include bread, pasta, sour cream, sauce, cereal, frozen meat/poultry/seafood, canned meat/poultry/seafood, and lunch meat."[4] For most home cooks, all these ingredients would count as items that could be used to create a meal "from scratch." Ready-to-cook foods (8 percent of the total), the final group of food purchases that require the touch of the home cook, are dishes that are already prepared and primarily require heating and serving; they include frozen entrees, frozen pizzas, and prepared soups and chili.[5] The remaining part of the budget was spent on ready-to-eat meals, fast-food meals, and sit-down meals and snacks purchased and consumed outside the home.

Over the past century, the time spent on kitchen work has also decreased. During the 1920s, the average amount of time Americans spent cooking each day was three hours; by the late 1960s, this had dropped to two hours per day. And the downward trend has continued; scholars estimate that in the 1990s, the average time spent on active cooking was less than an hour per day. The most recent American Bureau of Labor Statistics study, the 2013 "American Time Use Survey" (a nationally representative survey providing estimates of how, where, and with whom Americans spend their time) puts kitchen work at an estimated forty-eight minutes per day.[6] At an even more granular level, the survey indicates that individuals in the United States are now spending an average of twenty-seven minutes per day on home cooking (seventeen minutes for males, thirty-seven minutes for females), and another seven minutes on food cleanup and other kitchen tasks (three minutes for males, eleven minutes for females).[7] Many meals are made every day, but home cooks are less often responsible for preparing them, and when they do cook meals, they spend less time making them.

The need to source nourishment no longer entails the obligation to create a nourishing meal for yourself or others. For example, Sarah's thoughts and actions are not constrained by her gender or social expectations. Sarah, a young single woman living in Boston, agreed to be observed and videotaped while making dinner. Her meal is a cabbage, potato, and kielbasa dish; the recipe is from a friend, and Sarah has made the dish once before. She is nervous having someone watch her cook, which leads her to talk about a friend, a chef, who was recently filmed doing a cooking demonstration as part of a television show. She says that her chef friend told her that the cooking process seemed so different when doing and explaining at the same time. Even though she has no professional training and she does not cook all that regularly, Sarah isn't afraid to provide explanations, and she doesn't mind imagining herself as a chef. She does not ascribe her culinary knowledge to her mother or grandmother; rather, she relies on professional cooks. She regularly watches shows on the Food Network and recently read Anthony Bourdain's *Kitchen Confidential.* Her aspirations as a cook are influenced by those who now make our meals: "I think in general now, it [gives you] cachet to be friends with a chef. They're the cool person at the party." As she bustles around her small galley kitchen in an urban apartment, pulling out a knife, measuring the sugar and salt, washing and then cutting up the cabbage, Sarah admits that her worry revolves around messing up the recipe. As the session continues, she explains less and less and instead talks more about her choices around making meals. She has not cooked much over the previous weeks ("but I end up spending so much [money] on crap") and so is making a large portion of the sausage dish to eat for dinners and lunches over the course of the week. Both her knowledge and her practice rely on a set of porous boundaries between the private and public spheres; she has a "the world is my oyster" sensibility about making meals.

Sarah enjoys food and is a curious and relatively confident cook who does not feel constrained by a certain identity or the need to cook every day. Rebecca also has an unencumbered relationship to meal preparation, as her statements about cooking at home or eating at a restaurant testify. Does their flexible, catch-as-catch-can approach reveal and reflect long-term transformations of how, why, where, and when we cook? Over the past century, Americans (if considered in totality, as the national surveys mentioned above have done) have gained many more choices and thus certain freedoms when it comes to answering the question "What should we have for dinner tonight?" Sarah and Rebecca's power to choose whether to labor to buy ingredients and prepare a meal at home after a long day at work reveals so many of the social and cultural shifts experienced by Americans, especially American women. Sarah and Rebecca are not simply or solely female home cooks; they work and have money and a sense of autonomy. There are also many other people who can be relied on to acquire food that has been transformed from whole ingredients to dishes to make a meal. Both Sarah and Rebecca are free to choose how, where, and when they will have their breakfast, lunch, snacks, and dinner.

How can such freedoms be explained? Changing gender roles and responsibilities; new realities when it comes to wage earnings and the overall cost of living; and the changing organization of social life are all crucial factors. But what about the everyday aspects of Rebecca and Sarah's liberation, those most directly related to their decision to eat out or order in as often as cooking their own dinner? These involve understanding the wider horizons of food choices available to Americans each and every day.

It has often been argued that the greater array of possibilities when it comes to home meal preparation in America can be explained by transformations in technology, which facilitated the shift away from people and to machines. Thus, all new manners of making food—for example, the way chickens are raised, killed, plucked, boned, packaged, breaded, fried, and then shipped to be sold in a distant retail outlet—have allowed machines to replace humans. This argument also associates these changes with the rising power and influence of the "food industry," the businesses—and increasingly the multinational corporations—that make the packaged and processed foods that now dominate supermarket and convenience store shelves. Critics of the contemporary food system link the rising availability of such options with a decline in home cooking.[8] To some extent, this is true (and those consequences will be explored in later chapters). However, machines alone cannot make the chicken and other ingredients become a platter, tray, or box of fried chicken or chicken Cordon Bleu. And our decisions, as reflected in Rebecca's comments, do not always involve turning to packaged and processed foods. Machines are an important part of our food system, but when we sit down to eat, whether in a restaurant or at home, many human hands continue to be involved in producing the meal on the table.

Also, there remains a tendency to assume that eating food that has been cooked for you (whether by people or machines) is a relatively new phenomenon, linked to the rise of industrial modes of production and the development of mass-scale processed food, an unfortunate by-product of the food industry. However, even with the advent of mechanical feather pluckers and a robot capable of removing chicken legs from chicken breasts and then filleting the breasts, people have continued to labor to put food on someone's table, even if it is not exclusively their own. Over the course of the past century, it has become easy, almost *easiest*, to buy our way out of the everyday chore of making meals by moving the acts of cooking away from ourselves and our daily lives, and to figure out the best means of letting cooking be an activity other people do. In the contemporary history of cooking, machines and the associated industrial mode of production are key figures. But additionally, other *people* help us to cook or not to cook.

Relying on the emergence of "technofixes" to explain the long-term rise in the expenditures of Americans on meals made outside the home erases an equally powerful reality: this shift is also due to consistent efforts to have other people cook for us, first inside and now outside the home. From the founding of the Republic, people of means have always been able to find someone else to make meals for them. We might be a nation of eaters, but we have never really been a nation best represented by the motto "In every house resides a cook." In fact, looking closely at labor documents, cookbooks, and other treatises on American domestic life from the past century (and earlier) reveals that the idea that other people cook for you has existed, and continues to exist, not merely as a *suggestion* but rather more fully, as an *assumption*. Rebecca's choice to eat at restaurants and the reality that many hands touch our food might be a case of old stew on new plates. Innovation and technology alone have not permitted us to be primarily a nation of eaters. Rather, as has always been the case, the labor of cooking remains central to our particular national history of getting dinner on the table. But not everyone, or even every woman, is a cook. During the same period that we have reduced the amount of time we spend in active home meal preparation and increased our annual expenditures on food prepared away from home, there has been a significant increase in the number of paid cooks, which has helped make such freedoms possible. American meal preparation has always relied on an invisible army of laborers. This invisible army has allowed many Americans to consume many of their meals without making any effort to acquire ingredients, plan, and cook.

> Recipe for Cheese Custard Pie (4 Servings)
> In Switzerland we had a vile tempered cook named Marguerite. Her one idea, after being generally disagreeable, was to earn enough to own a small chalet on some high peak where she could cater to mountain climbers. While she was certainly not born with a silver spoon in her mouth—although it was large enough to accommodate several—I am convinced that she arrived with a cooking spoon in her hand. . . . The following Cheese Custard pie was always served in solitary state. Its flavor varied with Marguerite's mood and her supply of cheese.[9]

Irma Rombauer knew her audience. The first edition of *The Joy of Cooking* was published in 1931, and she wrote it in large part because she had a reputation among the bourgeois residents of Saint Louis, Missouri, for being a wonderful cook and hostess. Her introduction to the recipe for Cheese Custard Pie reveals certain givens about cooking at that time: making a meal was a must, but if you could afford to have someone else do the work, albeit grumpily, there was no sense of social admonishment. In fact, many middle- and upper-class Americans widely assumed that having and managing a home *required* household help. Since the earliest days of the founding of the nation, slaves, country girls, and new immigrants worked as domestic cooks for more wealthy families, preparing the everyday meals. Rombauer mentions several domestic servants as sources for her recipes in her breezy introductions; these women were clearly as crucial to the creation of this nationally beloved tome as were her friends from the social clubs and well-off neighborhoods of Saint Louis. Her introduction to the custards section of the book charmingly conveys the importance of the sweets course for Americans: "A family I know had a colored cook who always urged them, when they were children, to eat sparingly of the meat course and to leave a little room for the 'hereafter.' I have prepared so many, many 'hereafters' for children and grown-ups, that I feel like Christopher Morley's heroine, who made an anthology of the loaves of bread she had baked."[10] However, Rombauer's matter-of-fact mention of the "colored cook" hints at other truths about American cooks and cooking: Above all, if at all possible, try to have other people cook *for* you. Also, your race, class, and ethnicity might make a great difference in whether you are cooking and whether your cooking labor is for your own family or for someone else's (or both).

The obligation to prepare a meal for the family, to keep the domestic household running smoothly, has always required women to *think* about dinner, but such responsibilities have not always required them to use physical labor and culinary skills to get it on the table. Historically, a woman was able to satisfy her domestic obligations to provide meals if she could afford to bring somebody (usually also a woman) into her home to cook for the family. The American approach to cooking has always involved certain flexibilities in the connection between the cook and the eater. This might be due to the disruptive qualities of the nation's history and culture. The genealogies of so many American citizens involve migrations, disjunctures, and reinventions. Such mobility had consequences for American cooking and cuisine. These include what was cooked and who did the cooking. Often, long-standing embedded and embodied culinary traditions and expectations were severed. More importantly, multitudes of migrants streaming into cities and towns and looking for employment made it fairly simple to find someone else to cook for you. At the same time, so many people's choice of domicile was determined by mobility, particularly in terms of economic opportunity in expanding urban areas, and thus fully functional domestic settings were not available to everyone. Despite the persistent cultural assumption that meals are made by women for their families, there is plenty of evidence to contradict it: boardinghouses, taverns, restaurants, canteens, cafeterias—whatever might work to feed the many Americans moving from other nations, from the country to the city, from birthplace to workplace. One could say that throughout most of America's history, *many* hands have made our food.

The reasonableness of bringing in others to cook is intrinsic to the American culinary tradition (although being able to make this actually happen is variable). In fact, during the nineteenth and much of the twentieth century, managing domestic servants and teaching them both moral and household economies was central to the identities of many middle- and upper-class Americans. Certainly, the Beechers thought having domestic servants was a normal and necessary practice for households of a certain class:

> Again, American women must not try with three servants to carry on life in the style which in the old world requires sixteen; they must thoroughly understand, and be prepared *to teach*, every branch of housekeeping; they must study to make domestic service desirable, by treating their servants in a way to lead them to respect themselves and to feel themselves respected; and there will gradually be evolved from the present confusion a solution of the domestic problem which shall be adapted to the life of a new and growing world.[11]

The Beechers felt that there were a number of "domestic problems" that needed to be addressed. As the nineteenth century progressed, they argued, women were falling short in both their aspirations and their actions. Once a woman found someone else to cook for her—considered a right of the educated and moneyed classes—the obligation was to teach her cook, to transmit the social values and obligations involved in creating a proper American home, to *elevate* domestic work. Yet the Beechers' frustrations with American women went beyond lazy supervisors who were unwilling to instruct their servants in the domestic arts and extended to those women who seemed to be perfect candidates for servant cooks. As they put it, "Beyond all doubt, the labors of a well-regulated family are more healthy, more cheerful, more interesting, because less monotonous, than the mechanical toils of a factory; yet the girls of New England, with one consent, preferred the factory."[12] These country girls were rejecting domestic work, which had historically helped them support themselves, in favor of manufacturing work, partly for social reasons and partly for financial reasons. The Beechers believed that it was because these girls preferred to be with "their own station" rather than working for families where they would be "by the side of others of their own age who assumed as their prerogative to live without labor."[13] During the second half of the nineteenth century, domestic ideals and domestic realities seemed to be moving further apart with the emergence of new opportunities for paid work for women, particularly in the newly emerging and expanding manufacturing sector.

These realities were not identical for all young women seeking employment. Paid domestic cooks were still in demand, and women could be found to do the work. African American female cooks had essential roles in numerous American households, especially in the South.[14] This was not always by choice. As John Egerton points out: "Throughout 350 years of slavery, segregation, and legally enforced white primacy, the vast majority of women of African ancestry in the South—and many of women of European lineage who oversaw their work—lived lives tightly circumscribed within hailing distance of the region's domestic kitchens."[15] These women, "who did much of the cooking in early American kitchens," contributed greatly to the emergence of the specific skills and knowledge necessary to making a "proper" American meal.[16] The African American men and women authors whose cookbooks are beautifully documented in Toni Tipton-Martin's *The Aunt Jemima Code* demonstrate complex culinary practices and systems for effectively making meals, whether these men and women were working as domestic servants, caterers, or chefs. The stereotype of African Americans as docile servants who are always willing to serve permeates the texts and images of many cookbooks Tipton-Martin surveys (many are similar to the 1927 *Mammy's Cookbook*, the cover of which features a smiling African American woman with a headscarf). She argues, however, that these books contradict another set of pervasive beliefs about African Americans cooks, which she labels the "Aunt Jemima Code." Namely, this code assumes "that all black cooks, chefs and cookbook authors worked by natural instinct."[17] In fact, the opposite argument can be made: the building blocks of American cuisine—the skill and knowledge required to plan and cook meals each and every day—were learned, created, and reproduced first and foremost by paid cooks, expert practitioners at their craft.

Perhaps the skillfulness of cooks who do such work as an occupation rather than as an obligation has been hidden from view due to powerful cultural assumptions about the *moral* implications of domestic tasks in American homes. The moral high ground was always the final destination for reformers like the Catherine Beecher, Harriet Beecher Stowe, Mary Lincoln, and Fannie Farmer. These women believed that the noble goals of domestic life were under assault, and these beliefs remained consistent from the late nineteenth century until well into the twentieth century. But these claims kept losing ground in the court of public opinion, partly because of expanded employment choices for poor women that allowed them to work outside of the domestic realm. Their antipathy toward cooking for others eroded the cultural commitment to domestic life; somehow, emerging social values and economic opportunities had turned domestic work into a universally dreaded obligation, even for poor young girls who, if they did choose to work in other people's homes, could find their lot improved—social, morally, and economically. Much to the dismay of reformers, domestic cooking had become a chore for *everyone*, whether they were cooking for love or for money. The tension between making meals and making moral citizens was always more complicated than the domestic ideals transmitted.

But fear not—American women of means were able to identify new groups of women looking for paid employment and thus willing to work in another woman's home. Historian Rebecca Sharpless demonstrates that domestic servants did not completely disappear when new jobs became available manufacturing such consumer goods as shoes, dresses, and so on. Rather, new cooks were quickly recruited after farm girls scurried to mill towns and expanding cities to take on factory work. In the North, recent immigrants, especially Irish and Italian girls, were recruited as domestic servants.[18] In the South, Sharpless points out a continuation of African Americans cooking for white families after Emancipation: "Skilled cooks found themselves in demand. White women might be willing to clean their houses or care for their own children, but they eagerly sought workers to take on the task of food preparation."[19] Domestic service (of all types) remained the most viable employment option for African American women and was seen as an improvement over field work, although as Sharpless notes, it was not necessarily ideal: "Cooking was one of the avenues open to them. The work was hard, the hours long, and the pay meager."[20] It was also during this period that a differentiation between domestic cooking and other domestic tasks such as cleaning and childcare emerged, and "women who cooked often commanded higher wages than maids or nurses."[21] Until new opportunities opened up after World War II, African American women from all over the South were the cooks in countless Southern homes.[22] The shift away from many domestic servants to few (if any), although a clear trend, was also a long-term process.

In 1953, a hundred years after the Beechers published their directives to upper-class American women, and a little over two decades after Irma Rombauer put pen to paper to write *The Joy of Cooking*, Julia Child received this feedback on one of the earliest drafts of her soon to be nationally renowned cookbook, *Mastering the Art of French Cooking*:

> What really makes me want to stand up and cheer, and at the same time fills me with a wild new hope, is what you say about the servant problem. Nobody can cook as she wants to, lovingly, while coping with children, housecleaning and all that. Food is what suffers first—and that's why we depend more and more on sliced bread, frozen foods, pressure cookers. . . . Nobody has more than a part time servant any more, except the rich.[23]

The letter was from Avis DeVoto, the wife of writer Bernard DeVoto, who became a champion of Child's work to create a thorough and accessible cookbook about French cuisine for American home cooks. Almost a century after the Civil War, readers of *Mastering the Art of French Cooking* still dreamed of hiring several people to maintain their households and assist them with all the necessary housekeeping chores (including cooking). The culinary tradition of letting other people cook remained at least an ideal, a path to making good food for your family and becoming a successful hostess.

DeVoto presciently points to a substantive change in cultural values regarding the obligations of cooking. If you couldn't find or afford a domestic servant (although this was still preferable) there were now new ways to have others do the cooking; these methods simply did not happen inside your home. Now you could bring in prepared food to replace bringing in household help. Managing a household and figuring out what to make for dinner each night remained an important concern, but social conditions had changed from before World War II, part of a long-term transformation of who did the cooking and why that began with the end of slavery and the rural migration to urban areas in the late nineteenth century. DeVoto herself discussed her struggles with cooking to Child in the early days of their friendship:

> Truth is, I am only a part-time cook. I have a maid now only three days a week (why will they get married and move out?) who does all the cleaning and cooks our dinners on the days she is here. She has worked for me a long time and I have taught her to be quite a good cook, if I do say so. The rest I swing myself, and it is great fun when I have time, which I seldom do.[24]

It's clear that DeVoto was knowledgeable about cooking and even enjoyed it, but she also embodied the bourgeois American woman's dilemma at the time: given the difficulties in finding people to hire as domestic cooks, a woman's job now included figuring out new ways to be responsible for all the meals and still be a part-time (or episodic) cook. Nobody wanted to give up their autonomy and have the obligation to cook constantly rather than intermittently.

DeVoto may have described an important truth about the tension between the real and the ideal when looking at cooking *in action*. In her boast about teaching her maid to be a good cook, she speaks to a certain reality about Americans: knowing how to cook and actually cooking are not always perfectly aligned. Our enactments are neither permanent nor constant. Clearly, this tension has existed for a long time. Perhaps fittingly, both Harriet Beecher Stowe and Catharine Beecher "promoted domestic ideals but each distanced herself from their daily execution."[25] Beyond their work admonishing American housewives to be leaders and teachers for their domestic servants, Harriet was the author of the bestselling novel *Uncle Tom's Cabin*, and Catherine founded a school for young women. In a letter to a friend in her early days as a wife and mother, Harriet wrote, "I mean to have money enough to have my house kept in the best manner and yet to have time for reflection and that preparation for the education of my children which every mother needs."[26] A good dinner, carefully prepared at home (but ideally by someone else), was a goal for all these women authors, from Beecher and Beecher Stowe to Child, even though their lives and domestic travails spanned the nineteenth and twentieth centuries. The symbolic resonance of the home-cooked meal—whether it was made using a coal stove or a gas range, whether it included johnnycake or cheese soufflé, whether it was made daily by a female member of the household or a live-in domestic servant, or more occasionally by a maid—has remained significant far beyond any historical particularities.

Interestingly, these bestselling authors of culinary and domestic treatises—Catharine Beecher, Harriet Beecher Stowe, Mary Lincoln, Fanny Farmer, Irma Rombauer, and Julia Child—all presented the same solution in their extremely successful publications: liberate women by elevating domestic work. What does it mean that their intended audience—middle- and upper-class women with duties as a mothers, wives, and hostesses—were never expected to always actually do the cooking? Perhaps these women all belong to the same lineage. Their attitude remains constant: If I can buy my way out this daily chore, why shouldn't I? None of the authors mentioned (champions of home-cooked meals across multiple generations) really assume that all of the everyday cooking should be done by the woman of the household. However, when a woman was in the kitchen cooking, they hoped to empower her and elevate the household meals because they believed that cooking was fun, or cooking was noble, or cooking was sophisticated, or cooking could build a virtuous society. Thus, they all believed that cooking was vital knowledge because of what was achieved *beyond* nourishment. To them, the reality that this was not always a necessary or desirable everyday task was of secondary importance. Perhaps this is not a paradoxical attitude but rather part and parcel of everyday American meal preparation, as culturally axiomatic as serving meat, vegetables, and starch for the evening meal. The finished meal holds greater cultural resonance and significance than the process leading up to its completion.

COOKING FOR OTHERS: NOT A FAD BUT A TREND

From the Beechers' three servants to Avis DeVoto's part-time maid, Americans clearly have a long history of employing someone else, or being employed to do the cooking, in some manner. Categorizing cooking as an occupation (something other people do for you) should not be seen as a unique outlier when telling the story of American cooks and cooking in America; rather, this category is central to the culinary tradition. It might be even more universal, part and parcel of the maintenance of many cuisines. Historian Rachel Laudan argues that the increasingly global shift from rural to urban residency, first in Europe and now almost everywhere, initially helped create both supply and demand for domestic servants. The reasons were varied but also consistent:

> Driven by the mechanization of agriculture, poor wages, and/or bad living conditions, men and women sought their fortune elsewhere, whether they

> were English displaced by enclosures and farm machinery, Irish fleeing famine, Japanese and Chinese escaping political upheavals and food shortages, blacks in the US moving northward from an impoverished south, or Mexicans seeking to make money to send home to buy land for a house.[27]

Young women who migrated to urban areas from the countryside could most easily find jobs in domestic service; many were employed as "plain cooks." These women did not come to the work especially knowledgeable at the outset; rather, it was assumed that they could be trained by the mistress of the house. If your obligation was only nourishment, shortcuts could alleviate the tedium, but if making meals was your occupation, the johnnycake or cheese soufflé were the conditions of your employment.

If the process of *making* the meals helps to define a culinary tradition—creating the conditions for the transfer of knowledge, the honing of skills, and the reproduction of values—then those who do the cooking matter. A lot. Thus, as Laudan points out, the poor girls and women who found employment in wealthy and middle-class urban households were those making the meals that defined the culinary traditions of each region and nation. These cooks created continuities in culinary practice that might not have lasted if the cooking was being done solely as an obligation, part of the daily round of chores.[28] Moreover, the skill and knowledge related to cooking has never truly been a universal practice: gender, class, and race have long differentiated cooks from noncooks. Perhaps any cuisine exists due to the work of a few, even if the fruits of such labor are enjoyed by many.

In the American context, having others do the cooking for you remains a consistent option, but over the past century, the *locations* for paid kitchen work have multiplied. The overall trend has been a decline in paid cooks working in the domestic, private sphere and an increase in paid cooks working in the commercial, public sphere. Even after the number of paid domestic cooks went into a general decline after World War II, women did not necessarily stop cooking for a living; they just found new locations to ply their trade. The legacy of others cooking on our behalf persists, but where it occurs has not been fixed or constant.

Fairy Bell Hewlett, a lifetime cook in Oxford, Mississippi, started cooking at thirteen in the kitchen of the plantation where her family resided.[29] She was born in 1936. Her mother was employed as a household cook, and her father was a sharecropper. Her grandmother had been a washerwoman, and her grandfather had been a slave. She started cooking after school because she was big enough to start working, or so her mother said. In an oral interview, she talks about her first day cooking at the plantation. The man of the house requested oyster stew, but she had no idea how to make the dish. Hewlett says, "I cried, I cried, I cried, and then I found the cookbook, and finally I found oyster stew in it."[30] When her interviewer asks if she remembers the name of the cookbook, she protests, saying, "No, sir; I said I didn't want to ever make any oyster stew anymore." Eventually, her entire family moved from the plantation into Oxford, where her father built a house in Shelley Bar Hollow, a black neighborhood. By 1952, when she was sixteen, she moved on to a job in the University of Mississippi's cafeteria and then spent the rest of her career working as a cook in Ole Miss sorority and fraternity houses.[31] She worked as a paid cook at Ole Miss for over forty years.

So, why has there been such a persistent neglect of the many generations of paid cooks who first worked in homes and then worked in commercial settings all over the United States? The cultural emphasis on the virtuousness of the final prepared meals over the process of *making* meals partially answers the question. Another reason may be the marginal social status of most of these women. Another explanation (certainly not unrelated to the long history of hidden female labor) could be the impulse to "lump" cooking into the larger category of domestic food consumption, which means that we do not analytically separate *cooking practices* from *eating patterns*. The practices and people involved in *making* food are sidelined when contemporary investigations only on American "eating habits," a continuation of the American preoccupation with results over process. This leads to an emphasis on the types of meals consumed, the number of products sold, and lists of types of locations where people eat these meals and goods. Moreover, these statistics are based on assumptions about the people that make up a household and do not take paid domestic servants into account.

The graph displayed in the introduction (see figure 1) charts a seemingly inevitable increase in meals purchased and consumed in commercial, public venues. And when such undeniable changes are linked to the long-touted American domestic ideal of a single household containing both cooking practices and eating patterns, claims that a decline in cooking skill and knowledge has followed the rise in industrialized food production systems seem logical. But the focus on the amount of money spent, without providing the context of such expenditures—the who, what, where, and why—erases other, equally compelling, alterations to American cooking and cuisine.

For example, a close look at the changing employment status of women over time shows that while commercial expenditures for food kept rising, the number of women employed as domestic servants kept declining. Did the women working in homes cooking and cleaning and caring for children all go work in factories and leave domestic chores behind? Or were they employed in new ways to help other people not do the dreaded domestic chores? Although the dominant narrative about the state of American home cooking might not take such a push and pull into account, there is an important story of substitution to be told.

Unraveling the paid cook's story from idealized visions of domestic meal preparation and consumption is the first task at hand.[32] The second task is to not confuse correlation and causation. It is the case that over the course of the twentieth century, there has been an increase both in the number of locations for purchasing food prepared outside of the home and in the number of meals consumed outside of the home. These trends, however, do

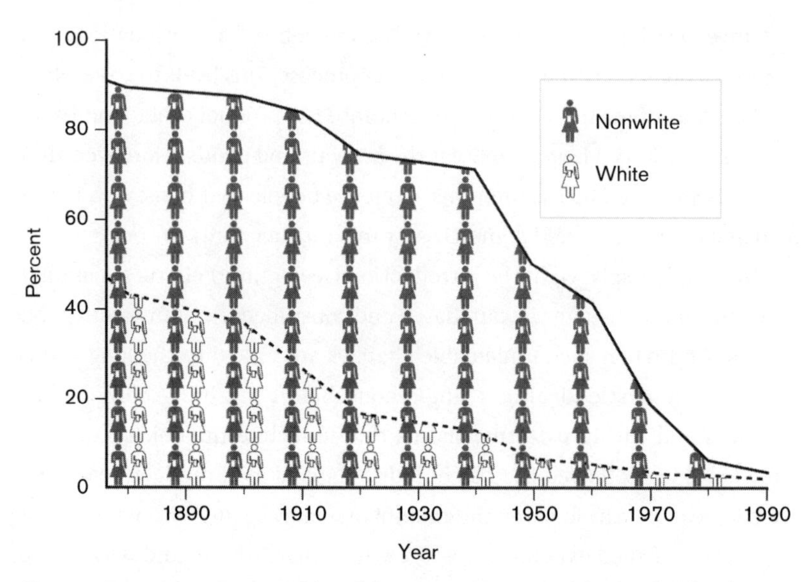

Figure 6. Domestic servants and farm laborers as percentage of the female labor force, by race, 1870–1990. *Source:* Sobek, "Occupations" in Carter et al., Historical Statistics of the United States, pages 2-138 and 2-139.

not necessarily *cause* a decline in cooking skill and knowledge. Domestic servants remained part of households, making meals at least some days of the week, through the 1950s, which means that many women remained paid domestic cooks even as new choices for eating meals emerged. And there are also many more cooks who are now employed outside of the home; cooking still happens, and meals continue to be made.

The key questions, then, are: Who were the cooks—in people's homes, in restaurants and hotels, in hospitals and schools—working for remuneration during the twentieth century? How did they ply their trade? If we don't answer these questions, the American embrace of having other hands making daily meals will remain unexplained. The maintenance of any culinary tradition over multiple generations will also not be fully understood. Among food scholars, the academic neglect of cooking as an occupation is in part due to the difficulty of finding adequate empirical sources. There are three main reasons for this: first, the fruits of such labor are ephemeral; second, the labor is considered mundane; and third, there is considerable slippage between noncompensated and compensated labor when it comes to this practice. This army truly is invisible from view, both in the past and in the present.

Figure 6, computed from a number of data sets that are part of the large-scale work *Historical Statistics of the United States* (2006), reveals the long-term trends in American female employment in domestic service with graphic simplicity. Throughout the nineteenth and early twentieth centuries, domestic service was a major form of employment for all women, but particularly nonwhite women. However, much cooking activity has not been captured for posterity. In United States census data, unpaid domestic labor is not recorded as industry, labor force participation, or occupation. Moreover, occupations are more difficult to quantify than jobs, because an occupation encompasses a social identity as well as an economic activity. That said, the numbers are clear: women, especially nonwhite women, have a long history of domestic service. In 1900, there were an estimated 1,136,829 nonwhite women employed in all census-listed occupations (those listed included professionals, farm laborers, clerical workers, sales workers, and domestic servants). Of this total, 566,897 were domestic service workers, about 50 percent. In 1940, there were 1,621,856 nonwhite women employed, and 912,459 of them were domestic service workers, about 55 percent. For most of the twentieth century, paid work for women was work in other people's homes. This number only really declined after 1970, when there were 248,687 nonwhite women in domestic service (and these are only domestic servants with documentation; those paid in cash and not reported were not counted), in no small part due to the gains made by the civil rights and feminist movements.[33]

In *Revolution at the Table: The Transformation of the American Diet*, historian Harvey Levenstein asserts that between 1880 and 1940, all American upper- and middle-class families employed servants; the main variation was in number and type. Few wealthy families employed less than four, and "relatively few middle-class households seemed to have been able to operate on a servantless basis. By 1880, almost one quarter of all urban and suburban households employed at least one servant."[34] The increase in middle-class households starting in the 1880s was partially due to the creation of new white-collar occupations. Meanwhile, these newly bourgeois families needed to assert their social status; expectations of sophistication were now added to those concerning moral virtues. The prevailing standard for home-cooked meals shifted, especially cooking for guests, and brought new expectations about the type of food to be prepared in the home, another variant of the Beechers' call for keeping one's house in the proper manner. These fancier meals were hindered by the ongoing "servant problem," or the difficulty in getting help committed to achieving these new standards. From the 1890s through World War II, a number of strategies were developed to help households maintain paid cooks who could get breakfast ready and also put together a multicourse European-style meal for guests. One involved teaching domestic servants how to cook—or rather, how to cook properly. The Boston Cooking School hosted classes for domestics. Although the domestic science movement was primarily dedicated to valorizing domestic work for middle-class women (now increasingly in charge of their own kitchens) efforts were also made to train the domestic workers they still might be able to employ. All the women in a household who were either supervising or making the meals needed to feel better about (but also be better at) the everyday domestic chore of cooking and feeding American families.

But with more and more industrial manufacturing jobs available to all, the next solution was "to bring . . . service into the world of modern capitalism by putting it in a contract basis, specifying hours of work, tasks to be fulfilled, and so on."[35] This was difficult to accomplish with live-in employees, as this form of labor did not conform to the increasingly commodified and standardized routines of the modern world of paid labor. World War II was the death knell for such work; during the war, the demand for all women to do work outside of the home effectively created another great migration from the kitchen, this time to the shop floor. By the 1970s, the domestic realm as a site for wage labor was increasingly irrelevant for *all* women when compared to other locations for paid employment. At the same time, there was a commensurate decline in the amount of money Americans spent to employ domestic servants.[36]

By the time Irma Rombauer had revised the third edition of *The Joy of Cooking*, in 1943, she too spoke to the transformation of the identity of the "domestic" cook:

> My roots are Victorian but I have been modernized by life and my children. My book reflects my life, and as you may see by its timely contents, I have not stood still. So I am bringing you not only much that is old and memorable but also much that is new. Many simply prepared dishes, low in cost, have been included to *meet the change in our domestic homefront* [emphasis mine]. Every effort has been made to encourage the cook in her daily grind by lifting everyday food out of the commonplace.[37]

And in a pithy confirmation of the long-term trends outlined here, Rombauer had this to say in the preface to the 1951 edition: "In the last few years the revolutionary changes in household equipment have given rise to the quip: 'Discharge your cook and hire an electrician.'"

As Rombauer's cook Marguerite and others testify, a long legacy of compensated labor for foodwork predates our ability to purchase prepared meals at grocery stores, food chains, truck stops, and pizza shops. If the assumption that cooking among Americans exists solely as an unpaid domestic duty gets removed from the analytic process, and with it the confusion of correlation and causation, what can we identify as important long-term trends in cooking as an *occupation* in contrast to cooking as an *obligation?* As the evidence of the necessity of employing servants, especially cooks, indicates, making meals has long been a type of paid labor, one that resolves the everyday necessity of providing sustenance. Finding evidence of those "other people" cooking for a wage as well as their motivations for taking on this work requires investigation, because locating the cook's tale in the American story of everyday meal preparation and consumption is no easy endeavor. Cooking as an *occupational* task has been too often neglected in the telling of American culinary history. Such neglect is partially due to the tradition of considering the work performed in the domestic realm as outside of or irrelevant to the domains of commerce and politics and also of linking cooking to many other labors performed by women, which have been left to the dustbin of history. At the same time, when work categorized as domestic in nature does shift into the public sphere, the function remains trivialized, and those who do it are seen as helpmates to those with occupations more valued for action and import (the histories of the legal and medical professions, e.g., have been substantially documented by sociologists, historians, and others, while histories of cooks, chefs, restaurateurs, butchers, and other food workers are meager at best). Also, the cook's work, whether domestic or public, has traditionally not been perceived as an occupation associated with power and privilege; therefore, when cooking is categorized, if at all, it is identified as menial labor performed by people of low status.

One possible conclusion, given the decline in domestic service between 1880 to 1960, is that socioeconomic changes combined with technological innovations meant that having other people cook for us was ultimately no longer relevant to American culture and cuisine. But is this true? Did other people stop cooking for us? No. But now, knowledgeable cooks, like Fairy Bell Hewlett, make our daily lunches, which we consume at or close to the workplace; these cooks also prepare our "I am too tired to cook" dinners at the end of the workday. The level of cooking skill and knowledge held by

Americans may be remarkably consistent over time, but this expertise now resides in the minds and hands of paid cooks cooking in commercial kitchens rather than in those of black slaves, farm girls, recent immigrants, and others, like Marguerite, Fairy Bell, and Avis DeVoto's part-time maid. When domestic cooking and eating habits are left so strongly associated, the increased consumption of food produced in public domains (i.e., outside the domestic sphere) might be interpreted as providing a completely new type of occupation, commissary cooks and restaurant chefs as a version of the emergence of new work opportunities in response to new consumer practices and technological innovations, such as software programmer, TSA agent, and call center customer service provider. However, to make this assumption would be to erase the history of many American cooks.

Much of the contemporary critique of American cooking practices and eating patterns tends to concentrate on trends in the food industry; the increases in purchases of entire dishes and meals already prepared in industrial settings and then preserved in some manner (e.g., frozen, sous vide) are significant. Clearly, companies and corporations contributed to the American culinary landscape over the twentieth century. Historian Amy Bentley, for example, focuses just on the industrialization of baby food. Commercially produced jars of pureed carrots and peas create new solutions to a short developmental moment in a person's lifetime of eating, but even these small meals are enmeshed with changes in home meal practices and culturally familiar moral and maternal claims.[38] The increased importance after World War II of industrially made, prepared foods (extended even to baby foods) clearly helped resolve what DeVoto called the "servant problem." However, the introduction of new players, like Gerber, and new products, like small jars of apple sauce and pureed carrots, that are made on a large scale and manufactured by machines, does not mean that other people have not continued to cook *for* Americans; rather, what develops are multiple means of substitution to facilitate the necessary transactions involved in making meals. A wife and mother can buy the Gerber baby food to have her babysitter feed her baby while she and her husband go out to dinner at a restaurant with friends.

THE INVISIBLE ARMY, REVEALED

So, not much is known about the history of cooking as an *occupation*—that is, cooking as a form of compensated wage labor associated with certain tasks. Concentrating solely on food industry statistics shifts the focus to food as commodity rather than cooking as a practice, resulting in a lacuna that erases lots of skilled cooking activities and forms of culinary expertise. There have been targeted investigations of certain groups of paid cooks, but much remains to be analytically well understood. What are the larger trends in both domestic and public spheres and what implications do these have on the cooking skills and knowledge understood to represent a shared cultural practice across these domains?[39] In *A History of Cooks and Cooking*, Michael Symons ranges across time and space to tell the cook's story. He argues that the low status of cooks and inattention to their knowledge and skill can be traced (in the West) to Plato's dismissal of this type of work, pointing Socrates to claim in *Gorgias* that "cookery 'isn't an art at all'. It is a 'kind of knack gained by experience' that is aimed at 'gratification and pleasure.'"[40] He then reviews all the contributions cooks have made to civilized society, refuting Plato's claims and also building a case for the cook's tasks. Despite such dismissals, the occupation of "cook" has been around for a long time, as revealed in documents discussing commercial cookshops found as early as the 1300s in urban areas globally, including in China and India.

In North America, the story of commercial cooking does not extend so far back; the earliest enterprises—saloons and taverns—followed European colonization. In the eighteenth century, taverns were "legally bound to provide food and shelter for man and horse," and although they were segregated by gender, race, and class, they were available to all in colonial cities.[41] These venues offered food, but the meals were served informally; in a sense, they were extensions of the family meal, now being dished up to the community of workers or boarders who had no other place to eat. Restaurants became more typical beginning in the mid-nineteenth century. They offered a more "civilized" eating experience in which the meal took center stage, but the price demanded a middle- or upper-class clientele. Krishnendu Ray, in his exploration of class and ethnicity in commercial eating establishments in New York City, aptly points out both the universal presence of restaurants, with options for all, and clear differentiations between them: "In the 1850s, dinner at Delmonico's would set the customer back by at least two dollars, which was two days of a manual laborer's wages. That was in contrast to the sixpenny working class eatery and the twelve-cent chop house for the commuting working classes."[42] Over time, the ever-expanding scope and scale of such enterprises helped to create the "sovereign consumer," the result being that meals were no longer prepared in bulk to be shared among many (as in most taverns); rather, individual choices led to individual consumption patterns (as in most restaurants).[43]

The story of commercial cooks reflects the power of European colonization and European culture and simultaneously its reliance on, as Ray puts it, the "immigrant Other." American middle- and upper-middle-class households and commercial food enterprises really rely on waves of immigrants (forced or not) seeking gainful employment as paid cooks in this "promised land." These immigrant cooks have been able to gain employment making food at all kinds of establishments, from informal street stands to elaborate hotels. Chefs (or, to use the more traditional term, *chefs de cuisine*), the male cooks who oversee large kitchens in hotels and restaurants, are part of an occupational structure that emerged from the European apprenticeship tradition of the early modern period. Up until the 1800s, the *chef de cuisine* was responsible for running the kitchens of members of European royalty, often supervising many cooks and other kitchen workers. As with other domestic servants, a *chef de cuisine* would join the royal household as an apprentice between the ages of thirteen to fifteen. Many of the French chefs who are still heralded as the best representatives of the much-storied French haute cuisine worked their entire careers in royal households. For example, La Varenne, author of *Le cuisinier françois* (1651), worked for the Marquis d'Uxelles, among others.[44] There was a strict hierarchy in these kitchens, and all who labored to make the meals, simple or grand, could be called domestic servants, although there were status hierarchies among these positions as well. European cities, from the medieval period onward, were sites where cooks cooking for those beyond a single household could be found. In England, paid cooks, bakers, and butchers all had guilds, organized both as mutual benefit associations and governing authorities. In London, the Worshipful Company of Cooks was founded in 1311 and ultimately included cooks, pastlers (makers of pasties), and pie bakers.[45]

In the United States, royalty, needless to say, did not have the same power as it did in Europe, and thus the history of "haute" cooking in America is situated in early hotels and restaurants. Due to constant waves of migration, especially into cities, kitchen work became part of commercial enterprises in urban areas starting in the eighteenth century. The migrations of people to cities for work, the density of urban areas, the often cramped living quarters, and the lack of ready access to arable land conspired to make urban areas natural sites for public cooking and eating.

Influential hotels and restaurants of this era included the Revere House Hotel in Boston, the Fifth Avenue Hotel in New York City, Delmonico's in New York City, and Antoine's in New Orleans.[46] These were large and complex enterprises that required a large staff to cook the menus of terrapin, *macaroni a l'italienne*, and oysters prepared many ways, or as historian Paul Freedman puts it, to create a culinary aesthetic of "Frenchified English" meals.[47] Many of these dishes can be found in nineteenth-century cookbooks as well, indicating that this type of fine food was also being served in the homes of the wealthy, cooked by domestic servants. By the late nineteenth century, more options became available as freestanding Chinese and Italian restaurants became increasingly popular in urban areas; more recent migrants to American shores owned many of these establishments.[48]

Immigrants both worked as commercial cooks and became instrumental to the rise of commercial eating establishments, usually those defined as "ethnic" eateries. Ray investigates the connection between immigration and occupations in commercial cooking by examining United States census material. In his review, he documents that in the mid-nineteenth century, "the foreign-born numerically dominate certain occupations, such as domestic servants, hotel and restaurant employees, hotel-keepers, saloon-keepers and bartenders, traders and dealers in groceries, bakers and butchers."[49] In his presentation of selected occupations over the course of a century, certain continuities are traced. In 1900, people listed as foreign born still worked more often as bakers, brewers, and boardinghouse and restaurant keepers than as lawyers, teachers, and doctors.[50] Interestingly, in 2000, almost 30 percent of bakers were foreign born, but 30 percent of physicians were foreign born as well. The largest percentage of foreign-born workers were employed as chefs and head cooks (over 30 percent).[51] Ray's argument about the import of the race, class, and ethnicity of commercial cooks (in New York City, in this case), resonates with the larger changes from domestic to commercial venues where other people prepare our meals: "There is a long-term pattern of ethnic succession. Foodwork done by German and Irish immigrants in the mid-nineteenth century was carried out by Italians and eastern Europeans at the end of the nineteenth century, who in turn were replaced by Latinos and Asians at the end of the twentieth century."[52] Perhaps it is our cultural burden, an impulse of the American "melting pot" identity, that history does not support our categorical assumptions about who cooks, where they cook, and why they cook. We like to imagine that once an immigrant arrives on our shores, a singular story will unfold, but there are really many tales to tell.

FROM SERVANTS TO COOKS: THE AMERICAN STORY

In the twenty-first century, it may no longer be culturally acceptable (or feasible) to rely on the enslaved cook or her descendants, the mammies and maids so matter-of-factly discussed in earlier cookbooks, to make meals in American homes, but the occupation of cooking has persisted and actually expanded since the 1800s. It remains primarily hidden, a form of menial labor done by marginalized people in difficult and demanding circumstances. Despite such erasures, there is a long and storied history of Americans having other people cook for them as a solution to the perennial problem of what to have for dinner. What has changed is the way this is perceived: now, having someone else cook for you is categorized as an everyday solution for many citizens rather than an expectation of the more privileged. Making meals has increasingly become part of a job description and is identified as a distinct occupation rather than bundled together as a form of servitude. There are multiple people to rely on when seeking to outsource the daily obligations of nourishment and nurturance, including the short-order cook at the diner, the lunch lady at the elementary school, and the commissary cook at the Whole Foods.

The multivolume work *Historical Statistics of the United States* provides insight into cooking as a type of occupation.[53] This massive enterprise uses U.S. census data to provide quantitative data about five broad areas of American life: population; work and welfare; economic structure and performance; economic sectors; and government and international relations. Each area is delineated and explained in detail, supported by numerous tables generated using the Integrated Public Use Microdata Series. Within a long list of occupations provided by the census data, a specific table can be created focusing on major groups that are involved in transforming whole ingredients into dishes or meals: craft workers, proprietors, and domestic service workers. Even the categories used for the census provide new insights into the *practice* of cooking (and baking).[54] As historian Matthew Sobek, the editor of the chapter "Occupations" points out, occupations are different than industry or labor force participation, other measures of contemporary work. He makes the following distinction: "Industry is concerned with the kinds of goods and services produced, whereas occupation relates to the specific characteristics of the job a person performs, regardless of the product involved."[55]

The United States Census Bureau's statistics on labor occupations reveal the changing location of kitchen work over the course of the twentieth century. In the census data, a clear demarcation is made between "private household workers" and "service workers." Within the private household worker category, there are a number of intriguing distinctions outlined that reflect the complexity of paid labor that occurred in households, such as one between workers "living in" and "living out," and another between housekeepers and laundresses. By 1950, "babysitter" had become demarcated under the category "domestic service worker" (a shift from the earlier-named "private household worker"), and it got larger and larger between 1950 and 1970, while the subclassification that captured domestic work beyond childcare consistently declined. Census data reveals that although the occupational categories had shifted again by 1970, the general trend remained the same: more and more employed kitchen labor was occurring outside of the home.

A review of major occupational groups in *Historical Statistics of the United States* shows that in 1940, there were 2,111,314 domestic service workers (of which 93.3 percent were female). Up until this point, this was one broad census category, and the particular household tasks performed by everyone employed were not clearly differentiated. This year appears to reveal the peak of this occupation, which experienced a subsequent steady decline, with a total of only 521,839 in 1990. During the same period, people who reported their occupation as cook (excluding private household cooks) increased from 300,088 to 2,106,500.[56] So, does this mean that the number of people employed as cooks could in fact have been consistent and constant throughout these fifty years, just that their workplaces had changed? Instead of cooking in private family homes, these cooks were working in school cafeterias or restaurants.

The decline of domestic service as an occupation and as a solution for middle- and upper-class families who hope to have other people do their household work was not the death knell for the occupations of paid cooks (or bakers). After World War II, paid cooks did not lose their relevance to American culture and cuisine. Their workplaces shifted and their cooking practices adapted to the new locales. During the twentieth century, newly emerging fast-food restaurants become a source of employment for cooks. Fast food was a new paradigm characterized by quickly prepared meals that can be eaten in a restaurant setting. Fast food is considered a uniquely American invention; McDonald's often gets credit as the first fast-food establishment, but some food historians identify White Castle, founded in the 1920s, as the original.

Another form of paid kitchen work that became increasingly important over the twentieth century was cooking in and for social institutions dedicated to the care of others, such as schools and hospitals. Part of paid cooking's long-term shift away from domestic settings and into the public sphere lay in new ideas about how to feed children, the ill, and the elderly. As these groups no longer resided exclusively in the home and spent more time in larger social institutions, feeding them became less and less the sole responsibility of families. For example, to differing degrees, depending on cultural practices, feeding children and young adults became either the sole or the partial responsibility of educational institutions. Higher education that involves students boarding in dormitories with cafeterias is now the norm in the United States. Feeding groups in such settings has become big business and a major mode of employment, and it has also created new requirements for cooks' skills and knowledge.

In this setting, the work overlaps somewhat with the model of restaurant and hotel cooking (many of the methods of procurement and preparation are the same) but a major difference lies in the organization involved in the transformation of ingredients from the raw to the cooked and how the prepared food is served to the diner. In institutional settings, much of the food is prepared in advance, a process known as "batch cooking," rather than each individual meal being cooked when it is ordered. This approach is in fact closer to fast-food preparation, although the greater variety of choices institutions offer for every meal period as well as the array of dishes prepared over a menu cycle require a larger set of culinary skills.

Current occupational statistics demonstrate the differentiation of cooking as an occupation: a set of clearly delineated tasks requiring different types of expertise. Such precision is a far cry from earlier categories that included cooking. The *process* involved in getting food to the table has become increasingly delineated and institutionalized. In some ways, the more frequently that paid cooks work outside the homes of individual families, the more the process can seem radically transformed; how do the elements of care and nurturance persist in these more clinical production settings? However, many of the tasks that need to be carried out by paid cooks working outside the home—such as planning, prepping, and transforming raw ingredients into palatable dishes—are no different from the tasks involved in getting dinner on the table in any given household. And while the demands of cooking on a grander scale and for more diverse (but perhaps no less demanding!) consumers do make commercial cooking more of an associated than identical enterprise, the goals of these tasks remain startlingly static: a meal must be planned, ingredients must be procured, and basic components must be integrated into final dishes. Herein lies a paradox between change and continuity: the scope and scale changes when the cook's location of

TABLE 1

Occupation Employment Statistics—Cooks and Food-Preparation Workers

Type of cook	Description	Total employed
Chefs and head cooks	Direct and may participate in the preparation, seasoning, and cooking of salads, soups, fish, meats, vegetables, desserts, and/or other foods. May plan and price menu items, order supplies, and keep records and accounts.	129,370
First-line supervisors of food preparation and serving workers	Directly supervise and coordinate activities of workers engaged in preparing and serving food.	884,900
Fast-food cooks	Prepare and cook food in a fast-food restaurant with a limited menu. Duties of these cooks are limited to the preparation of a few basic items and normally involve operating large-volume, single-purpose cooking equipment.	520,010
Institutional and cafeteria cooks	Prepare and cook large quantities of food for institutions, such as schools, hospitals, and cafeterias.	404,890
Private household cooks	Prepare meals in private homes. Includes personal chefs.	380
Restaurant cooks	Prepare, serve and cook soups, meats, vegetables, and other foodstuffs in restaurants. May order supplies, keep records and accounts, price items on menu, or plan menu.	1,150,760
Short-order cooks	Prepare and cook to order a variety of foods that require only a short preparation time. May take orders from customers and serve patrons at counters or tables.	193,170

SOURCE: Bureau of Labor Statistics, "Recent Occupational Employment Statistics: 35-2000 Cooks and Food Preparation Workers," May 2015.

employment moves out of the home and into restaurants, hotels, schools, and the like, and the knowledge needed to become a paid cook becomes more specified and specialized, but meals still need to be made, and people still need to be fed.

HOW DID WE GET HERE?

As the U.S. occupational statistics reveal, paid labor for kitchen work in homes tended to be bundled with other domestic tasks before World War II. A black maid working in a Southern white household, for example, was expected to clean, cook, do laundry, and oftentimes help take care of the children. Over the course of the twentieth century, with the rise of nondomestic service workers, a more precise differentiation of these domestic duties emerged.

The visual tables created from the raw census data that appear in each section of *Historical Statistics of the United States* reveal the changes in domestic cooking and eating practices as well as transformations in cooking as an occupation that have occurred over the past one hundred and fifty years. The drumbeat, or perhaps the spoonbeat, of all these cooks, working in so many milieus, demonstrates why a reconsideration of the argument that there has been a decline in cooking skill and knowledge is in order. Can a new understanding of making modern meals in America emerge? In particular, do these graphs allow for a visual and numerical understanding of the growing distinction between *obligation* and *occupation* when it comes to making meals for Americans?

The daily obligations of taking care of the household—cleaning, shopping, feeding, and nurturing—could be all be completed by paid employees, and taking care of these tasks was a popular job, especially from 1880 to 1940. The occupation of domestic servant started to decline, partially due to the invention of new machines that made many household tasks much simpler and less labor intensive, and partially due to new job opportunities, including factory jobs. Machines could not completely replace the work of the maid, the

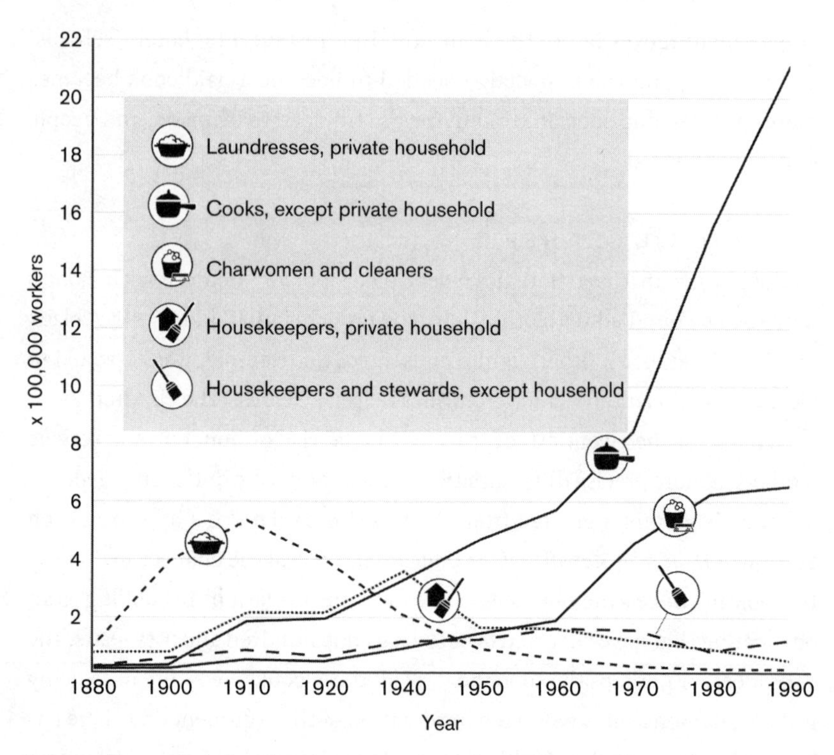

Figure 7. The number of workers in service occupations, 1880–1990. *Source:* Susan B. Carter et al., *The Historical Statistics of the United States: Millennial Edition*. Census data for 1890 and 1930 not available.

laundress, and especially, it appears, the cook. In fact, between 1900 and 1990, two million more Americans took up the occupation of cook; with each decade, more people cook on the behalf of others, whether at restaurants, elementary schools, hospitals, or the grocery store's prepared foods kitchen.

As indicated in figure 8, there are a number of occupations concerned with preparing and consuming food where employment stayed fairly steady over the course of the twentieth century, particularly bakers and millers. Baking, especially producing the bread, rolls, and other baked goods so cru-

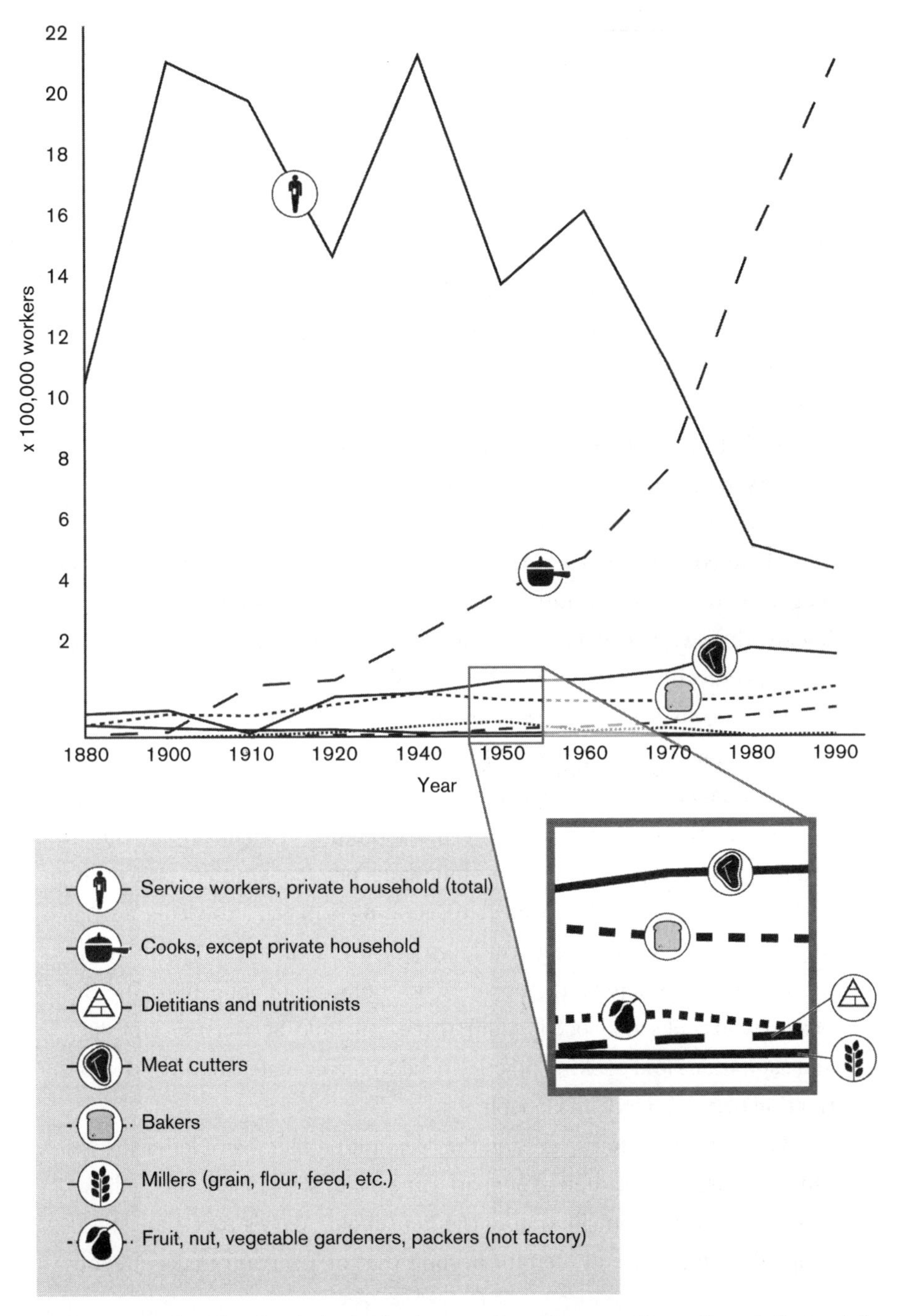

Figure 8. The number of workers in food-related occupations, 1880–1990. *Source:* Susan B. Carter et al., *The Historical Statistics of the United States: Millennial Edition*. Census data for 1890 and 1930 not available.

cial to the American diet, had long been a task households outsourced to small enterprises, especially in cities where many people lived in small apartments without copious space for large stoves and ovens. The increase in the number of people employed as cooks during the same period, however, is truly remarkable, from approximately 200,000 in 1920 to 2,000,000 in 1990.

Figure 8 reveals more details about the changing demographics of occupations and the occupational shift out of the domestic and into the public sphere. The "bubble" of housekeepers and laundresses mirrors Levenstein's claims that the dominant period for American households employing servants was from 1880 to 1940.[57] The steady increase of charwomen and cleaners combined with the exponential increase in cooks (not including private household cooks) starting in the early 1900s reveals the beginning of the long-term occupational shift from workers who did general private household work to workers who carried out these sorts of tasks in a way that was more specifically categorized and differentially organized. A cleaning lady, for example, now came into the home and was paid a daily wage. More and more often, meals were purchased and prepared outside the home.

What happens to cooking in the midst of such occupational transformation, and what does that mean to any understanding of American cooking in action? Close analysis confirms the following: one, cooking as a paid occupation has existed for a long time; two, cooking skill and knowledge are not located in a specific *place* (e.g., the home or the tavern) but rather in certain categories of *person* (e.g., the person who cooks out of obligation, and the person who cooks as an occupation); three, any links between social values and aspirations and cooking practice need to incorporate this analytic distinction between place and person.

When Avis DeVoto expands on the "servant problem" in a letter to Julia Child, she uses the example of her part-time maid, Mary. She seems ambivalent about Mary's contribution to the household. Mary's part-time status coupled with a sense of identity beyond that of a servant makes DeVoto

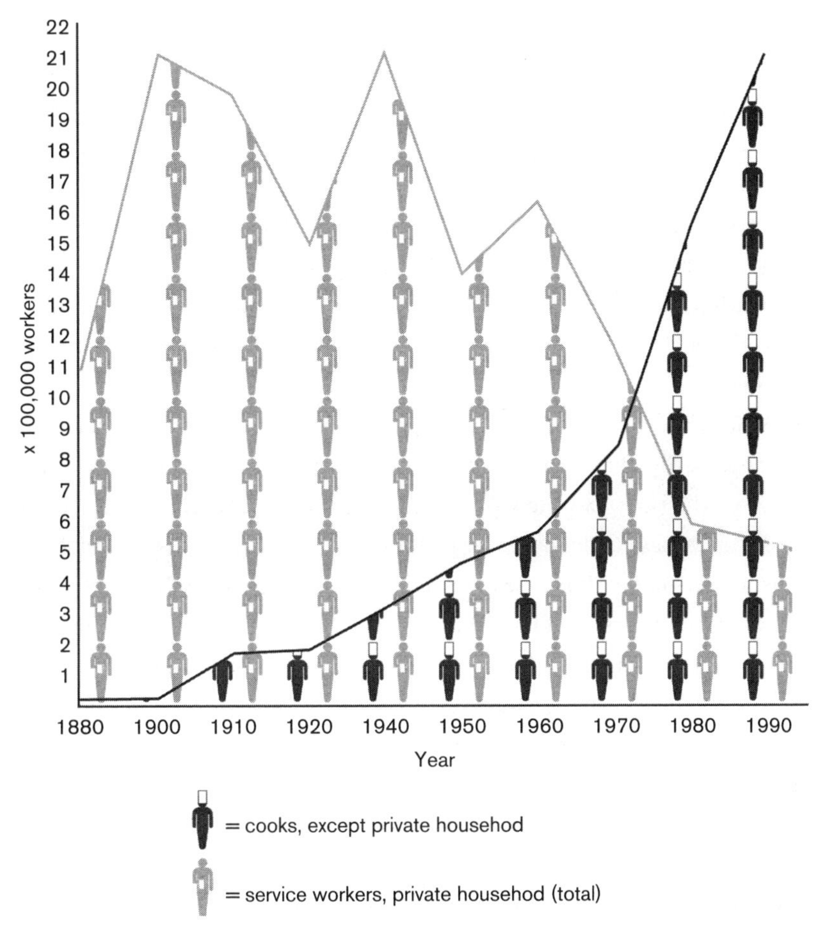

Figure 9. The number of household service workers and nonhousehold cooks, 1880–1990. *Source:* Susan B. Carter et al., *The Historical Statistics of the United States: Millennial Edition.* Census data for 1890 and 1930 not available.

pause: "I pay Mary eight dollars a day for three days a week—she comes at ten, cleans the house, serves us dinner at six-thirty—a perfectly horrible hour—because naturally she wants to get home to her husband, and he is more and more demanding, so that she is torn between us."[58] DeVoto does not complain about Mary's performance of her occupational tasks; rather, she seems to struggle with the accommodations she has to make for Mary's other responsibilities. As the job of household cook becomes an occupation like many others, the cooks now have two jobs to fulfill: cooking as paid work (for other families) *and* cooking as a chore (for their own families).

Meanwhile, the social obligations related to cooking and eating well did not necessarily abate. In one of the early reviews of Child's manuscript, which at the time had the working title *How to Cook French*, the reviewer used this tension to advocate for Child's new approach: "This is a book for housewives—not for hostesses. It is a book for people who will do the cooking themselves. Mrs. Child, unlike most Americans who seize on the opportunity of cheap service in Europe, does all her own work and serves as well as cooks."[59] The distinction between categories of person—housewife versus hostess—reveals both the long history of hidden domestic labor and a new servantless future for home cooks, who continue to have complex social obligations when it comes to serving dinner.

KNOWLEDGE IN ACTION: IS COOKING REALLY IN DECLINE?

The fact that cooking is fully established as an occupation and that cooking is something that many Americans pay other people to do makes this a category that explains and reflects our everyday actions. Looking carefully and closely at the occupation of paid chefs and cooks might be a more fruitful means of considering social changes in many aspects of meal preparation than looking solely at transformations in technology, or the concentrated

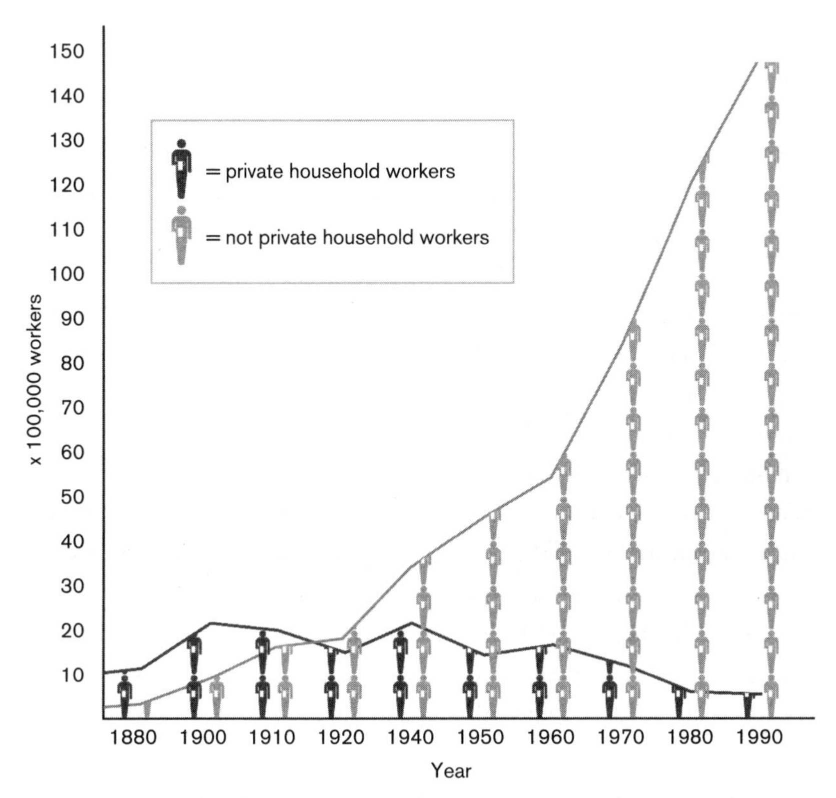

Figure 10. The number of private service workers versus commercial service workers, 1880–1990. *Source:* Susan B. Carter et al., *The Historical Statistics of the United States: Millennial Edition*. Census data for 1890 and 1930 not available.

power of the food industry, or the individual failings of home cooks. The great increase in paid cooks in relation to everyday enactments of American meal preparation influences practices and perceptions in profound ways, from the shifting landscape of what defines culinary expertise to the transformations in the structure of meals. Furthermore, the actions of these cooks reflect a changed reality in Americans' relationship to where certain meals are consumed and what is considered a culturally appropriate meal structure. Lunch has ceased to be a meal usually prepared and eaten at home, a victim of the model of industrial work and the changing structure of the modern workday. Lunches are mostly packed or bought, either on-site, from a food truck, or at a restaurant. Breakfast has shifted from being a primary hot meal to a secondary cold meal, sometimes consumed at home but just as often purchased at the takeout window of Dunkin Donuts or at the nearest Starbucks, while waiting for a cappuccino.[60]

So, what of the dominant narrative that cooking is in decline because home cooks don't cook and that home cooks used to cook everywhere, every day, and in every type of household? Can we trust this assumption? Not really. Yes, there have been major changes in the production and consumption practices of Americans over the past century. We spend more money on food prepared outside the home, we spend less time each day preparing our meals, we eat fewer meals at home, and we have more diet-related disease issues. But all these changes cannot be singularly attributed to a decline in cooking skill and cooking knowledge. The dexterity needed to make scrambled eggs and biscuits or tomato soup and grilled cheese still resides in the hands of many, although not in the hands of each and every American.

Perhaps the culprit is the organization and structure of modern life. In multiple discourses (occurring in cookbooks, historical and contemporary media, interviews with cooks, etc.) there exists a pervasive sense of lack and loss as to what we *can* and *should* do in our domestic lives. Almost seventy years ago, Avis DeVoto complained that she did not have time to cook. This perception of "time poverty" is now the backstory of almost all narratives about the challenges of putting food on the table in all American households—rural and urban, rich and poor. Sociologists Angela Meah and Matt Watson attribute this narrative to a more pervasive sense of loss: the need to abandon certain ways of life in the journey to becoming modern. In this narrative, home cooking is much more episodic than in earlier times because it *needs* to be, given the expansion of daily demands, and skills and tasks related to meal preparation are given up so that cooking can be fit into modern life.

During the interview with Rebecca, one exchange demonstrated the episodic nature of making meals. In her case, choosing whether cook or order takeout is a down-to-the-wire decision that she makes even on nights when she intends to cook. The interviewer asked, "Do you think it's one of those things where you break down and say let's just get takeout tonight, or is it something that at the beginning of the week, you plan out [when you will go out]?" She responded:

> Oh, I never plan it. I never plan it. If I had enough energy I would cook everyday. It's just like, I come home and like, usually it happens after twenty minutes of us starting, looking at [the] fridge, opening the cabinets, being like, "I really don't want to make, even pasta." We don't even eat pasta that often. Usually what we make is an hour-long plus meal, and maybe that would be different if we had more convenience foods around, but we are just not into that. So, it's deliberation, and then it leads to, "Okay, then let's just get takeout."

Contemporary home cooks like Rebecca consistently identify "time" as a significant barrier to making meals at home. In another interview, Claire, who was not quite sure whether it was worth it to make her butternut squash soup from scratch, said, "What will deter me from cooking is the time factor." In fact, a sense of time poverty is what makes or breaks her decision to cook: "The number one problem with going through the entire cooking process is time." When asked to elaborate, Claire said that she sees the various steps involved in going from thinking about making a meal to actually making it as onerous, so why bother? The steps she mentioned were deciding whether she needed a recipe, figuring out if she needed to go grocery shopping and, if she did, making a grocery list, going to the store, coming home, unpacking her items, and then preparing the meal. Another participant, a mother of four, explained, "Sometimes there's not enough time to be as natural and organic as we'd like to be." She went on to say, "I can't do things that are really complicated, otherwise I would [have had to have started] cooking an hour ago, and that takes up my entire afternoon, which honestly isn't on my agenda these days." These comments were echoed by almost everyone, and the solution was just as consistent: the time and bother it takes to prepare food justifies being a food consumer but not a food producer. As Mary, a mother of two, put it, "Let's say I got home late, and I just don't feel like cooking. . . . Sometimes you're like, 'Oh, I could go for some Indian,' [and we get takeout]." Or, in a classic American response, another participant said, "I'm lucky because [with] my husband and my kids, if I come home and I don't feel like cooking, they're happy with a pizza."

The tension between an impoverishment of time and the varied obligations required to successfully make a meal is consistent and constant when all our participants make everyday decisions. Perceptions of time poverty in relation to cooking have been documented in numerous other studies. Nicole Larson and her colleagues, for example, found that "the most common barrier to food preparation was lack of time, reported by 36% of young adults."[61] This can be associated with the social gains that have released women from their identity as having been "born to cook," which has allowed housewives and domestic servants to move out of the home, as they are literally no longer confined to the domestic space. Cooking practice has therefore been altered, no longer bound by the same social conditions and expectations explained and addressed in books like *The American Woman's Home* and classes run in schools like the Boston Cooking School.[62] It's possible that this could result in a "deskilling of domestic cooking," a concern that has been articulated by many.[63] But it can be argued that the categorization of cooking is continuously changing based on the food environment and the contemporary milieu. Modern culinary knowledge includes new navigational skills: at the everyday scale, it is not the burden of doing but the quandary of whether to do it yourself that preoccupies many home cooks. The challenge now involves juggling various solutions to the problem of getting dinner on the table: Do you opt for systematic means of provisioning? Do you choose not to plan at all? Do you engage in active cooking or passive purchasing? There are so many ways to provide for yourself and your family so that everyone is nourished.[64] At the same time, the cooks in the Indian restaurants and French bistros where Americans get their takeout meals and celebrate Saturday date nights do possess cooking skills and knowledge.

After Rebecca left the job that required her to work until 8:00 p.m. every night, she cooked more at home and ate out less. In some ways, though, she kept her expectations for ease of preparation and exotic tastes. One evening, she used a Thai Kitchen stir-fry rice noodle kit that came with all the required ingredients save for fresh vegetables. She remains a navigator and an eater more than a cook.

Among all our cooks, those with the least intense set of obligations outside of the home were those that cooked most regularly. For example, one participant, a sixty-seven-year-old retired woman, cooked dinner seven nights per week and only ate out when she was on vacation or when she had plans that interfered with regular meal times (which only happened one to two times per month). Time poverty and stage of life do seem to make a difference in a person's decision to cook in or eat out; another study found that more advanced age had a significant positive effect on time spent preparing food, probably because these folks are retired or have less time-consuming jobs.[65]

If the evolution of cooking is more clearly articulated as a shift from obligation to occupation, perhaps more precise definitions of cooking skill and the status of such skills can be developed. Perhaps there are as many people who are skilled and knowledgeable cooks today as there were seventy years ago. A consideration of the enactment of such skills and knowledge, and any relationship between making a meal and where, when, how, and why that meal is consumed requires investigating all types of cooks, both in the home and outside of it. Such distinctions might help curb an alarming tendency to associate the supposed phenomenon of "decline" with the social categories of class and race. As Meah and Watson point out, "Concerns about the dearth of cooking skills among the 'lower' classes can be traced back at least 200 years, when calls were first made for the poor to be educated in the basics of cooking."[66] The contemporary concern about the decline of cooking skill and knowledge may be another iteration of using specific individual practices and norms as a proxy for larger, more complicated questions of social organization, social obligation, and social propriety.

During the twentieth century, the constantly expanding possibilities for having other people cook for us frayed the tethers between women, domesticity, and cooking, even while such restraints were not equally shared. However, another dimension has been added: these decisions *sometimes,* but not *always*, involve household members, or someone working for the household, engaging in the productive labor of cooking. We can still find the "evidence of the hand" or the continuation of cooking as a moment of food production in American culture, but there are more categories of cooking left to explore. In particular, the female head of household needs to be recategorized from "born to cook" to "born to figure out how to feed people." The domestic obligation really revolves around problem-solving: the fact that there are always hungry mouths to feed is the weary load of all humans, but especially all women. Resolving this issue by cooking all the food for a single meal or many meals using what we now label "fresh," "raw," or "whole" ingredients is but one choice. Having a single member of the household cook all the meals to feed their family has long been just one possibility out of a set of options available to Americans.

The focus on women as having social and moral obligations to be competent everyday cooks seems remarkably consistent with the preoccupations of the Beecher sisters, even though they lived in a different era, when women's rights were minimal and their domestic responsibilities significant. The possibility of doing work other than caring for the household and the invention of electricity transformed women's lives. If good meals are a reflection of a good society and we eat so many meals outside the home, why don't we pay more attention to those meals and their cooks?

CHAPTER THREE

Cooking Is an Art

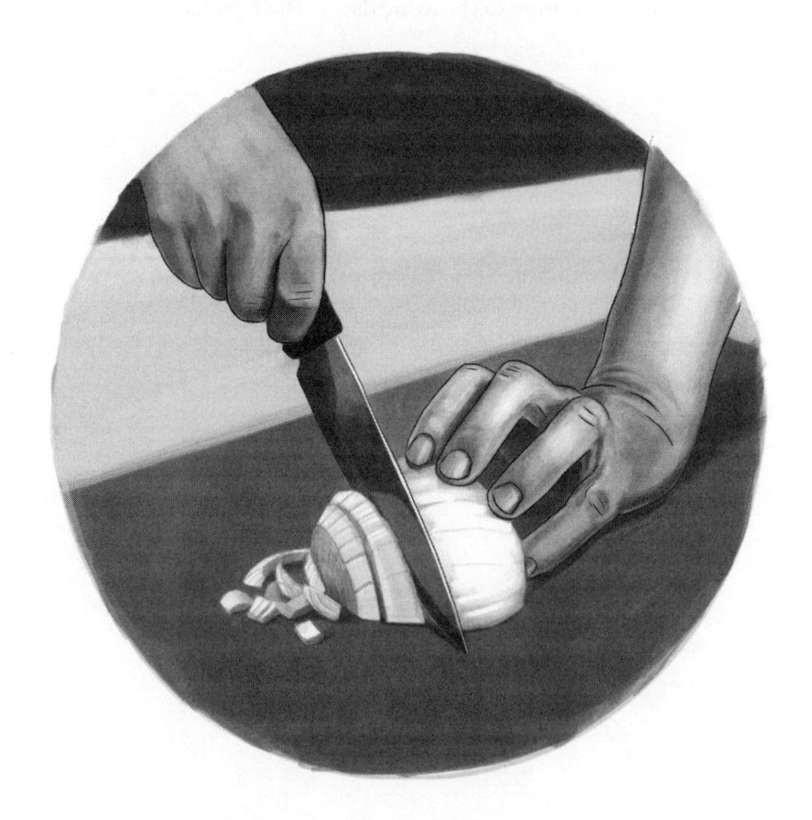

Cooking can be creative, and it can also have aesthetic aims, allowing a person to transcend the monotony of the task, the deep sigh that emerges when she realizes that, yet again, today, just like yesterday, people need to be fed. There are many tricks to accomplishing this, such as performing a certain identity (e.g., trained professional chef, home cook inspired by celebrity chefs), choosing to cook for certain events (e.g., a dinner party, a ritual celebration for a religious holiday), or possessing a certain manner of mastery (using culinary ingredients as if they were paints, using knives or other kitchen tools with the same ease as musician plays her instrument). These gestures and intentions involved in cooking change the context and therefore the results. Determining what makes a dish or meal into a moment of sustenance that is simultaneously mundane and exceptional is not easy. Modern commentators and critics struggle with definitions of artistry when considering a painting or a performance; what happens when we try to apply this concept to a meal? What are the manners of evaluation, the means of comparison, between two meals, say, a bowl of macaroni and cheese and an entire cold poached salmon coated with a dill cream sauce and served on a platter? To assert that artistry can be part of making a meal, and to include American home cooks as well as professional chefs, this category of cooking as art is best explored as follows: a dish or meal reveals virtuosity when the cook identifies the acts of cooking as a creative process or when the cook possesses an internalized aesthetic standard (or both). In the enactment of processes with such aims, not every cook necessarily embodies the same standard, but the cooking is perceived as *going beyond* performing functional tasks, becoming an act with creative or aesthetic aims.

In these moments, cooking is not a chore. The burden of obligation is somehow overcome. The cook's actions in these instances are different. What emerges is still a meal—an object or objects destined to inevitably disappear down the gullet—but all the steps, from planning to shopping to chopping to serving, need to considered in light of varied yet consistent expectations of creativity and artistry. Over the course of our ethnographic research, a number of cooks articulated their awareness of the creative potential in making a meal. Such possibilities, however, were enacted with great variation. The common core involved the transformative *possibilities* in these particular moments of making a meal. A certain revision, even transcendence, occurs because seemingly mundane actions are expressed in a different register. In other words, as philosopher Bob Valgenti puts it, in these moments, "To cook is not only a transformation of the ingredients into a particular dish, but a transformation of that dish's very meaning within the ever-changing contexts of its preparation."[1] Such a metamorphosis is the result of internalized standards; although these are not necessarily uniform, creative cooks all have some type of aspiration that spurs them to contrive meals that are beyond the ordinary.

Jerry, who has embraced cooking in retirement, looks to the Renaissance ideal of individual expression and identity to explain his decisions about what and how to cook. Carol, a young, single professional, strives to bypass the drudgeries of being a home cook by using organization and innovation to incorporate a creative energy into the work she puts into making meals. Peter, who has long been employed as a cook in commercial settings, enacts discipline conforming to professional expectations of an aesthetic standard. Sylvia, a recent émigré, works with clear confidence, displaying a set of competencies gained from witnessing others repeatedly make a certain cultural dish and then reproducing it herself over and over again until her aspirations and aims are in harmony. Sarah, a working mother, does not always use an aesthetic standard when she makes a meal; however, she is a "weekend warrior" culinary artist, using more leisurely days to cook beyond obligation and function.

When creative and aesthetic interpretations are understood as crucial to the process of cooking, artful food emerges through a dialogue. The cook articulates, in mind or in body, a certain aspiration that then comes to fruition in a certain dish. Peter, who trained at a culinary school and is a longtime professional cook, does not pronounce the tricks of the trade he has learned as he works; rather, the way he chops an onion or makes a chiffonade of basil are so integrated into his aesthetic that they are merely means to the end of preparing the meal. His artistry rests in the relationship of his *vision* of the meal and the *work* he does to enact it. In Peter's case, the intersection of his aesthetic standards and professional training means that all his home-cooked meals involve artful practices, whether he is preparing an elaborate meal for guests or a quick and casual dinner for his family. In one instance, the odds and ends left from a dinner party serve as an inspiration. He begins the meal preparation by rummaging through the refrigerator. He had company staying at his house and had entertained his guests the night before, so there are a lot of leftovers to use as the base for the meal. "We have had a lot of company," Peter explains, "so [tonight] we are going to have leftovers. We are going to make some soup, grill some bread, and make a salad." In a sense, his aesthetic involves using a set of constraints to guide his decisions: the items already in the house and the conventions of trained practice. He describes creativity as "being flexible. . . . [It's when] you go with the flow and you do [what you] need to make it [the meal] happen." One of the ingredients Peter finds in the refrigerator is a bowl of chicken stock. He made it the night before with the parts of a whole chicken he didn't use for the dinner party. Peter's decision to let the ingredients guide his choices for the meal reflects creative interface between what is valuable and what is possible.

Cooking as a creative process and as enacting an internal aesthetic standard are particularly fluid categories of experience. Temporality—the right or best time for creativity—is variable both within each individual cook's repertoire and between various cooks. The ability of an artful dish or meal to be a distinguishing characteristic of a cook's reputation is crucial to a professional chef but optional for a home cook. The aesthetic aspirations to be achieved with any meal are not fixed in time or place but rather are mutable, responding to cultural, social, and economic contexts. As such, in the contemporary American context, the boundaries between public and private spheres are especially porous. Today, shared understandings of these ideals move easily between domestic and commercial kitchens and are transmitted by numerous social networks: friends and family, television shows, social media, and magazines and cookbooks, among others. Artful dishes and meals are made, savored, and categorized in the push and pull between our private and public engagements.

Aesthetic standards emerge through shared disciplines of practice, and due to his training as a chef, Peter's cooking also conforms to professional norms. The integration of an external standard into his everyday practice can be as simple (or complex) as chopping an onion or crushing a clove of garlic. Peter, who graduated from the Culinary Institute of America, chops his onion exactly the way thousands of culinary students have been trained. First, using a paring knife, he cuts off a small part of the top stem end and then peels away the papery outer skin. Once the slippery skin is removed, leaving the white layers, he switches to a larger chef's knife and cuts the onion in half, right down the center, through the root end. He then puts the flat side of the onion half on the cutting board and carefully makes several horizontal cuts stopping just before the root. His left hand rests on top of the onion and presses down to make sure it does not slip. He grips the chef's knife tightly with his right hand, keeping his hand as close to the blade as possible. He makes several vertical cuts next. The onion is now almost entirely cross-hatched; the surface is no longer smooth. He then places the knife parallel to the onion and cuts across the entire surface and toward the root end, leaving clean half-inch squares of diced onion on the cutting board.

When preparing a different meal, Peter crushes garlic for a grilled chicken dish. He uses the large, wide-bladed chef's knife for a number of tasks, the first of which is to cut off the root ends of the garlic cloves. After peeling off the outer skin with his hands, he uses the knife horizontally, pressing the flat end of the wide blade down onto the cloves to crush them. Next, he brings the knife back to a vertical position and chops through the garlic and then quickly flips the blade to use the flat end again, pressing the cloves one more time. Finally, he scrapes the blade under the crushed, chopped garlic, lifting it up and pushing it into a bowl in one fluid movement. His hands and his knife work together, as if partners in a choreographed dance.

Jerry, a retiree who started cooking regularly only late in life, uses his knife much more hesitantly when he chops onions for his soup. He holds the entire knife in the air above the onion and cuts straight down rather than keeping the tip of the blade on the cutting board and lifting the back of the blade in the air to obtain leverage (as Peter does). When he moves the knife down to chop, it hits the onion but slips. He holds the knife at the back of the handle rather than close to the blade, and he *pushes* rather than *glides* the blade into the onion.

Peter's aesthetic and expertise are the result of what Richard Sennett calls "trained practice," which is in contrast to "the *coup de foudre*, the sudden inspiration."[2] Jerry's aesthetic sensibilities are more clearly aligned with the Romantic ideal of artistry, the burst of brilliance. These notions are central to his culinary artistry. To describe his cooking style to friends, he says, "I use the analogy of a painter. . . . A painter is a creative artist, and the painter does not paint by numbers in the little box. . . . A painter paints and mixes his different colors, and sometimes he has to throw it [his work] away, sometimes it's okay, and sometimes it's very good." The capacity for self-expression, more than the appreciation of the audience or the mastery of techniques, informs his process and internal standard.

For Peter, all cooking, be it artful or obligatory, involves a constant process of moving toward mastery: "I think you're always learning while cooking, no matter what you do. . . . And the ingredients are always different. . . . I think you are always learning as long as you have the basic concept of how to cook correctly. It's half the battle for most people; some people are afraid to take a recipe or not take a recipe and just try." The first step is mastering a set of shared skills, and with those in hand—or, as Peter demonstrated, in the hands—creativity and artistry can emerge. Peter's artistry lies in a constant negotiation between received knowledge (e.g., the culinary school truisms about the best way to cut an onion) and embodied understanding. In his case, *actions* make artful food, or in Tim Ingold's words, "To know things you have to grow into them, and let them grow into you, so that they become a part of who you are."[3] There is a grace and precision to Peter's movements that is quite distinct from Jerry's more hesitant use of the knife; Peter's culinary artistry happens while he is cooking, or in the doing. The contrasts between Peter's and Jerry's actions highlight the mediations constantly in play between cooking knowledge, skill, and identity. A dynamic always exists between an internal perception and types of external sanctions, even if what *happens* is not in any way identical. Peter has been formally trained yet always feels as if he has more to learn. Jerry always responds primarily to his own intuition. But they are both culinary artists, and their practices reveal another level of complexity to classifications and their ability to contain human endeavors. In this case, categories *in action* may not be in concordance with obvious definitions of that category. Or perhaps the creative and aesthetic can never be rigidly defined within the home; perhaps the processes involved in making such a meal at home constitute a type of tinkering, moments of bricolage. At times, actions like chopping an onion fulfill the mundane, and at other times, they attempt to achieve something more exceptional. Peter and Jerry consistently make such moves, albeit unique and varied, in their "purposeful process of transformation or metabolization."[4]

Thus, the relationship between intention and action is not uniform for all cook-artists. The consistency lies in an expectation and a sense of aspiration toward a standard that comes from somewhere and is somehow articulated by the cook. If categories of practice themselves are products of time, place, and identity, so too are the evaluations that deem one cook an artist and another a hack. Defining cooking in this manner allows for the possibility of creativity and artistry on any given day for any given meal. As long as a standard is held up—in mind and body—artful food is created.

There always remains, however, a tension between self-expression and social obligation, because we cook primarily for others, not just for ourselves. Jerry never categorizes his cooking as a chore or associates his artful cooking with external social expectations:

> [Think of someone like] Picasso. . . . I like to think of [him] as a typical example of going through stages where at one point he was doing wonderful portraits, then he would do something else, and so forth, and he could also sculpt, so he was using his artistic creative abilities in a lot of different ways. Well, I think that when I cook, it's the same way. I want to use the creative artist I have in me whatever there is and not rely on somebody else. . . . The Rombauers or Julia Childs of the world are great, and I enjoy reading about them, but I don't want to stick to what they say is the right proportions of this or that.

When Jerry cooks, his actions are a form of individual expression and are not constrained by obligations of any type, such as a certain way of preparing the food or a particular audience that he needs to feed. According to Jerry, his cooking is not bound by customs or rules and so is somehow *purely* a creative act; his aspirations are not bound by rules of practice but rather reflect individual expression. At the same time, in comparing himself to Picasso and distancing himself from Irma Rombauer and Julia Child, Jerry acknowledges that like other categories of cooking, artful cooking is expected to involve informed knowledge that is linked to social standards and cultural contexts.

Carol also defines her cooking, especially the cooking she does for dinner parties, as a form of individual expression not mediated by the demands of others: "I guess the part about cooking that I love is seeing something that I've never done before come out. [I] like the final product. . . . Once I've used a recipe once, I never use that recipe again. I always adapt it." Yet Carol's culinary artistry does not have the constancy articulated by Jerry. Her circumstances—she is single and childless, thus not bound up with domestic and family obligations—give her space for making artful meals: "For me it's not yet a chore because I don't *have* to cook for people." When Jerry compares himself to a painter, arguing that both a cook and a painter can be understood as creative artists, and Carol compares herself to her mother and others more bound by obligation, they reveal the fluidity of modern American cooking. As cooks become increasingly less contained by expectations of constancy, it is in the *actions* of making a meal that they can shift their identity and expectations, and ultimately the perception of the meal itself. Jerry and Carol are episodic cooks whose creative and aesthetic culinary efforts are fluid yet crucial to their own self-perceptions as to what defines them as cooks.

For Jerry, the definition of cooking as a creative art is based on an assumption that "artfulness" comes from individual intuition and expression. His cooking inspirations emerge when his ideas interact with a set of ingredients and an array of equipment, allowing him to play and invent a dish. When he cooks, he uses many cooking implements, often in unpredictable ways. When he makes a chicken soup, he introduces me to what he calls his "tools of the trade." He opens up a drawer next to the stove that is full of dried spices from a well-known mail-order spice company. He says, "This is my box of paints." He picks up different spice bottles and then decides what to put into his soup pot. He points to his blender. After he boils all his soup ingredients (including a whole chicken, bones and all) for some time, he "blenderizes" them all and puts that concoction through a sieve to get his final dish. Later on, he introduces me to his "secret weapons": standard-issue spray bottles, the type used for household cleaning tasks. He uses them to mix marinades, which he then sprays on many different types of meat and fish. Jerry shows us his technique for making striped bass, explaining, "I just made this up in my head." He starts with a fillet, which he places on a sheet of tin foil. Next, he chops several sprigs of dill and spreads them on top of the fillet. He adds butter and extra virgin olive oil, salt, pepper, and a little Tabasco. His voice rises a bit as he says, "Now I will show you my great secret. . . . I invented this years ago." He reaches up into a cabinet over the stove and pulls down a spray bottle. This particular bottle contains a mixture of four wines: sherry, Madeira, Marsala, and port. He spritzes the entire fillet with it. He explains why: "Again, it is like mixing paint. If you have all blue, or yellow, or green, or black, it's not very good. But if you can find a way to mix those colors, then you have something good." He then folds the foil over the fish to make a tight packet and puts his creation in the oven to bake.

Jerry's understanding of cooking as an art is inspired by the belief that art is created by the solitary painter, working alone, seized by a *coup de foudre;* it is more about expression than technique.[5] Of course, Jerry's theory of artistry as an expression of individual talent is not sui generis. He follows a long Western tradition of valorizing individual artists and their acts of genius, a tendency to highlight individual talent that has been passed on in undergraduate art history classes for generations. When he compares his cooking to Picasso's painting, he is really placing himself within a certain genealogy of defining artistry, a line of thought that sees art as an expression unconstrained by normative assumptions or even technical competencies. According to this narrative, the "Rombauers and Childs" are inconvenient because their cookbooks rely too much on instruction and prescription; in other words, their aims are not congruent with those of Picasso, since their approach is based on the notion that one must always *learn* to cook rather than simply *express* cooking talent. In keeping with this sensibility about creativity and artfulness, Jerry also relies on certain assumptions about aesthetics articulated by philosopher Immanuel Kant, who saw aesthetic judgment as indicative of individual perspective and talent rather than as a form of analysis or understanding mediated by social values or social organization. The trope of the tortured, brilliant, potentially great artist stymied by unappreciative audiences and a lack of patronage arose from such a singular definition of art and artistry.

ARE AESTHETIC STANDARDS ALWAYS SOCIAL STANDARDS?

However, if, as Priscilla Parkhurst Ferguson aptly puts it, "Constrained by the insistent needs of everyday life, . . . domestic cooks work the ordinary,"[6] can we accept Jerry's categorization of himself as a painter of food? Should we? Our struggles with cooking in modern life—our ambivalence, our decisions to outsource some or all of the steps involved in making a meal, our indecisiveness about what makes food good—might lie in our current *expectations* of what should happen when we cook, what Frances Short calls the "creative cooking ideal." Short's research in England, a crucial (and early) systemic analysis of people's domestic cooking skills, refuted the analytic drumbeat insisting that modern life had rendered Britons useless or clueless cooks, arguing instead that cooking is a complex practice that changes depending on the context. She pointed out that current definitions of cooking skills were vague and inconsistent. For a proper definition, it is not sufficient to detail practical and technical abilities; conceptual, creative, and organizational abilities must also be included.[7] At the same time, she felt that the increasingly porous boundaries between public and private food and the rising influence of the chef as a culinary standard-bearer created expectations for home cooks that were too grand. In a sense, Short believed that the creative and aesthetic standard was as much to blame for changes in the perceptions and practices of her participants as the (often accused) increased access to industrially or commercially prepared food.

In this sense, Jerry's assertion might more accurately reflect the relatively recently elevated status of commercial or professional cooks: not only does he call himself an artist with food, but when he is making a meal, he comports himself like a chef on the Food Network. His artistry might arise from his self-professed identity rather than any unique skill or talent on his part. In her recent analysis of the power of food media and celebrity chefs in contemporary society, Signe Rousseau points out that although there is little

Figure 11. “The Cooking Lesson,” 1911. Art and Picture Collection, New York Public Library Digital Collections.

evidence that watching cooking shows translates into practical knowledge, celebrity chefs "have more and more influence over those who hold . . . power and they certainly have a significant impact on a growing number of individual consumers."[8] She argues that chefs have joined other experts—especially those involved in matters related to food, health, and the environment—who are engaged in the work of improvement: "They [celebrity chefs] promise to make us better: better cooks, better carers for our families, better shoppers, better entertainers."[9] Contemporary chefs are more than really good cooks; they function as impresarios, elevating home cooks like Jerry as well as themselves in the process of performing what might otherwise be considered pedestrian acts. Chefs demonstrate virtuosity, and home cooks follow along. The changing social status of cooking, or at least certain categories of the practice, has empowered Jerry; he can comfortably define his cooking as creative and artistic, making analogies between his decision to make a certain soup and Picasso's blue period. Increasingly porous identities and boundaries enhance the possibility of domestic culinary artistry, allowing for "something of the professional's skill . . . to make its way into the domestic kitchen. Some portion of the artist's pride in culinary creation has to make it to the dining table at home."[10] Thus, perhaps cooking can be a creative act and type of performance that occurs in domestic spaces, insofar as achieving the "creative cooking ideal" now has larger cultural resonance and approbation. Jerry's artistry is but one of a number of possibilities within a cultural milieu that increasingly accepts and even promotes creative moments of transformation during cooking while also assuming broad agreement that the practice should have aesthetic aims.

Thus, if cooking always transpires within a set of social relations, culinary artistry as created by an individual genius does not exclusively define the category, but it can be used as a form of identity. Apparently, definitions of cooking as an art are multiple and frequently contradictory. If social relations and social obligations function as the "glue" that binds all categories of cooking practice, Jerry's explanations make sense but do not fully capture what happens. As with other aesthetic practices, cooking defined as an art also needs to be socially acceptable: rules, habits, and traditions must be followed by those who cook and accepted by those who eat. Classic dilemmas around the social acceptability of dishes and meals involve the parameters of edibility. Examples abound. In Mexico, for instance, there is a long-standing tradition of consuming insects—in Oaxaca, an appetizer of a taco full of *chapulines* (fried and spiced grasshoppers) certainly adds an aesthetic dimension to a meal. Serving this at a dinner party in parts of the United States might be gamely received, but would it be deemed an artful choice?

Certain social conditions also need to be met for a cook to be considered an artist of food or the creator of artful dishes and meals. If artful cooking involves the possession of a certain aesthetic standard, the standards of home cooks come from four main social codes: normalized forms of practice, shared customs and traditions, values of creativity, and expert communities. Each one of these social codes creates the conditions for a certain aesthetic standard; the cook adopts a standard and displays it when cooking an artful dish. But there is a *tension* when it comes to the best ways to reproduce and reinforce creative and aesthetic standards when comparing home cooks and professional cooks or chefs. This tension emerges because the home cook has less at stake; the social milieu of a private home will accept a luxurious shrimp risotto one night and a workaday spaghetti and meatballs on another.

In Parkhurst Ferguson's exploration of professional expertise, she states that for American professional cooking to be identified as a creative and artistic profession, certain social conditions need to be in place: "For cooking to attain the prestige of a 'real' profession, it has to come first—before the people involved, before concerns about nutrition. . . . Cooking must be prized for its own sake rather than for what it can do. . . . The preparation of the food like the presentation of the meal must be more than a means. It must be an end in itself."[11] When chefs discuss what differentiates their meals from the countless other meals being consumed around the world, they focus on the artistry—not just in "mixing the paints," or inventing a dish, but also in the larger context of the meal.

For trained cooks and chefs, multiple senses must also be engaged when preparing a meal. The look, the smell, the feel, and the taste of the food are all important—all the senses matter. Also, food needs to be presented with care, because making art requires not only a certain identity or fidelity to a type of process but also a particular *reception*. Only then can the final result can be deemed a piece of art. The diner cannot be forgotten, for a chef's artistry can only be fully appreciated when it is consumed. Literally. Chefs cook for larger and more diverse audiences than home cooks, and without these audiences, there is no display of artistry; professional chefs cannot be artists by themselves. Professional chefs carry a certain burden when it comes to cooking a meal: any action perceived of as an expression of creativity (versus an obligation) is dependent on being accepted by an audience. The chef's identity is dependent on such social approbation. In that sense, it might be more accurate to compare a chef to a jazz musician. Both produce ephemeral experiences that can happen in homes or on the streets. But in the case of these *professionals*, someone needs to be willing to listen to Wynton Marsalis play jazz, or in fact be willing to pay for the pleasure of listening to his music, for it to be elevated beyond an everyday practice or a part of a certain cultural tradition or bounded musical community. In the same way, someone with a reservation for dinner at Babbo in Greenwich Village needs to be interested in engaging with the theory and practice of Mario Batali's artful food and willing to eat his beef cheek ravioli and crispy bronzini. Even if Batali had an audience of family members or other domestic partners to consume his food, it would not be enough to raise his practice to art.

To maintain his or her creative and aesthetic standards, the professional commercial cook must constantly convince others to engage. The home cook has more options. Nowadays, though, when the choice is to engage creatively, to move beyond the mundane, a professional chef like Mario Batali increasingly not only embodies but also transmits such aesthetic ideals and standards. Chefs have become the primary teachers of artistic cooking because they now not only represent but also reproduce the category in an ever-widening circle of contact with Americans—both in restaurants and in homes. Over the past twenty years, Batali, who is just one of many chefs taking full advantage of the transformations in American culinary values and practices, has built a multimedia empire with eight restaurants and the food emporium Eataly (now found in five American and six Italian locations), while hosting multiple television shows on the Food Network. The cultural saturation of cooks such as Batali means the "creative cooking ideal" inspiring (or overwhelming) home cooks often emerges from watching him make homemade ravioli or reading about his adventures in Italy in books such as *Molto Gusto* and *Molto Italiano*.

Another possible definition of artful cooking, which Parkhurst Ferguson hints at in her analysis, involves identifying certain culinary practices as those that uphold any and all professional aesthetic standards. These standards are upheld when a cook is trained to master specific professional styles and make certain dishes and meals. Thus, a trained chef, such as Peter, does not "invent" his or her meals; rather, the chef works within a culinary paradigm that is deemed aesthetically appropriate by society and reinforced by professional standards. Another, overlapping, definition aligns artful cooking with certain aesthetic sensibilities. A meal cooked by a chef looks and tastes unique in certain ways because socially dictated expectations relating to a meal's aesthetic quality inform what appears at the table. These aesthetic (and in the case of culinary art, multisensory aesthetic) judgments, as sociologist Gary Fine defines them, "are grounded in social relationships, face to face negotiations, social structures and organizations and are found throughout society."[12] Fine's fascinating ethnography of professional cooks in four different restaurants explores, among other things, the types of aesthetic judgments inherent in their everyday cooking practice and argues that aesthetic standards emerge from social contexts. Jerry's justification for the sui generis nature of his culinary artistry is that "art defines itself." This idea, when seen through the lens of a sociological theory of aesthetics, is illusory.[13] What is missing? The social dynamic between the cook and the eater, as well as the inherently social nature of any culinary process. Thus, to properly define an artful practice, there must be a focus on the *response*, because "an aesthetic object, or act, is intended to produce a sensory response in an audience."[14] Understanding the aesthetic dimension of cooking through this definition allows for an integration of cognition (what is imagined), affect (what is felt), *and* intention (of both maker and recipient).

If this definition of cooking as an art holds true, a certain dilemma arises. Is the cook required to meet the sensory expectations of the eater? Or is it simply the fact that the cook holds certain sensory expectations and a concept of quality in mind while cooking that makes all the difference? And where do ideas emerge about fulfilling expectations of what makes a "good" dish—a dish that is aesthetically pleasing across multiple dimensions? In traditional theories of aesthetics, the ability to be discerning when making an aesthetic evaluation of an object is crucial. Again, there is a constant dialogue between internal desires and external judgments.

CREATIVE AND AESTHETIC STANDARDS: SOMETIMES OR ALWAYS?

The shape and tenor of these dialogues may mean that the definition of artful cooking by home cooks and professional cooks ultimately diverges. Home cooks are not required to categorize their meals as artful based on uniform aesthetic standards. These standards do not determine Jerry's or Carol's identity as artistic or creative cooks because they are neither essential nor static. Less is at stake for home cooks. The risotto and Caesar salad listed on the dinner party menu Carol puts together and proudly displays to her guests also feeds and nurtures them, and they will remain friends, no matter the creaminess of the risotto or the ratio of salad dressing to lettuce. This is not so for the professional cook; such standards are crucial to pleasing his customer and maintaining a good public reputation. As an episodic American home cook, Carol, the day after the dinner party, might decide to go out for dinner and consume someone else's aesthetic aims or to quickly throw together a salad without much aspiration or enthusiasm.

Chefs trained in the culinary arts are taught that certain standards are required to create "good food," and so their aspirations are (at least theoretically) constant. Throughout the history of trained American chefs cooking for publics in restaurants, hotels, and other venues, such concepts of quality have been profoundly influenced by the French culinary tradition, especially French haute cuisine, food prepared for elites. Up until twenty-five years ago (and to some extent through today), the dominant standards for preparing food deemed to have aesthetic quality in such locales came from French haute cuisine, especially the ideas of French chefs of the early twentieth century, notably Auguste Escoffier. Escoffier and his colleagues helped institutionalize a group of aesthetic and technical standards that came to dominate commercial cooking and culinary education for over a century. The reasons for French dominance in both the discourse and practice of professional cooking are complex, but the "simple answer is that French chefs have dominated as the masters of the practice and as the primary instructors in the culinary knowledge necessary in fine dining restaurants, hotels, and clubs since their very inception."[15] In the American public sphere, when dinners were made, eaten, and understood to be more than ordinary, the accepted aesthetic standard was culturally defined *and* disseminated by these cook-artists.

So, artful cooking, like all types of cooking, always requires attaining knowledge and skill, but all cooks do not learn the same forms of knowledge or the same set of skills. For those training to be professional cooks in Europe

Figure 12. French chef Georges Perrier, photographed at Le Bec-Fin, his renowned restaurant, in Philadelphia, Pennsylvania. Photograph by Carol Highsmith, circa 1990–2000, Library of Congress Prints and Photographs Division.

and the United States, there traditionally exists a unique integration between a certain culturally based set of practices and types of aesthetic standards. Artistic cooking, professionally defined, came foremost from the principles, methods, and techniques of French haute cuisine. Thus, the historical emergence of public spaces where people could purchase and consume food and participate in a shared sensory experience converged with the articulation of ideals or expectations of aesthetic quality from a certain cuisine. Interestingly, the professional standard was closely guarded, perceived to be a means of distinguishing professional cooks from home cooks; the social conditions for obtaining the standard were perceived as bounded by certain social settings, commercial and not domestic. Restaurant meals are often called a type of performance; making and serving a meal is a group endeavor and almost always a shared experience. The perception that artful cooking presents itself in restaurants differently than at home might be like comparing what happens when you go to a concert hall to hear a full orchestra perform Mozart's Requiem versus when you play the first movement at home on your piano.

The five foundational elements of French haute cuisine are stocks, sauces, knife skills, cooking methods, and pastry.[16] The sensory expectations involve subtle tastes, complex combinations of ingredients, and spectacular three-dimensional presentations. In the French culinary tradition, learning and mastering the foundational knowledge and internalizing the associated aesthetic expectations necessary to make coulibiac of salmon or steak with a Béarnaise sauce removed these dishes from the quotidian, giving them the status of artful food. These standards, in turn, separated the trained cook from the cook taking care of an everyday chore. For those training to be paid cooks, the journey from novice to apprentice to master involves following a certain path, one that is fairly narrowly drawn. And French culinary traditions created the road map.

However, the hegemony of the French aesthetic standard in professional culinary practice should be questioned. As is the case with all culinary practices, the julienne cut and the definition of mother sauces are not *naturally* good or right but rather part of a set of standards that has been codified and reproduced, often for the benefit of certain groups over others. Perfectly competent cooks are maligned and incredible ingredients and techniques are ignored. And given the quotidian and universal nature of cooking, the possibility for artful cooking can be cast as forever present, anywhere, with anyone, in numerous forms; in regard to creativity and artistry, French haute cuisine does not cover all the possible territory. The issue lies in a dynamic between any individual's act of artful cooking and the creation of her perception of an aesthetic standard that emerges from social context.

Tensions exist within the culinary profession when artful food is defined: Must all chefs acquiesce to French culinary hegemony? Contemporary chefs like Batali and Marcus Samuelsson (an Ethiopian-born chef who trained in Europe and is now cooking in Harlem), respond in the negative. Julia Child's and Marcus Samuelsson's reflections on the French culinary aesthetic reveal long-standing tensions between act, expectation, and standard. Child dedicated her career to teaching Americans, especially American housewives, the French way with food. Her personal awakening began when she moved to France with her husband and attended Le Cordon Bleu. She became zealous in her efforts to communicate the sense of pleasure and accomplishment she felt when she mastered French cuisine. She was a missionary: her dream was to teach people both why and how to aspire to the French culinary aesthetic standard. She understood the ways that cooking knowledge and skill were changing, the decline of domestic servants, and the fact that women were taking on the role of social hostess as well as family cook. She took advantage of this era of social transformation (the 1950s and 1960s) to create a new conversation between an aesthetic standard and a group of cooks. As she says in her foreword, "This is a book for the servantless American cook. . . . Anyone can cook in the French manner anywhere, with the right instruction." The book remains in the classic cookbook genre as a manual for instruction; however, she wanted to offer knowledge and skill that would elevate everyday cooking, bring artistry to the act, enhance food beyond sustenance, and improve home entertaining. As she concludes her plea, her long-term desires are clear: "Cooking is not a particularly difficult art, and the more you cook and learn about cooking, the more sense it makes."[17] When it comes to becoming a cook-artist, Child says, "Vive la France."

In *Yes, Chef,* Marcus Samuelsson's memoir of his culinary journey, he explores the allure of the French haute cuisine standard while simultaneously rejecting its hegemonic nature. He begins by recounting his experiences of learning to cook in Sweden, both in culinary school and in restaurants. During one of his early apprenticeships, he worked with Swedish chefs, making both traditional Swedish food and the standard "fine dining" dishes found throughout Europe. He learned the professional aesthetic standard, often throwing his mother's and grandmother's practices into doubt. He describes how the time he spent working at Tidbloms, a high-end restaurant in his hometown of Gothenburg, Sweden, started this process:

> My first week, I learned how a proper fish stock was made. Where my grandmother threw a mishmash of bones into a pot with water and chopped red onions, mixing salmon and haddock and letting it cook at a furious boil, Tidbloms only used finer, more delicate fish, like turbot and sole. They added fresh thyme and parsley, peppercorns, white wine, and the white part of the leek, cooking it slowly, barely simmering, coaxing out flavors rather than bludgeoning them.[18]

He had learned how to cook a fish stock while growing up, as fish cookery is fundamental to Swedish cuisine, but now the context had shifted, and something else—his emerging professional identity, an intersection of knowledge, skill, and concepts of "artful" preparations—was at stake.

Eventually, his ambitions propelled him beyond Sweden, and he ended up in a very traditional kitchen in a large Swiss hotel in the tourist town of

Interlaken. It was run by a German in a strict, hierarchical fashion, and so Samuelsson started out picking herbs in the garden, then moved up to *garde manger*, and eventually was promoted to *chef de partie*. But for the extremely hardworking and ambitious Samuelsson, the gold standard was working in France: "I had to get to France. Anyone who wanted to know greatness had to go to France. Yeah, I found French food too heavy and rigid and fussy sometimes, with technique overshadowing flavor, but there was no question that it embodied excellence, history, and craft—three qualities that appealed to me."[19]

After several years of moving from job to job, Samuelsson completed his journey as a culinary apprentice, but he started to question the pressure to conform to a certain standard to become a chef and to gain prestige and status within the professional culinary world. As he traveled around the world and began to develop an identity as a black chef originally from Ethiopia, he realized that there might be new ways to train, new techniques for artful cookery, and new systems of prestige to develop. He ends this section of his memoir with a telling (and compelling) passage about his thoughts after spending time in Asia: "I tasted coconut milk and lemongrass in hundreds of preparations, sweet and savory, and I thought, This is it: This food has as much integrity and power as any French food I have ever eaten. Why did people fly in Dijon mustard when they could make their own, fresher and better? I started to ask myself, Who lied? Who started the lie that France has the greatest food in the world?"[20]

Samuelsson goes further, clearly delineating his desire to create a new aesthetic standard: "That question ran through my head every time I bit into something new and that changed my notions of what 'good food' is. Then that question was replaced by a second: Who's going to make the people realize that food dismissed as 'ethnic' by the fine dining world could be produced at the same level as their sacred bouillabaisses and veloutés?"[21] It could be argued that the shifting patterns of who cooks and where that cooking has taken place have created opportunities for someone like Samuelsson to espouse a new aesthetic standard. With the decline of domestic service (especially since the 1950s), formerly the main means of employment for paid cooks, and the expansion of public venues serving meals, many cooks no longer working as individual servants for middle- and upper-class families could bring their internal aesthetic standards into larger communities of those who cook and those who eat. Many of these domestic cooks were immigrants, and their traditions began to play a larger role in the public culinary sphere. In the many decades between the publication of Child's *Mastering the Art of French Cooking* and Samuelson's *Yes, Chef,* artful cooking, in the home and in restaurant kitchens, shifted in form and content while retaining fidelity to aesthetic aims.

STANDARDS IN ACTION

When Amelia, a student-assistant who had trained at a culinary school and subsequently worked as a cook in Vermont's leading fine dining restaurant, watched the video ethnography of Jerry's meal preparation, she was horrified. Jerry's recipe for making soup does not conform to the rules of stock making as rigorously delineated in the curriculum of culinary schools. For example, students are instructed never to boil the stock because it will cause the bones to break down and cloud the soup and always to use raw meat because the stock will be more flavorful. Amelia's evaluation of aesthetic quality emerged through her training and experience, and her evaluation is a shared one. Fine also points out the long tradition of valorizing stock as crucial to the *fonds de cuisine.* Of his experience doing participant-observation in restaurants, he says "Cooks . . . are proud that they produce their own stock, avoiding canned broth or powdered stock."[22] In this type of culinary system that combines sensory and technical sensibilities, to trample on the received wisdom about making stock (or any soup based on stock) is to dismantle the very foundation of the entire edifice, to deny Escoffier's point that "stock is everything in good cooking." In learning how to be an artful professional cook, you must follow the dictum, "There can be no skilled work without standards."[23]

Jerry's artful cookery does not fit into the category of practice disseminated by Julia Child, enacted and then rejected by Marcus Samuelsson, and fully internalized by Amelia. Although almost seventy-five years elapsed between Julia's, Marcus's, and Amelia's apprenticeships, they traveled within the same universe of expectation and action while being inculcated with the French aesthetic standard. Jerry's practice is more difficult to contain because he does not imagine it working within a shared universe of values, nor does he feel compelled to internalize any set of expectations in relation to his artistic expressions. However, his approach may in fact reveal a shared set of values about artful cookery. These values coalesce around ideas about creativity. In this characterization, creative cooking involves ignoring or bypassing standards or other forms of shared expectations. Although a professional aesthetic standard may influence the practice of a home cook, it does not necessarily determine its artfulness. Presumably, there is less at stake in terms of identity, approbation, and long-term livelihood.

ARTFUL COOKING AND CREATIVE EXPRESSION: INTERNALIZED STANDARDS OR EXTERNALIZED INTUITIONS?

Jerry sometimes starts his stock or soup with a raw chicken, but he often uses a cooked chicken carcass. He then throws any leftover vegetables and stuffing he has into the pot. One of his tricks is to add a can of Campbell's cream of celery soup—"I do this to add a little body." For Amelia, one of the most difficult moments of watching Jerry cook is when he says to boil the soup (at one point he says that it should be boiled for one and a quarter hours, at another point he says four hours). How could Jerry boil all those ingredients rather than let them simmer, long dictated as the best technique for making a chicken stock? (This is similar to the reaction Samuelsson had when he learned how to "properly" prepare stock at Tidbloms.) Another challenging moment for Amelia is when Jerry points to the Cuisinart blender and says, "Then I put all the ingredients, including the chicken bones, vegetables, and spices into a blender." He then pushes this blended mixture through a colander to produce the final thick soup that he serves for dinner. This tramples on Amelia's aesthetic sensibilities (developed in culinary schools and restaurant kitchens). Jerry's decision to blend *all* the ingredients into the soup without first sifting out certain parts (especially the chicken bones and carrot tops) is profoundly counterintuitive to her. Jerry's practices defy her culinary paradigm for defining artful practice. But Jerry is not bound by any such rules. He concludes his exegesis on making chicken soup, reiterating his theory that "cooking is like art. I never use a cookbook. I only use what is in my head."

Like Jerry, Carol prides herself on possessing creative cooking knowledge and skill: "I strive to be creative. . . . It's one thing to be a good cook, but I really want to be creative." She is more of a rule follower than Jerry and is very careful in her techniques and especially in organizing both her time and her cooking space for maximum productivity. Creativity for her resides in adapting recipes to her tastes: "I really do it with everything. With a vegetarian chili recipe, I think, no, I want to have more vegetables in there, and I want it to be spicier, and I want to throw in some red pepper, and I want to put in curry powder because I want to get that kind of flavor. . . . I don't veer off in terms of cooking time and things like that." She credits her creative ideas to the influence of other good cooks, saying that she "steals their recipes," but she gives her friends credit when she entertains others.

Carol differentiates her dinner party cooking from the ordinary cooking of her mother because she chooses all aspects of the meal—why she is making it, when she makes it, to whom it will be served—rather than being trapped by necessity or obligation. The organization and execution required to formally serve others a meal resembles the work of a *chef de cuisine:* it involves planning, cooking, considering the service and the expectations of guests, and so on. Her artful cooking is intuitive *and* systematic.

She takes an instructive tone when discussing making the risotto for the dinner party, but less one of a celebrity chef than of an executive chef: "The key with this spinach is, it takes only *one minute* to cook," she explains, and later, "You must taste the difference between regular and extra virgin olive oil." She discusses the importance of flavor to a stock, but in doing so, she, like Jerry, confounds the expectations of professionally trained cooks. She buys a can of low-sodium broth for her risotto but then complains about how much salt she needs to add to make the dish palatable. Amelia comments, "The thought never even occurs to her that she could just as easily make her own stock, to her liking, and keep it in the freezer."

The complexity of categorization, especially when it comes to cooking that rises above the ordinary yet remains a meal to be eaten in the home (just like any ordinary day), involves both the impetus for an aesthetic standard and the enactment of such a standard. Amelia's critiques of Jerry's and Carol's cooking practices are examples of this tension. However, there is solidarity between artful cooks—including Amelia, Jerry, Carol, and the cooks and chefs observed by Fine—whether they are professionally trained or not. This shared sensibility lies in their relationship to recipes. As Jerry frequently points out, he does not really follow rules but rather general guidelines: "First of all, I very seldom use a cookbook. . . . Measurements we usually try to avoid, in other words, how much of this and how much of that. I think a lot of it is instinct. You never want to oversalt, for example, but many recipes say 'a pinch.' Well, what is a pinch? A pinch to you might be different than a pinch for me."

Among the cooks and chefs Fine observed, he identifies a tension between following a recipe, using a recipe as a guide, and internalizing processes so there is no need for a recipe at all. He considers the ability to traffic between different strategies to primarily be the provenance of the professional cook, but with cooks like Jerry and Carol, who are confident and ambitious, similar tensions also emerge. Like the chefs in Fine's research, they consult recipes, but they "ignore them, interpret them, and move beyond them to creative autonomy."[24] Fine argues that home cooks tend to follow recipes as if they were "orders." Professional cooks, on the other hand, rely on "memory and experience."[25] Jerry, however, sounds a lot like Fine's cooks, even if his practices might not quite fit within the professional paradigm: "I think using a cookbook is fine. I'm not opposed to it, but once you get to know it instinctively, . . . once you get past that hurdle, then you can start [to work on your own]." He also acknowledges that cooking, like painting (or like playing the piano, another analogy he uses during an interview), is a learned skill, but he clearly does not think it should be uniform or mechanical work:

> Well it's like mixing colors if you're going to paint. You don't suddenly [go] bingo. God doesn't suddenly give you insight into when you mix yellow and blue it makes green. So you [need to] play around or go to a professor or take a course in it. . . . So I'm not opposed to cookbooks. [But] once you get past that learning curve, . . . somebody's not going to tell me how much thyme I have to put in that soup to make it right because I sort of instinctively know.

For Amelia and Peter, artistry involves understanding and mastering skills and expectations set by others. A chef must literally become *part* of a culinary system—in body and mind, in what he or she knows and does—before there is a possibility of making artful food or being a culinary artist. Custom and tradition may inform these skills and expectations, but in culinary training, the individual cook is judged by whether he or she upholds an abstract (if not objective) standard.

Another way to explain artful food is by gauging the quality of the dishes and meals prepared by how they reflect or embody certain cultural traditions.

The attainment of mastery remains the goal, as is the case with professional cooks and the French aesthetic standard. But in this context, the individual cook reproduces, more or less competently, skills or expectations learned by watching others who have mastered the culinary expectations of their culture or tradition. Often, the aesthetic standard is implicit rather than explicit. Such an explanation overlaps with the cultural foundations of French haute cuisine—dedication to a set of ingredients, methods, and techniques—but here, such fidelity emerges from *familial* cultural traditions.

Sylvia, an émigré from Russia who is in her late twenties and recently single, displays a comfort with the practice of cooking that is the result of internalizing a system of action. As with Peter's kitchen choreography, she is comfortable in her workspace. She keeps the main counter where she works very organized. The ingredients for the dish she is preparing are pushed to the back of the counter, from left to right in order of use for easier handling. She does not place any ingredients on her cutting board other than those that she will be directly working with; the majority of the board stays clean, free of extra tools or ingredients. Sylvia spent time in the United States as an exchange student in her teenage and college years and finally emigrated when she was in her twenties. In Russia, her mother did all the cooking, even when Sylvia lived at home while attending university. Her active interest in cooking emerged after she had relocated, when she wanted to recreate the meals of her childhood:

> I was missing my ethnic food, Russian meals, and I tried to make it, and I also tried to expose my family, my American family, to what it is like, what the food, what the meals are like in Russia. I made Russian beet salad, which is potatoes, onions, carrots, pickles, and beets, and it's all [dressed] with vegetable oil or sunflower oil. And meat dumplings. So it's just the simple dough with, I make two kinds of stuffing, meat, I mix pork and beef and onions and some spices sometimes. And mushroom filling, just mushrooms sautéed with breadcrumbs with butter and an egg to hold it all together.

She goes on to explain that she made these meals without a recipe: "For those meals, I just knew it somehow. When you see it, you know the right proportions." Her comfort and creativity in cooking these dishes comes from kinesthetic and sense memory; by witnessing the act of making Russian beet salad multiple times and through bodily practice—from her cutting techniques to her tasting evaluations—she can make it too. Unlike Peter's decision to be trained as a professional, she did not make an *active* choice to be trained in Russian cuisine. The strong Russian food culture and the continuity in everyday cooking practices shaped her understanding and ability to reproduce these dishes in a creative manner. In the twenty-first century, the strength of a culinary system involves a high level of competition from a global-industrial supply chain that can provide multiple options for the cook, such as a wide array of ingredients not specific to geography, many preprepared dishes, meals that only need to be heated, and so forth. When Sylvia was growing up, Russia's communist regime meant that Russian cuisine was less dictated by such competitive foodways; her culinary palette was quite narrow, which, in a sense, permitted greater possibilities for mastery of a particular aesthetic standard.

Before she begins to make dinner, she quickly consults a Russian cookbook. She then moves into the kitchen and starts to cook. Her first actions are organizational. She pulls out all the ingredients necessary for a Russian tomato and cucumber salad that was a childhood staple. She explains that in Russia, they didn't have access to lots of vegetables, and this salad used those that were available: cucumber, tomatoes, green onions, and dill: "And we would add sunflower oil and sour cream. We did not have prepared dressings." When she has lined up all the ingredients at the back of the counter, she then reaches for two bowls, a cutting board, and a paring knife. She confidently picks up the knife, gripping it near the blade. She puts the flat side of the cucumber down on the counter and slices it in half length-wise and then uses the knife to peel the cucumber. In a gesture very familiar to cooks around the world (but definitely not part of French-style professional culinary training), she grips the cucumber in one hand. She holds the knife in her other hand and slices the cucumber into smaller pieces by moving the knife through the cucumber, toward her body. The cucumber is next to her body and far from the flat surface of the counter. Slice by slice, the cucumber gets smaller, and the pieces fall into the bowl directly below. She cuts the tomato in much the same way. She adds a dollop of sour cream, seasons the salad with kosher salt, stirs thoroughly, and then refrigerates it. There is no hesitancy in her thoughts or motions.

As a cook-artist, Sylvia enacts another aesthetic standard, one that involves improvised practices, or the ability to be creative within a set of external rules or constraints. Anthropologists Maryann McCabe and Timothy Maleyft, echoing Ingold and Sennett's views, argue that culinary creativity should not be categorized according to the Romantic ideal of "novelty and genius as if anything creative were singular and unrepeatable with its source in the individual"; rather, they contend that artistry can emerge in everyday cooking, tweaking a recipe or responding to cues—in the ingredients or from the audience.[26] Jerry certainly articulated innovation as part of his definition of culinary artistry:

> Talk about creative, I've created a dish, which is a summer dish, which is a salmon. . . . [I take] a fillet of salmon and cook it in the normal sense in the oven with some olive oil and maybe a few herbs, and then I cool it. . . . I created this dish which is then putting it in jelly, [and] I would put sour cream and pickled ginger, and so when the salmon comes out, there it is in this marvelous jelly, and then there's the ginger, the pickled ginger nobody knows about how you use that, it has the sour cream and a little wine, and I have some herbs, and it's a wonderful dish in the summer—very easy to make. I didn't look that up in a cookbook—just one day it sort of came to me.

In McCabe and Maleyft's study of forty-eight female home cooks, many of the women displayed innovative cooking practices, both because they had a desire to express creativity within the constraints of a required everyday task and because they wanted to bring new sensory experiences to their audiences, which in most cases were their families. These artful cooks, like Fine's professional chefs, always considered the eater as they prepared food. These women also often adapted recipes. For example, one woman found a pork tenderloin recipe online and then substituted cinnamon for cumin because certainly members of her family did not like cumin.[27] They searched for new recipes to make in order to ameliorate sensory boredom, a privilege of modern Americans, who are no longer required to consume the same foods every day. McCabe and Maleyft point out that culinary artistry creates positive sensations for everyone in the family: "The sensuous experience of cooking involves that cook and other household members. Through seeing, smelling, tasting, stirring and mixing ingredients, a cook produces a meal and enjoys the sensuality of cooking. At the same time, the family gains sensuous pleasure from the smell of food wafting through the home."[28]

In the Western aesthetic tradition, the tension between art as the enactment of external standards and art as an experience of a creative impulse has a long history. In fact, for most philosophers of aesthetics, cooking could never be categorized as an artistic practice at all, given that food fulfills base needs and is primarily experienced through the senses. Immanuel Kant made these issues clear. Kant's first premise about aesthetics is that it should be grounded in a notion of disinterestedness. Thus, aesthetic appreciation must be "only directed at the experience of the object appreciated."[29] The problem with food is that it satisfies base desires. Hunger makes "anything palatable as long as it is edible."[30] Kant believed that pleasure should be a *consequence* of our sensory engagement; senses other than sight were inconsequential to the making of art. According to this understanding of food, art, and aesthetics, the process of making the food is irrelevant; what is crucial is the food after it has been made into a dish—an object to be appreciated and savored. Kant's line of argument has influenced the generally heightened focus on the visual aesthetics of food, especially in cases when people intend food to transcend the quotidian and want to be awarded social approbation for their artistry.

Philosopher Emily Brady pushes back on the traditional Western philosophical distinction of higher and lower orders of pleasures. She thinks that smells and tastes can be incorporated into traditional forms of aesthetic theory. As the same time, she acknowledges that they "have a place in our more ordinary aesthetic responses."[31] She argues that these senses have been neglected in the development of aesthetic theories of food due to the predominance of the visual. Smells and tastes are more "bodily" senses; they bring experiences inside of us and are thus considered to be in the "realm of the crude."[32] In fact, she claims that people make sensory discriminations all the time during processes of cooking and eating: "Our everyday lives are infused with this kind of appreciation, in choosing the best ingredients for dinner, appreciating our daily route to work, and so on. One aroma is lovely, another stinks, one taste is vibrant, another dull. That we make and defend judgments like these indicates our capacity for aesthetically appreciating different smells and tastes."[33] In her fascinating meditation on the intersection of philosophy and taste, Carolyn Korsmeyer argues that taste cannot be understood either simply in the mind or simply with the body: "A study of taste and its proper activities thus takes us into territory involving perception and cognition, symbolic function and social values."[34]

The cooks participating in our study affirmed Korsmeyer's point that sensory actions and aesthetic standards are not static and absolute but rather fluid and responsive. For them, tasty and tasteful food may not happen every day, and the episodic quality of making artful food was due to varying expectations and constraints. In this context, constraints were identified along two axes. The first involved the obligation of cooking; the second concerned figuring out an unusual or different meal to prepare. The first constraint refers to the pressure of the quotidian. When Sarah is asked if she enjoys cooking, she responds, "I don't enjoy it every day. I almost have two different kinds of cooking. There's the cooking I do to get people fed, and then there's the cooking I do that I enjoy." She goes on to differentiate the two types of cooking in terms of the organization of her time: weekday cooking and weekend cooking. When she cooks on the weekend, she can take the time to experiment and even be playful:

> You take the pieces that you want, and then you put them in various combinations, and then you see what you get in the end. Sometimes, a lot of times, I experiment. One of the things I bought this weekend was some shrimp, and I'm going to figure out how to do shrimp scampi. I've got all my recipe books, and at some point we're going to make this shrimp scampi. For me, that will be a fun sort of creative process.

The recipients of her weekday and weekend cooking remain primarily her nuclear family, so she always cooks for others. However, she is less focused on her family's approval when less pressed for time: Of her experimental weekend dishes, she says, "If I can actually get the teenagers to eat it, it will be a great success, but even if they don't, if I'm pleased with it, that will be an accomplishment." Sarah wants an audience, but its members do not control her sense of artistry.

Like Fine's cooks, Sylvia, who is recently single, also identifies the importance of an audience in her determination of which category of cooking she might adopt on any given day:

> I have to be in the mood to cook something, and I usually don't like to cook for myself. So [if] it's for someone, for my friends, for example, I'd be more motivated to make something tasty and different. . . . I consider my friend's tastes, and preferences, and allergies, and things like that. For myself, I may be lazy. I'll skip a step or two, maybe an ingredient. [But] I'll try to make more than the one-course meal sometimes when I have friends over. For myself, it would be something simple.

She, like the other home cooks expressing artful cooking through creativity and innovation, displays confidence and a willingness to move beyond her typical methods. However, like trained cooks, she needs an audience to see cooking a meal as above and beyond a chore. Cooking a meal is standard; creating a meal to share, savor, and perform is not.

ASPIRATIONS AND DISAPPOINTMENTS: EXPERTS AND THEIR PUBLICS

What about the many culinary artists—the chefs that appear on television, in magazines, and in other media—who serve as coaches, ideals, and interlocutors for home cooks as they create menus and prepare meals? What role do they play in creating standards, fostering creativity, and reproducing customs and traditions? Even if you do not regularly go to the restaurants that make the dishes and meals that define culinary artistry, you can know this food. You might not experience the featured dishes through direct sensory engagement—tasting it, smelling it—but you can watch these meals being prepared on television, see what they look like in magazines, and even follow along via blogs as others eat them. Cookbooks increasingly rely on both images and text in order to convey instructions and suggestions for how to cook. *The Joy of Cooking* and *Mastering the Art of French Cooking* were considered innovative in their day because they included black line drawings that illustrated certain techniques, ingredients, and pieces of equipment. Now, it is standard practice for cookbooks to provide full-page, full-color images of finished dishes, solidifying aesthetic expectations without offering much guidance on meeting them successfully. Many Americans now classify cookbooks as belonging to a coffee-table genre, in the same category as an illustrated history of Renaissance painting or an account of Shackleton's voyage to the South Pole with photographs. The recipes are secondary to the images, which are beautiful, noble, exotic, and ultimately not attainable.

This visual rather than multisensory form of consumption destabilizes the cook, valorizing product over process.

Maybe culinary aesthetic standards are being primarily enacted through the frame of performance because of technological transformations, especially forms of video media. First, there were the cooking shows. Now, blogs, webcasts, Instagram accounts, and other types of media create a visually saturated environment for imagining artful food. Frames of reference and sources of inspiration come from everywhere and everyone. TV presenters, teachers, cookbook authors, podcasters, bloggers, family friends—wherever you look, there's someone with a recipe and an opinion. The circle of influence gets larger and larger, and more voices contribute to what makes food "good" and a meal beyond the ordinary.

Julia Child was the first American cookbook author to make the transition to culinary media maven. But as media scholar Dana Polan points out, before Child's public television show, *The French Chef* (which first aired in 1963), there were cooking shows on American televisions, shows that wanted to "both provide the basic didactic goals of teaching how to cook certain recipes and dishes and to help educate middle-class housewives on how to entertain."[35] The advantage of adding the medium of television to the didactic discourse on cooking was that, "for better or for worse, television finds you where you are. It is a public medium that uncovers each person in the privacy of the home."[36] Child's media success had much to do with her personality, but Child also understood that television, and especially cooking on television, integrated professional and domestic culinary worlds. She used television to teach home cooks to cook artful food and understand French cuisine as an art form. And as many food scholars have pointed out, traditionally, most kitchen knowledge was orally transmitted, by mothers to their daughters or by chefs to their apprentices.[37] In the contemporary United States, this is no longer the case, and this may have something to do with the phenomenal success of *Mastering the Art of French Cooking* and its companion television show, *The French Chef.*

Meanwhile, the documentation of kitchen work in many forms of media continues to expand. There are now newspaper sections, magazines, pamphlets, recipe cards, cookbooks, cooking shows, websites, and blogs all devoted to kitchen work. A notable trend in teaching how to make a certain dish, exploring a certain culinary culture, or providing how-to tips, is the increasing importance of trained and paid cooks and chefs as experts over knowledgeable home cooks. To be called an expert cook is less and less the provenance of women like Irma Rombauer, who cooked at home but developed a larger reputation for being an excellent cook and was thus considered capable of sharing wisdom and expertise. A cook's knowledge increasingly needs to be learned from people who cook beyond the everyday chore. Celebrity chefs capitalize on their expertise, which they have honed in the many new sites for cooking that evolved over the past century, such as restaurants and other public venues. Examples include Jacques Pepin and Pierre Franey at Le Pavillon and Howard Johnson's, Emeril Lagasse at Emeril's, Mario Batali and his multimedia and multirestaurant empire, and Rick Bayless at Tobolabampa and Frontera Grill.

The audiences of these chefs need to be taught about *both* culinary skills and aesthetic aspirations. Their socialization into a set of standards means these ideals are intrinsic to what they teach. Ideas and expectations about the possible ways of making artful food are exponentially greater for today's home cook than they were for cooks of previous eras. Teresa, who is originally from Trinidad and Tobago but now lives in an urban area of the Northeast, expresses ambivalence toward this expanded horizon of possibility. Her experiences with cooking while she was growing up were much more constrained, and so she identifies these new possibilities as opportunities but also finds them confusing to her everyday cooking practice: "I never cook with cookbooks. . . . I find it's hard to follow cookbooks. . . . When I grew up, I don't think there was one cookbook in that house." She likes to cook from experience and intuition, and she talks about her turnip soup with pride: "I'm from Trinidad and Tobago, and in Tobago, every Saturday the meal was soup, almost seven out of ten homes will make soup on a Saturday. I don't know why. . . . Mark [Teresa's husband] likes my [turnip] soup. His brother suggested that I could sell my soup." However, other possible ways of making "good" dishes and meals impinge on her ability to see herself as an artful cook: "William and Sonoma, they have classes that they offer, and I wanted to take some, and Mark was the one who talked me out of it. [He said,] 'You are such a great cook, you don't need cooking lessons.'" During a taped cooking session, she discusses her desire to be more imaginative about cooking fish, an important part of her family's diet: "I saw this guy—who is that crazy guy? . . . A celebrity chef. He has a reality TV show, *Hell's Kitchen*. He was on Jay Leno, and he was showing Jay how to cook [fish]. I would like to learn those types of techniques." Her husband chimes in, saying she already knows how to cook fish, but she continues to demur. His support is not sufficient. Pleasing herself and pleasing her domestic audience is not enough for her to consider herself an artful cook. There are bigger and broader culinary standards to be met.

Teresa's ambivalence indicates that moving cooking beyond the category of a chore might create too much of a good thing. Categories of practice shape as well as contain what happens in the kitchen and what it means. Cooking does not have to be chore—it can also be an art—but making that transition means that there are so many more possible ways to make good food but also so many possible ways to *not* make good food. Teresa's family's traditions do not satisfy her expectations any longer, nor do her husband's protestations that she should consider herself a good cook. She has to consider Gordon Ramsay's opinion too.

What gives a celebrity chef such as Ramsay the authority to define artful food, not only for professional chefs but also for everyday cooks like Teresa?

Does "expertise" make a cook an artist? Some home cooks articulated artful cooking as primarily involving creativity and innovation, but this was not the case for everyone. Those cooks who possess a professional pedigree (or some type of unique expertise) hold more and more sway in shaping the category of cooking as an art. Chefs are now considered the best guides for educating home cooks who aspire to make artful and "good" food. As more chefs become multimedia stars, there appears to be a general cultural acceptance that these professionals now define "culinary mastery" both inside and outside the home to the extent that questions of "authority" haunt the category of cooking is an art. There is acting with authority, there is being understood as an authority, and there is defining your culinary identity with authority.

Jamie Oliver, a restaurateur and chef from London, belongs to this club of influential star chefs, although Oliver's efforts demonstrate another quality of the contemporary culinary discourse. It is now possible for a celebrity chef to wield influence over all domains of contemporary kitchen work. The audience for proper cooking skill and knowledge now extends beyond the home cook. Oliver first attained international prominence with his cooking show, *The Naked Chef*, which premiered in 1999 and focused on simple preparations and attention to the quality and provenance of ingredients. This led to a series of books designed for the home cook, including *The Naked Chef* (1999) and *Jamie's Dinners* (2004). Oliver, who also owns the restaurant Fifteen in London, then started to turn his attention to the food served at schools all over the United Kingdom. In his documentary series *Jamie's School Dinners* (2005), Oliver chronicles his attempts to change the way food was prepared and consumed at a large public school in Greenwich, outside of London. Oliver, a self-professed "lad" who was in a rock band and learned how to cook in his father's pub, has said of restaurant cooking, "Cooking in the real world, when the shit hits the fan, it's horrible." These days, with the cultural power of celebrity chefs, he has the right to, as Signe Rousseau puts it, make an intervention that is "sanctioned by invitation" and to interfere with other cooks and in other kitchens.[38]

Oliver now effectively has irons in the fire in almost every category of contemporary kitchen work: homes, restaurants, and schools. As Oliver's empire indicates, the borders between public and private cooking have become completely porous. But Oliver's manifesto about the importance of "tasty meals with fresh ingredients" marks a shift in the stance of a trained chef. The goal is to help with the cooking chore rather than to elevate the home cook by teaching the knowledge for more creative practices. Family gatekeepers, it appears, can no longer be trusted. Like Irma Rombauer's friendly exhortations and Julia Child's casual approach on her television shows, part of Oliver's appeal is his commitment to democratizing cooking and his casual and approachable demeanor. At the same time, emphasizing certain styles of cooking and making them more accessible also transforms aspirations and expectations and thus shapes the form and content of cooking categories.

Today's home cooks can take on numerous identities while chopping onions and stirring soup. At its most basic, making food is creating something for human nourishment, and although food is necessary for survival, we also imbue dishes as well as meals with meanings. Such meanings are not necessarily universally held or universally positive, and as David Sutton points out, "When this concept is applied to cooking, one could say that in transforming materials or ingredients into forms—the cooked dish—one is also engaged in a process of self-transformation, into that of the competent or incompetent cook."[39] Determinations of competence, however, are not straightforward. The possibilities for self-transformation, I would argue, always occur within existing social categories, shaping the standards of evaluation. Teresa wants Gordon Ramsay's assistance in order to become competent; Gordon Ramsay needs Teresa in order to flaunt his expertise. If cooking artful food occurs not merely in the act of Jerry or Peter or Sylvia transforming ingredients into cooked dishes but also in the enactment of social expectations and standards, competent cooking in one context could be deemed incompetent in another. Jerry's artistic creation of a blended soup is an aesthetic travesty to Amelia, but does that matter? Jerry has a theory of action, he is perfectly confident about his decision to put the entire chicken, bones and all, into the blender, and he appears satisfied with the results.

There is another way to understand the conflicts between Jerry and Amelia and Teresa and her husband, one that requires more inquiry into the concept of *skill*. Is all artful cooking skillful? Or does skillful cooking elevate a dish or meal from everyday sustenance to a multisensory experience called art? If competent cooking requires a facility with the relationship between the objects—ingredients, methods, techniques, dishes—and the final dishes and meals, perhaps Peter and Sylvia reveal the possibility that cooking is a craft as much as it is an art. The beauty of their practice lies in its fluency, for "skill development depends on how repetition is organized."[40] They have clearly worked with the garlic, onions, cucumbers, and tomatoes they use in their dishes many, many times. They also use the knife as a tool with an ease of action borne of repetitive motion. However, the dishes Peter and Sylvia make are in no way out of the ordinary, somehow technically exceptional, unusually creative, or an extension of a particular culinary identity. How does the craft of cooking work in our saturated landscape of culinary possibilities?

CHAPTER FOUR

Cooking Is a Craft

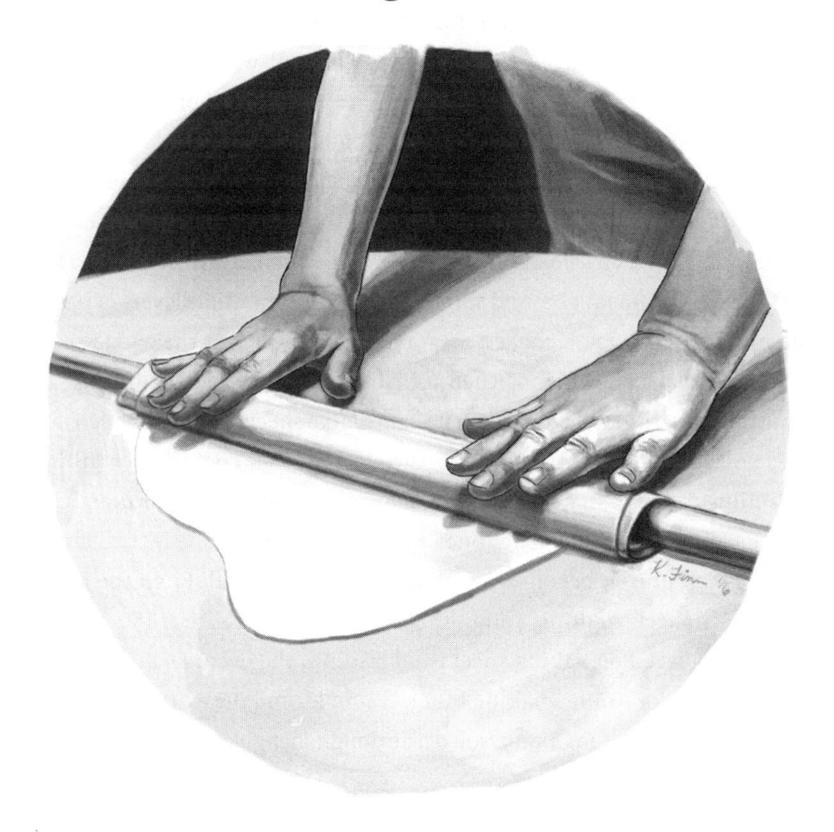

Anina emigrated from Bosnia to a small town in rural New England in the early 1990s. She became involved in her town's community and is also active in the statewide Bosnian community; 1,600 Bosnian migrants settled to this state between 1993 and 2001 (it is estimated that 20,000 Bosnians migrated to the United States between 1992 and 1995). She and her family ended up in a place with a very similar landscape and climate as her natal home, and she feels fortunate for this. Similar foods are foraged and cultivated in both regions: wild mushrooms, prune plums, apples, strawberries. Many traditional dishes, however, are not easily available or simply not available at all, save among other Bosnian refugees who settled in rural New England in the early 1990s, during the height of the civil war in their country. One such dish is *burek*, which Anina and her mother make often; its taste evokes memories and solidifies identities. To an outsider, making burek looks difficult, almost impossible. A small disk of dough is rolled out on a round, eight-foot table until it is as thin as a sheet of paper and the dough takes up the entire surface. This large, thin pastry is then transformed into smaller round spirals consisting of multiple layers of pastry and meat filling. First, a cooked meat mixture is placed at the outside edge of the pastry sheet, which is then rolled over and around the filling. The resulting long, thin roll is cut away from the large sheet of dough, which now has a new outside edge. The process—the placing of the cooked-meat filling, the rolling of the pastry over the filling—is repeated until all the dough has been used. Each six-foot-long, one- to two-inch-thick tube is then curled around itself until it becomes a twelve-inch round spiral. From the eight-foot pastry sheet, multiple spiral-shaped bureks are created. The finished bureks are placed on baking sheets and put into the oven. Each step looks daunting, but for Anina, making burek is simple, and the evidence is in her hands: her confident manipulation of the dough, her graceful use of the rolling pin.

Burek can be classified as a form of savory pastry or a meat pie. It is considered part of a family of pastries made from phyllo dough and linked to the Ottoman Empire; there are numerous phyllo-based pastries (both savory and sweet) made from Turkey to Albania to the Slavic countries, such as Bosnia. The burek made in Bosnia is distinctive for being rolled into a long tube, spun into spiral shape, and then baked. Other versions of burek are rolled into individual, shorter, cigar-like rolls or are baked in one large dish (most Americans are familiar with spanakopita, a rectangular spinach pie).

Anina makes burek in her home, primarily for special occasions these days. She learned how to make it by watching her mother: "I then tried it many, many times until I learned how to do it." She first makes the dough by mixing together flour, salt, and water, and she then lets it rest. She does not use a formal written recipe: "I just add some water to the flour." When she is ready to roll it out, she puts the disc of dough (which is about six inches in diameter) onto the middle of her round, eight-foot dining room table, which is covered with a cotton tablecloth. The tablecloth is thoroughly dusted with a light coating of flour. To roll the dough, she uses a long, thin wooden dowel (six feet long and about one inch in diameter) that her mother found in the local hardware store.

Anina starts the process of transforming the disc of dough to a sheet of pastry by rolling the dowel backward and forward across it. She then stretches the dough by rolling the disc onto the dowel (it spirals around and looks like a massive croissant). Once the dough is completely wrapped around the dowel, Anina flips it off and onto the tablecloth; the dough is now stretched and reversed. She repeats this process numerous times until a sheet of pastry emerges—first two feet in diameter, then three feet. At this point, it resembles a large island in the lake that is the round table. As the pastry gets larger, she changes her approach, stretching the sheet by rolling across it on the table and then flipping the sheet of dough onto the dowel so it looks like a towel hanging out to dry. It seems like the pastry could tear at any moment (it is now one eighth of an inch thick), but Anina's trick is "to make sure to add lots of flour [to the surface of the dough] so it does not get sticky." When the pastry is about four feet in diameter, she stops using the dowel for fear that the pastry will stick to it and tear. Instead, she covers the pastry with oil, squirting it out of a plastic squirt bottle and slowly and methodically moving it across the surface with her hands, and then uses her fingers to stretch the dough, reaching underneath the pastry and slowly puling the sheet of dough outward from center. This is painstaking work. Eventually, a paper-thin sheet of pastry extends across the entire surface of the table. At this point, Anina's teenage son comes into the kitchen to watch. He has yet to successfully make burek.

Finally, Anina starts to form the spirals. Beginning at one edge of the dough, she adds a line of small balls of seasoned and spiced meat. She then starts to roll the pastry around the meat, using up about a foot of the pastry sheet. Her hands function like rolling pin, moving the dough back and forth, but she also begins to push the pastry and meat roll toward the center of the circle, creating layers of dough around the filling. She then cuts the pastry, and wraps the tube of meat and pastry into a snail-like circle. The first burek is complete. She repeats this until all the pastry is gone.

CRAFT: SKILLS AND CONTEXTS

In the contemporary American context, cooking as craftwork can be understood in two ways: as the reproduction of a shared culinary repertoire or as the assertion of a set of culinary practices distinct from industrial processes. As in Anina's making of the burek, cooking with craft can involve the acquisition of a skillful practice learned by repetition and the education of attention. The way that Peter efficiently uses his knife to chop onions, mince garlic, and move both into a bowl and the way that Sylvia deftly peels cucumber and organizes her space also illustrate such a definition; their creative practice is aided by skill. When Anina makes her family's burek recipe, both her body and mind are so engaged. She "knows" the dough, the dowel, and the process of stretching, pulling, rolling, and oiling the dough from watching her mother make burek and from doing it herself, many times, over and over, the same way. Their craft lies in a particular type of virtuosity, a manifestation of embodied knowledge and practice. Cooking in this manner may be as long established as cooking out of obligation. For centuries, women have participated in a daily chore by making the foods their mothers taught them: tamales, moussakas, or whatever dish characterized their communities and their geographies. And these dishes have become more than sustenance; they are also icons of familial, cultural, and national tradition. In this definition, preparing these dishes upholds a larger way of life and certain ways of knowing and doing. The craft made plain by the tamale or moussaka reproduces "traditions"—shared repositories of knowledge, skills, and expectations that allow a dish to confirm a group's identity and validate the cook within a certain social community. In some places, such as the Greek island of Kalymnos, where David Sutton observed home cooks, the reproduction of tradition fully expresses this category.[1] Among Americans, tradition is acknowledged, but there is more to investigate to capture contemporary craftwork.

In a closer scrutiny of the American culinary context, cooking as a craft can be defined as an intervention into a food system that encourages Americans to purchase food that has been produced using industrial processes that rely on machine technology rather than food that has been crafted by hand. According to this narrative, craftwork is based on a certain identity, and when it comes to food, creating a dish with craft or being a craftsperson involves rejecting the more dominant paradigm, in which modes of preparation are based in manufacturing practices. As Richard Sennett points out, "The greatest dilemma faced by the modern artisan-craftsman is the machine."[2] Becoming identified as a culinary craftsperson often involves making a decision to explicitly bypass machines and the foods prepared by machines, which are now ubiquitous (and often inexpensive).

For domestic cooks, the dilemma of machine versus handwork is particularly acute when it comes to baking at home. When Claire was asked if she did any baking, she replied: "Not recently. I did in junior high. I would bake bread. I actually made a couple of cakes a few weekends ago, but I don't count that because they're delicious and they're from a recipe from my aunt, but it's cake mix, Jell-O pudding mix, oil, eggs, water, [and] rum. It's actually really good, but I don't consider that baking because it's not totally from scratch." Although she considers this cake recipe a good one that consistently produces a final result that tastes and looks pleasing, Claire discounts her role in the quality of the final result. Machines made the cake and Jell-O mixes; once an industrial process has intervened, it appears, Claire's actions are not as crucial. Home cooks often make a distinction between actions that are required to transform whole ingredients into dishes versus actions that merely facilitate dishes being made. In many ways, the problem lies in a perceived distinction between active and passive engagement. Looking closely at baking and at products and dishes classified as "baked goods" reveals our paradoxical relationship to crafting rather than assembling dishes and meals. Although Claire might "know" her aunt's cake recipe as well as Anina "knows" the burek recipe, she feels as if too many external processes were involved before she stirred the batter; she feels that she is executing but not crafting the cake.

Discursively, this distinction is often made with the phrase "cooking from scratch." This signifies that baking a cake involves a series of choices in regard to ingredients and techniques. Here, the process does matter, even if the result remains the same—in Claire's case, a rum cake. The recipe might be part of a family tradition and made repeatedly, but relying on a cake mix and a box of Jell-O means the cake is not "from scratch." Claire's questioning of the cake's culinary legitimacy reveals that there can be a moral dimension to cooking from scratch or not. For many people, cooking (or baking) from scratch appears to define a more authentic practice that leads to healthier dishes and a better lifestyle, and the alternative is seen as a compromise or even as a type of failure. For example, the Radical Homemaker movement exhorts participants to grow and make all their own food and thus become "net producers" rather than "net consumers," which is the normal mode of modern Americans. These homemakers identify traditional domestic tasks, such as growing and cooking one's own food, as a form of liberation. In this telling, craftwork even has transcendent potential; it is seen as a means of moving beyond the strictures of modern life.[3]

Although this movement is relatively small, positive sentiments toward a net-producer approach are more generally shared. In a recent study by Julia Wolfson and her colleagues that asked home cooks to define cooking (and baking), the concept "from scratch" was consistently articulated as necessary to any definition, either as a major presence or obvious absence. In an overall synthesis of responses from seven focus groups of racially and economically diverse participants, "Perceptions [of cooking] incorporated considerations of the importance of scratch ingredients, the degree of time, effort and love involved if convenience foods were used, and whether or not food was heated in some way."[4] The greatest consensus, however, was that cooking should be defined in relation to the cook's commitment to preparing food from scratch and the amount of "from scratch" ingredients used in the meal. "From scratch" is a signifying concept; it represents a set of propositions about how we should make food, which in turn mark our place in the world. In this way, the phrase condenses certain tensions between our aspirations and our actions in response to modern lifestyles.

Claire questions her skills because her family recipe assembles already processed ingredients, but where did she get her ideas as to what "counts" as a legitimate process to be proper baker? The significance of cooking or baking from scratch goes far beyond any single individual or any particular meal or dish, and so defining the phrase "from scratch" is not straightforward. Are there minimum requirements per dish or per meal? If someone pulls together various ingredients—the egg and oil that need to be added to a cake mix, for example—can the resulting dish be labeled as made from scratch? Would Anina's burek be classified by most Americans as "beyond scratch" because the virtuosity involved in rolling the dough makes the dish so much more than the sum of its ingredients? The difficulty lies in making sense of what "from scratch" means in a food environment where machine technology and industrial processes play a role in every cooking or baking step: mills grind the flour; large mixers take sodium carbonate and combine it with tartaric acid and cornstarch to create baking powder; airplanes fly vanilla beans from Madagascar after the beans have gone through the curing process; and finally, the KitchenAid mixer mixes the dough. Figuring out just what it means to bake a cake or a loaf of bread from scratch ultimately happens during the very processes of creation—the *transition* between knowing and doing. For many, the phrase "from scratch" serves as a culinary bridge of sorts, a multivocal symbol of the actions we aspire to as we navigate our culinary landscape and perform our culinary identities. One of the participants in Wolfson's study echoes the various choices consciously and consistently made by home cooks: "I have different categories of my cooking. I have home cooking—that's scratch. Which means I use every ingredient and it's done by hand. Then I have semi-home cooking, where I may use a box meal, you know, like Betty Crocker something. And then add my own ingredients to that. That's semi-cooking. So that's quick meals. . . . But most of the time, it's between semi- and home cooking-scratch."[5] These days, many other hands—and mixers, and conveyor belts—make most or at least some portions our meals, making cooking "from scratch" more desirable and yet also more difficult to define and realize.[6]

However, when home cooks discuss their ambivalence toward cooking and baking from scratch versus using foods that have been processed in some way to reduce the time and effort involved in preparing meals, they do not necessarily associate these feelings with a sense of defeat. Rather, as Laura Shapiro points out in her discussion of the new forms of processed foods that were introduced in the 1950s, when packaged mixes and frozen dinners became widely available to most Americans, the decision to use a cake mix instead of making a cake from scratch was seen as a liberation from drudgery and expectation. Shapiro argues that beginning in the 1950s, the

American processed-food industry allowed women to reimagine cooking and its associated definitions. Changing social conditions combined with new technological innovations to open up new ways of categorizing cooking, which led to new questions: "Do women like to cook? That is, are there any good reasons to cook from scratch, apart from habit, sentiment and the family budget? The question had never emerged before, but, suddenly . . . there was a glimmer of space between women and cooking, just enough to invite reflection."[7] When we look at it this way, the food industry did not entirely hijack cooking and baking from home cooks: "Cooking, it turned out, had roots so deep and stubborn that even the mighty fist of the food industry couldn't yank them all up."[8] Home cooks are receptive to the seduction of convenience, but it is a complicated love affair. TV dinners and boxed mixes are welcomed but also held at arm's-length, leading to a widening gap between perception and practice: the requirements of cooking from scratch do not have to be enacted each and every day, but people continue to believe that they should aspire to such methods and means.

When craftwork is closely examined, Claire's concerns or the visions of the Radical Homemaker movement might in fact revolve around specific culinary losses, such as the loss of certain insights and capacities. Virtuosity, the difference between Anina and her son, might be not be transferred from one generation to the next if members of both do not consistently make burek, bread, or pie. For them to make these dishes using traditional methods without any assistance from the food industry requires mastery of skill and refusal of options not to use such skills (e.g., Anina chooses not to purchase premade phyllo dough). As philosopher Michael Polanyi points out, our very understandings of aspects of daily life might require "perception as an instance of tacit knowing."[9] If we no longer cook or bake often or consistently enough to develop such integration between our perceptions and our actions, do certain qualities of culinary knowing and doing go into decline? We still want to make our grandmothers' burek, upma, stollen, karelas, or collards, but since we make these dishes only sporadically, do we know how to prepare them through instinct and intuition or only by carefully following a recipe card? The power of "from scratch" as a symbol lies not just in material evidence—that is, the existence of a finished dish—but also in the ability to *make* the dish, to know and enact the processes that transform ingredients into a finished product. In this light, cooking and baking "from scratch" holds at bay the compromises we make each day to navigate the demands of modern life.

Lisa, a single mother living in Boston, articulates both the dilemma and the reprieve brought about by the new choices now available due to machine technology: "I am not as big a baker [as a cook]. There's a definite distinction for me. Like, I wouldn't go home and say, 'I'm going to make a cake.' . . . I don't do that. But my cousin Susan loves the dessert end, where I like the food end. I never got into making pies or cookies. . . . I'll get the Duncan Hines brownies, and [my daughter] will make Duncan Hines brownies, and we're happy as a clam with them." The modern food environment allows Lisa to prioritize her from scratch cooking. She is proud of her ability to make tasty, healthy dinners for herself and her daughter; however, she easily and happily concedes the territory of baking to other family members, commercial bakeries, and boxed mixes. Lisa accepts the "glimmer of space" provided by the food industry. Anina, however, lightens her load by not always choosing the traditional practices; she does not make burek regularly but only on weekends and vacations. Historically, in Bosnia, women would make burek almost every day, but Anina says, "I don't have time."

Lisa's and Claire's self-assessments of their baking—which they considered to be somehow improper or incomplete because industrial processes were involved—echo the sentiments of many. As Sennett points out, "Since the Industrial Revolution of the eighteenth century, the machine has seemed to threaten the work of artisan-craftsmen. The threat appeared physical: industrial machines never tired, they did the same work hour after hour without complaining." He also argues that *all* contemporary craftwork involves reliance on some form of technology. We (radical homemakers aside) cannot and do not really want to return to a perceived state of grace, a time before the taint of the hum of machines and the click of the keyboard. Distinctions made between handwork and machine work might be artificial ones: "The modern machine's threat to developing skill has a different character. . . . An emblem of a large challenge faced by modern society [is]: how to think like craftsmen in making good use of technology."[10] Is it possible for Claire's family cake recipe, which combines cake and Jell-O mixes, but also other unique ingredients, like rum, to be prepared with craft? What if Claire, with the confidence of tradition and repetition, prepares the cake with a level of fluency similar to Sylvia's cutting of cucumbers and tomatoes for her Russian salad or even Anina's rolling of burek dough? Does it matter that machines milled the flour, ground the cocoa, mixed the ingredients, and poured the cake mix into a plastic bag and then inserted the bag into a box before Claire brought her traditions and aspirations to bear when stirring the oil and rum into the combined Jell-O and cake mixes?

CRAFTWORK AS RESISTANCE

Most American cooking and baking that is classified as a craft really constitutes an *oppositional* category. As discussed earlier, there are two forms of craftsman-like opposition to the standard order of culinary business. First are the actions that one can take *in spite of* the numerous and easily available technological and industrial means of moving ingredients from the field to the kitchen and from the raw to the cooked. Cooking from scratch denotes this tension, which is inherent in making meals. In differentiating types of cooking—making versus assembling—Americans create a commentary that both accepts and rejects the importance of technology, machines, and industry in the ways we cook and eat.

Second is the notion that craftwork involves a certain set of culinary actions found in principles of embodiment and mastery. Anina and Claire could both be considered masters of their particular traditional dishes; they know intuitively how to roll the dough and stir the batter to make the chosen dish "just right." This intuition emerges from repetition; this is knowledge through practice. The changes in our everyday obligations and the expansion of our culinary landscape allow for our episodic approach to making meals but also certainly conspire to put cooking as a craft at risk. Meanwhile, historically, cooking practices and social expectations around meals were more narrowly defined. In the past, the repertoire of a family cook's dishes was more confined by the limited availability of ingredients due to issues of storage, seasonality, distribution, cost, and so on. Weekly meals tended to follow a standard pattern, just like the rotational scheme Laura's mother used to rely on, with beans and franks on Sundays and tuna and noodles on Wednesdays. Meals for holidays, secular and religious, have tended (and continue) to be quite static: a family may make a type of special cookies each Christmas or the same hamantaschen recipe every Purim. These dishes are made over and over throughout a person's life and are also likely to be transferred to the next generation. Here, people's culinary skill comes from repetition and context. Today, home cooks who are known to be masters of their craft usually get acclaim for their specialty dishes, particularly those associated with ethnic or religious traditions, such as Anina's burek, Teresa's turnip soup, and Sylvia's salads.[11]

Making burek, cake, or a loaf of bread "from scratch" and "by hand" could be understood as expressions of resistance. In this telling, everyday cooks and bakers, when they choose not to buy frozen phyllo dough or store-bought cake, are making what anthropologist James F. Scott labels "gestures of the powerless." For him, small everyday acts by ordinary people can be analyzed as hidden transcripts that help to tell a story, a narrative about moments of insubordination toward structures of power.[12] For home and commercial cooks and bakers working in this manner, defining and enacting craftwork may in fact create bigger and deeper culinary roots, ensuring that the food industry does not sweep away ways of on-the-ground knowing and doing. In this analysis, machine technology and industrial manufacturing enabled the food industry but they have yet to disable all cooks. Such a notion of resistance might really be the underlying meaning of all modes of culinary craftwork.

The abilities that emerge with repeated experience and the contemporary means by which such abilities can counter other culinary trends have both domestic and public histories. Craftwork has long straddled the domestic and professional domains of American cookery. Among commercial cooks and bakers, the craft involved in the work they do is often intrinsic to their identity. But the most telling practice, the one that exists at the intersection of both forms of craftwork, lies in baking and baked goods; in these acts, the complexity of defining certain cooking practices as embodied, labeling certain ingredients as whole, and not relying on machines is revealed. How many American home cooks make their own hamburger buns, even if they clean, chop, boil, and dress the other components of their summer meals (the hamburgers, coleslaw, corn on the cob, green salad)? Hardly any. For that matter, how many immigrants make phyllo dough by hand for every burek or spanakopita they prepare once they are more assimilated into American life? Fewer and fewer, especially as newer generations become more acclimated to American perceptions and expectations, including time poverty, multiple choices as to where and what to eat on any given day, and the possibility of sourcing prepared food outside of the home. Anina's son has tried to make burek several times, but he is not very committed to figuring out his mother's techniques and tips to make sure the dough stretches out into a thin sheet of finished pastry. By the time he becomes the main upholder of his family's traditional foods, how often will he make the dish?

BAKING: A CONTRADICTORY AMERICAN HISTORY

It takes time and experience to make breads and pastries well. It is a fact of contemporary American life that commercial bakers and assembly line

Figure 13. "Bread Store, 259 Bleecker Street, Manhattan," New York City, 1937. Miriam and Ira D. Wallach Division of Art, Prints, and Photographs: Photography Collection, New York Public Library Digital Collections.

workers, not home cooks, are now those that know and make these products on an everyday basis. This modern reality—that we almost always bake by choice rather than out of necessity—enhances the importance of experiencing baking from scratch as a means of fighting back against an industrialized food system and preserving traditions. However, are these big or small gestures? Are they only recent interventions? The answers are not black and white. The truth is that, no matter our aspirations, there is a long history of having other people and machines bake our breads, cakes, and pies for us.

American domestic cookery appears to have a long history of including baking in the cook's repertoire, at least if the historical sources are cookbooks, teaching manuals, and other written forms intending to transfer culinary know-how to American women. Much of early American baking used dry heat. The main heat source was wood, and most food was cooked over a wood fire or inside or beside a wood-fired hearth. Radiant, rather than direct, heat is crucial to many forms of baking. Cornbread, spoonbread, Indian pudding, pasties, pies—all these recipes require dry, radiant heat, and initially they were cooked in enclosed pots placed directly in the hearth. Flatbreads and griddlecakes were cooked on top of the fire. At home, bread was often baked in Dutch ovens, deep iron pots with lids, which could be placed in the hearth or buried in the ashes of a fire. Beehive ovens, which use radiant and direct heat, were built next to the main hearth or in separate outbuildings of larger plantations or estates; they were fairly difficult to construct and thus more rare than the standard open fireplace. Up until the nineteenth century, most baking occurred inside the hearth or outside the home, in commercial bakeries, for example.

Despite the pride many Americans today might take in a special family recipe for cornbread, apple pie, or pita bread, much baking, especially bread baking, has long been a communal practice. In the past, the relatively large amount of resources needed to build and maintain a wood-burning oven meant that baking was as much a communal or commercial practice as a domestic one. There exists a long history of groups sharing ovens within culinary cultures that have traditionally relied on bread or pastry as a staple. Families would bring their loaves to the village oven to bake: "From ancient times, bread-making had been shared between the bakers' oven and that of the home. Baker's guilds operated in the towns; in the country, women met their families' needs by baking enough bread for up to a month in their own ovens."[13] There are several interesting differences between the American tradition of baking and those of our forebears across the globe. One was the less dense settlement patterns of the colonies: there were fewer towns and they were spread further apart. Another was the lack of an organized guild structure (or other types of associations) for professional bakers.[14] This combination meant that there were few communal ovens and only a few quirky systems of oversight of the craftsmen; early bakeries were ad hoc affairs.

Whatever the genealogy of the American bakery, between the confines of space, money, and time, getting your baked goods from somewhere else is as American as Boston brown bread. Even during the early days of the American colonies, there were commercial bakeries; there is evidence of them in the settlements of Plymouth, New Amsterdam, and New Haven by the mid-1600s.[15] Philadelphia had seven bakers listed in the 1700 census; at that point, the population of the city was 4,500.[16] Until the late 1800s, purchasing bread and other baked goods was not the norm for all Americans, but it was certainly common for those who lived in urban areas.

According to historian Katherine Leonard Turner, increased urbanization and the rising number of middle-class families who were not able to employ a full-time domestic servant meant that by the 1870s, there were "6,396 bakeries in the United States, roughly 1 for every 7,800 Americans." And this number kept increasing: "There were twice as many bakeries per capita in 1910 as there had been in 1880."[17] Although there was a long history of communal ovens in European villages and towns, this practice does not appear to have been prevalent in the nineteenth-century United States.

People with the economic means to have large hearths with beehive ovens were the primary home bakers. Turner argues that the working-class families that increasingly lived in cramped urban spaces with little or no kitchen space became the "vanguard of a trend toward the labor of cooking being transferred outside the home," and she notes that this trend was well established before the fluorescence of the processed food industry occurred during the 1950s.[18] She goes on to say that "bakery items were the most common choice for a worker who wanted cheap ready-to-eat food, such as the family's daily bread or pies and cake for quick snack or lunch."[19] The urban working class did not possess adequate facilities or equipment to make bread at home, nor did they have sufficient time, given that many women also worked in factories and service. Turner suggests that what ultimately became another barrier was a loss of knowledge and skill about baking bread, which meant that purchasing bread was the only option for many.[20] As Cathy Kaufman points out, baking might have been the first of the housewife's cooking chores to become disassociated from both gender identity and social obligations, for as the transition to the twentieth century occurred, "[women's] skills tended to shift from making things to buying things. A good loaf of homemade bread became less of a mark of distinction for homemaking."[21] The shift away from net producers when it came to baking was a long and winding story, not an overnight episode.

By the early twentieth century, larger-scale commercial bread production became the generally accepted norm in American towns and cities. This was particularly true in rapidly expanding urban areas, where the population density meant that people had to make due with more cramped living quarters, including small and inadequate kitchens. A general culturally shared assumption that home-baked bread was superior to the store-bought version began to decline, partly because the greater concentration of urban dwellers created improved distribution and enough demand to make commercial baking viable. By the twentieth century, people were still baking at

Figure 14. Barrio Bakery, Burlington, Vermont. Photo by Serena Parnau.

home in both cities and rural areas, but in urban areas, this practice was increasingly defined as an occasional choice while commercial baking was increasingly defined as the everyday standard: "As incomes rose in the early twentieth century, so did the consumption of purchased bakery goods: by 1930 as much as 60 percent of all bread was purchased, although many housewives still preferred to make their cakes and pastries."[22] By the 1950s, the majority of bread consumed in the United States was prepared by commercial operations.[23] The 1954 book *Baking in America*, a two-volume history of the contemporary baking industry written by William G. Panschar, a professor of business administration, and assisted by Charles Slater, asserts: "The baking industry in America today [1954] is a four and one half billion dollar industry. It supplies 95% of the nation's bread consumption and a major portion of all other baked goods."[24] The assumption that bread is to be bought rather than made continues today. In 2011, the total unit sales of fresh bread (loaves, rolls, etc.) was over three billion.[25]

These transformations lessened women's obligation to make their families, daily bread and also helped expand the occupational niche of the commercial baker. The lack of time, space, and wherewithal among more and more Americans probably helped as well. In 1900, there were 70,000 people classified as bakers in the United States labor census; by 1950, there were 125,000.[26] With more and more people involved in making not only bread but also all the other baked goods now readily available in commercial venues (bagels, tortillas, donuts, etc.) these numbers have steadily increased. In 2010, there were 276,000 people employed in the baking industry, either as bakers or production employees.[27]

Early commercial bread baking, although not monitored and mediated by a European-style guild system, was modeled on the small-scale village baker model. As Panschar describes it, "[commercial American] bread baking in 1850 was still plagued by age old difficulties. Bakeries were for the most part one-oven and one-man shops in which craft traditions still had a tight hold. There was no mechanized equipment. There was nothing but the baker's skill to determine the quality of his products."[28] Interestingly, when Panschar wrote this, in the 1950s, the fact that mechanization had successfully become intrinsic to the baking industry was considered a triumph: "By 1900 it was clearly demonstrated that factory methods, although accepted by only a handful of bakers, were not to be stayed by tradition."[29] He goes on to outline the transformation in the industry, seeing the period of 1900–1930 as crucial, due to both increased demand, "the housewife looked to the bake shop—and not to her own kitchen—to meet [her] demand," and what he calls the "triumph of technology."[30] Panschar identifies professional bakers as the main barrier to the transition to a fully industrial mode of production: "Imbued with what was probably the deepest of all craft traditions, the great majority of bakers simply did not wish to change their ways. Indeed, they actively fought any attempts to introduce mechanization. What perhaps is difficult to understand today, [is that] their pride of craftsmanship and their belief in their ability to produce high quality products were unshakable and inborn."[31] He goes on to quote from the vice president of a commercial mixer company reminiscing about trying to convince commercial bakers in the early twentieth century to purchase their equipment, as "few bakers could be made to believe that bread dough could be made any other way than by hand."[32]

Eventually, rising demand for bread and the increased mechanization of much commercial foodwork meant that bread baking did become almost fully industrialized. During and immediately after World War II, purchases of commercial bread and baked goods continued to rise: "By 1945 industry output was more than 50 per cent higher than it was in 1941; compared to 1939 it was 62.5 per cent higher."[33] By the 1950s, the reality that making bread and most baked items "from scratch" was not a daily choice had become as American as apple pie. According to a 2014 MarketLine industry report, industrial bread and roll production now accounts for 59.5 percent of the total bread sales.

The increasingly large scales of production put pressure on the neighborhood bakeries; mass-produced bread required larger venues for distribution and sales. Not only did baking shift almost completely outside the home over the course of the twentieth century, but the sale of commercially produced baked goods also shifted from smaller to larger retail venues. Supermarkets rather than freestanding bakeries now dominate as the primary means for obtaining our daily bread; 60 percent of the bread purchased each year comes from these retail establishments.[34] The craft of baking bread, whether as part of a particular tradition or as a response to an increasingly industrialized system of production, really does go against the grain. To bake bread with craft, roll phyllo pastry with ease, or make a family cake recipe from scratch is not really cultural common sense, even if Americans value these practices because they feel they uphold traditions, push back on the food industry, and reinforce familial connections.

ATTENTION AND INTERVENTION: REINVENTING THE CRAFT OF MAKING BREAD

Since the early twentieth century, baking has been as much a commercial activity as a domestic one, if considering the entire American populace (lumping together various regional, cultural, and ethnic traditions). The ease with which Americans can make the choice to *not* make their own bread (or for that matter, cake or tortillas) might be interpreted as clear evidence for a decline in knowledge and skill. To some extent, this is true. The ritual of weekly bread baking may have lasted longer in rural areas where access to commercial bakeries was limited or among more impoverished families who could not afford store-bought bread. It can be easily argued, however, that for at least fifty years, if not longer, both baking knowledge and skill have *not* been actively implemented on an everyday basis or uniformly transmitted from one generation to the next through repetition and experience. Claire's critique of her cake, therefore, might not reflect recent losses in "from scratch" home baking, and the use of cake mix and pudding might not be a result of a recent decline in the tacit knowledge of domestic cooks. Her ideal version of a cake may rarely be made in any home. In the case of everyday practices, especially baking bread, a concern about the decline in craft skill and knowledge might really be a consequence of the decline of commercial bakers with such expertise.

What is clearly a result of the almost complete shift from home-baked bread to industrially manufactured bread and the concomitant rise of larger-scale distribution systems is a decline in the availability of certain *styles* of bread. New innovations and technologies that introduce greater efficiency to the complex process of making bread have long-term effects on the appearance, taste, and texture of the everyday loaf and bun. Bread has become softer and lighter. The dominant texture is uniform—the crust, crumb, and interior of bread are almost identical. The appearance of an industrially made loaf of bread is more or less identical to any other industrially made loaf at any store. If you go to a large supermarket and peruse the bread aisle, you have a remarkably similar experience to looking at the nail and screw aisle at a hardware store. Only a sign or label can help you differentiate between a 1 1/4-inch and a 1 5/8-inch drywall screw or a Pepperidge Farm and an Arnold loaf of bread. This is also the case with other baked goods; imagine the boxes of doughnuts at the supermarket, each one identical in shape and size, covered with exactly the same amount of powdered sugar or chocolate glaze. Baked goods, no longer products made every day at home, are now characterized by the attributes created by different commercial modes of production rather than by the traditions of certain bakers or their unique baking skills.

The complexity of coming up with an accurate definition of baking "from scratch" becomes immediately apparent when we consider the contemporary distinctions made between "industrial" and "artisan or craft breads." The ingredients found in commercial breads are now associated with the pitfalls of our industrialized food system. Roy Blount even penned a pithy poem that connects types of bread, moral claims, and ideals of health: "Eaters of Wonder Bread / Must be underbred / So little to eat / Where's the wheat?"[35] Calls to minimize the additives included in industrially produced bread and to transform the methods of making it take up ever more space in the American culinary discourse. Many American consumers now want their baked goods to conform to a culinary ideal, although they don't want to be responsible for making such conformity and confirmation happen. In many ways, the calls to eliminate certain ingredients used to facilitate the mass-production of bread (e.g., preservatives and stabilizers) and to introduce others that are considered healthy and traditional (e.g., whole wheat and spelt flours), is an attempt to make commercially produced food appear to be made "from scratch" and thus alleviate our concerns about the impact of these ingredients on our body and our obligations to make and serve food for others and ourselves. The aspiration to make food from scratch haunts so many choices, even when the meaning is indeterminate, commented on by many, and never fully resolved. The multigenerational reality of commercial bread baking reveals the many layers of industrial processes involved at every step when going from wheat grain to finished loaf, even in terms of what gets defined as a natural ingredient and what might make the bread be considered to have been made "from scratch." The public's call for a product made from minimal ingredients, one that evokes a shop rather than a factory, is now cynically exploited, such as when a Dunkin Donuts' advertising campaign claimed the corporation was producing artisan bagels.[36]

The alliance between the types of ingredients used, concepts of purity, and a distancing from industrial forms of food production is a fragile one. Even ingredients that appear to be pure and whole, such as flour and yeast, have actually been mightily transformed before they end up in the mixing bowl, whether in the home or at the factory. This is certainly the case with yeast, the crucial ingredient in transforming an inert lump of flour and liquid into an airy, raised loaf with a crisp crust and soft center. Most home bakers today, when they bake a loaf of bread, perhaps challah to celebrate Shabbat or cinnamon rolls for Sunday brunch, use commercial yeast. This raw ingredient has already been manipulated; it is the result of technological innovations and was initially intended for commercial bread production. The yeast used today by most bread bakers (both home and commercial) is called "active dry yeast," and it is manufactured in large fermentation tanks using molasses as the base. To produce active dry yeast, large batches of a single strain of yeast (*Saccharomyces cerevisae*) are dried and then made into a powder; this renders the yeast dormant, and it can be reactivated by being soaked in warm water.[37]

In *Cooked*, an eloquent journey into the potential of making meals at home using craftsman-like methods, Michael Pollan compares commercial yeast to other industrially driven monocultures, acknowledging yet querying its contribution to modern baking: "Though commercial yeast is alive, its behavior is linear, mechanical, and predictable, a simple matter of inputs and outputs—which is no doubt why it so quickly caught on."[38] He sees the use of *wild* yeast as a relevant gesture of resistance, perhaps small when only done in his kitchen, but much larger, perhaps even a type of movement, when embraced by bakers who sell their loaves of bread to others. While he sees a certain beauty in the simplicity of modern commercial yeast (with very little assistance, this microorganism gets the job of leavening done), he is drawn to the vision of a new generation of commercial bakers who consider themselves artisans. These bakers are bypassing the ease of industrial systems and adopting the methods of traditional European bakers or bakers working in American towns and cities in the late nineteenth and early twentieth centuries. He attributes his desire to successfully make bread without relying on commercial yeast to an experience of eating bread made by Chad Robertson, the owner of the phenomenally successful bakery Tartine, located in San Francisco's Mission District. Robertson, who made "the best loaf of bread [Pollan] ever tasted," works each day between a state of control (he produces only a certain number of loaves each day, he follows a set of principles as to kneading, shaping, and baking the bread) and a state of chaos (he uses only wild yeast, he spends most of his time "managing fermentation"). He, and numerous other professional bakers across the United States, has taken up the call of those bakers who resisted mechanization in the early twentieth century, who sought to keep working by hand and rejected the ease and efficiency of the modern industrial bakeshop.

Bakers are the front guard of those who identify with craft as a form of resistance, who have been building a definition of cooking or baking as a craft that works *toward* tradition and *against* machines and industrial technologies (this front guard also includes cheesemakers, brewers, DIY hipsters, and radical homemakers). The contradictions intrinsic to such efforts are notable, yet they are to be expected in the face of the ubiquitous industrial processes that are involved in our food system from farm to table. For example, the growing number of American bakers who primarily identify themselves as craftworkers, like Chad Robertson, are reluctant to categorize commercial yeast as a whole or unprocessed ingredient. Using commercial yeast leads to the loss of too much variation in texture, taste, and appearance. Yet this crucial ingredient, commercially made, brings consistency and efficiency to what is otherwise a quixotic process for most home cooks. This poses a particular dilemma for artisan bakers when it comes to determining what can be labeled as made "from scratch," making the definition of craft complex, even for those who embrace the category as part of their professional identity. Home cooks rarely make bread (over the course of interviewing and videotaping over forty dinners, only one person was taped making bread, in that case, dinner rolls), and at this point, their tacit knowledge assumes the use of a commercial, monoculture yeast purchased in convenient small packages at the supermarket.[39] For most people, baked goods made with this ingredient still count as "from scratch," but not for a baker seeking to contradict the generic, industrial loaf of bread.[40] There are few ingredients used in baking that are untouched by technologies of production, yet certain standards need to be met, or at least acknowledged, for actions to reinforce the category. Yeast—where it comes from, how it is nurtured—symbolizes this tension that is at the heart of contemporary craft baking.

THE MANY MODES OF TRADITION: PERSISTENCE AS A MODE OF RESISTANCE?

Gerard Rubaud, formerly a member of the French national ski team and an apprentice to a French *boulanger*, and presently an artisan baker in Westford, Vermont, represents a certain renegade community of bakers that has emerged all over the United States during the past thirty years, committed to baking bread at a small scale, using certain craft practices, and especially rejecting the use of commercial yeast. His breads, made in small batches, leavened with wild yeasts, and baked in an enormous wood-fired brick oven, certainly tests the conventions of most American breads, which are mass produced, industrially made, enriched, fortified, and sold sliced.

Rubaud has spent years perfecting the art, craft, and science of making the rustic country bread he first learned to make fifty years ago in his hometown of Aix-les-Bains, France. He began his apprenticeship when he was twelve years old, working in a combined *boulangerie* and *pâtisserie* (bakery and pastry shop) that was typical of the time and place, with a storefront on the street level and a large wood-burning oven in the basement. "We made rustic country bread," he says. "We did not make baguette, which was for sissies [the Parisians who would come to the alpine region for vacation]." Over a half-century later, across the Atlantic Ocean and after a career at the ski company Rossignol, he makes a version of the same bread several days a week. He still loads wood into the oven to build a huge fire each day, tending and stoking it until it reaches just the right temperature, and he still uses the same basic recipe, feeding and nurturing his own starter instead of purchasing yeast. This starter, or *levain*, is derived from whole organic spelt and rye berries that have been freshly milled and then soaked in water.

Rubaud's mission is to continue the tradition of making bread based on natural fermentation. "The quality of the bread is all in the levain," he explains. Fermentation occurs when a levain, or starter, is mixed with wheat flour and water. The starter is made using wild yeasts that are either captured from the air or released when whole grains are freshly ground. Rubaud never uses commercial yeast. For him, breads made using commercial yeasts never have the taste or health benefits of bread made with a levain and poolish. Over time, Rubaud has perfected his bread-making practice to reflect his philosophy: "Fermentation is the most important step actually in bread making. It's what you choose and how you make it that will determine the rest of the production of the bread. Then the next step is your selection of ingredients." He points out that in good bakeries in France, only the most talented and experienced baker oversees the fermentation process.

Rubaud's process for making the levain truly marries art (intuition), craft (technique), and science (precision). First, he grinds organic whole grains (most grains carry wild yeast) and combines them with water and organic sea salt and malted barley. This firm levain is placed into a plastic bucket and carefully kept at a warm temperature for almost twenty-four hours. If all goes well, the wild yeasts will emerge from the ground grains. The underlying assumption is that a slow fermentation will allow for a greater development of flavor from the wild yeasts; the salt makes sure the fermentation does not happen too quickly. When the levain shows cracks, this means the yeast is alive and working. He then adds white flour, ground spelt, and red winter wheat as well as more water, salt, and malted barley. Next, he adds more water to the now larger bubbling mixture to create the right proportion of levain to the total amount of dough needed for a batch of bread. The proportions vary depending on the ambient temperature (more levain is needed in winter, and less in summer) and the total number of loaves desired.

Everyone who learns from Rubaud, seeking to be taught his vision of the craft of bread baking, becomes a disciple of the recipe for the levain. Rubaud advocates for a two-step process to capture the wild yeasts necessary to make the dough rise. The first is making the levain. Another step when moving from levain to the final dough is the *autolyse*, when one more round of flour and water is mixed and left to sit for at least thirty minutes. The levain is then incorporated, and the dough undergoes its first full fermentation. The next step is making the poolish, which requires another precise recipe: to three hundred grams of levain, you add a larger proportion of white flour, some freshly ground spelt and red winter wheat, and then water, salt, and malted barley.[41] The poolish enables the long and slow rise that facilitates the complex flavors, soft interior, and firm crust sought after by artisan bakers. After kneading this dough, further precise instructions must be followed to make sure it doubles in size. His craftwork demands experiential knowledge but also very knowledgeable action.

Rubaud uses traditional and modern tools to promote the creation of a moist and light loaf of bread. He hews to a narrow path when it comes to making his levain, but it widens as he moves on to the subsequent steps of making his bread. For example, he puts the dough into a specific wooden "cradle," a reproduction of an eighteenth-century French dough trough. Every batch of levain, and ultimately the bread dough, is nurtured and cared for like a newborn child. At this point, Rubaud is often working with over one hundred pounds of bread dough, which he will ultimately turn into several hundred loaves of bread. These will be baked in the oven at just the right temperature and emerge with a dark, caramel-brown crust and a wonderful yeasty aroma.[42] He understands the convenience of using commercial yeast, saying that "it has democratized bread making," but he does not appreciate the final result. However, he does not mind using a mechanical mixing machine to fully integrate the poolish with more flour. Such machines have been in place for more than a century; they were first introduced into commercial bread baking in the late 1870s, primarily to address shortages in skilled labor and the difficulty of kneading large batches of dough.[43]

Rubaud, now over seventy, works at all hours of the day and night to nurture the perfect levain. Again, he understands that most American bakers use commercial yeast, "because this way they can . . . sleep better . . . and have a social life," but "for me, the hours are all sixty minutes, and whenever you take those sixty minutes doesn't matter." The pursuit of quality, perfection, and tradition motivate him: "I like the challenge in getting the fire at the right time and right heat and having all the variables for making the levain and shaping the loaves." He makes the same style of bread every day, over and over again. His craft of baking contradicts the dominant mode of industrial bread making, and crucial to his outsider status is that he embraces the repetition of the work—the tinkering, the process of repeatedly making and shaping the dough by hand—that it takes to obtain the consistency in quality he desires for his bread.

Rubaud also trains other passionate bakers in the hope that they too will embrace his methods of using wild yeast, levain, and above all, slow fermentation, for he "wants to bring back the neighborhood baker." Industrial bread made with commercial yeasts is readily available in the supermarket, but he feels that this bread contains many preservatives, is soft in texture, and often possesses little unique flavor. It is bread, but it is industrial bread.

Making the levain from wild yeast extends the mastery required to bake a loaf of bread, but it also integrates certain technologies of precision to a process often considered to be intuitive, at least as long as there has been a disciplined, repetitive practice in place. Making Rubaud's bread, like making Anina's burek, seems daunting for a novice. But Rubaud's insistence that only a scientific level of specificity and focus will make the fermentation process a success moves his practice into a particularly contemporary register for craftwork. Intuition and technique are never sufficient.[44]

BRINGING CRAFT INTO THE HOME

Mark, a professional and father of two, took one of Rubaud's classes in bread making, and he has been regularly baking bread inspired by the methods for his family ever since. His initial interest in learning how to make bread was sparked by the excellent artisan breads increasingly available to purchase in Vermont during the 1990s, a result of the burgeoning craft baking movement. His food environment exposed him to more than Wonder Bread and the supermarket bakery loaves of Italian and rye bread. The rural state of Vermont has an unusually high number of artisan bakeries for a very small population, but there are concentrated pockets of such bakeries scattered through the United States, especially in locales that attract people who want to intervene in the industrial food system (such as San Francisco, where Chad Robertson works). Mark wanted to learn how make these kinds of crusty loaves himself, partially as a challenge and partially as a means of saving money:

> It started because I wanted good-quality bread without having to pay an arm and a leg. . . . In 1995, I started studying out of cookbooks, and I made my share of bricks and crappy loaves and just straight white sandwich bread but nothing interesting about it. And then in 2000 or so, Alicia [his wife] gave me as an anniversary present an internship/workshop position with Gerard. I went to his place and tried to copy everything that he did.
>
> It started off as an economic thing, and then it additionally became fun. I enjoyed the craft of figuring out how to tweak it up to twenty more grams of this or a bit less of water there or what if I do a 72 percent hydration? So, I have been keeping notes of all the styles that I have done, and it has evolved over the years.

Mark has developed extensive notes and recipe sheets (tables, really) to maintain the precise rules of practice demanded by Rubaud. These notes and tables also enable him to be more confident during the complex process of cultivating and nurturing wild strains of yeast. His notes on the pre-fermentation process contain dictates to help deal with nurturing the yeast and managing temperature differentials:

> This is the phase in which to adjust the flavor. Poolish is soupy, levain is "hard" and is fed 2x day. To make a poolish—equal amount water and flour, perhaps a pinch of rye and 1/4 tsp yeast. Use approx. 25–40% poolish to total mass of batch. 25% in summer, 40% in winter. Firmer in summer than winter. Grind the berries and add water ASAP to get the wild yeast, which will oxidize if the flour is allowed to age.

His recipes for breads, which he has developed and adapted over time using the principles he initially learned from Rubaud in 2000, resemble lab notes. They help him manage all the unknowns when making bread. He does use a pinch of commercial yeast because the wild yeast imparted some flavors his family did not like, but he relies on Rubaud's long and slow poolish method to encourage a good rise and great tastes. His notes have four columns, labeled phase, data, basic recipe, and notes. The phase column gives the name of the particular step of the process. The data column contains the list of ingredients, and the basic recipe column shows the precise metric measures for each of the ingredients. The notes column focuses on the percentage of hydration, or the proportion of water to flours, information that has an impact on the taste and texture of the final loaf.

Although Mark is as convinced as Rubaud about the importance of levain and poolish to the overall quality of his breads, as a home baker, the social expectations of his family play a role in the types he actually bakes: "Basically, I make the bread that I like to make and I make the bread the kids like to eat. So, I haven't been too adventuresome making the dark ryes and the anadamas because the kids won't eat those. Or, they will eat them and then they will complain, 'This isn't your normal bread.' So part of it is feeding the kids, [and also] the kids love it." Craft or chore, we respond to our obligations.

His craft practice of bread baking, learned from Rubaud, has shifted and adapted due to his social obligations. His children do not love the bread he makes with the most fidelity to Rubaud's approach. They like a softer, slightly sweeter loaf—one that is more similar to everyday supermarket bread. His wife wants to make sure that there are enough whole-grain flours in the bread. He sees his bread baking as a mediation between "the bread that I like to make and that the kids like to eat." His social obligation, now a general household principle, is to always have bread available in the house. He makes six loaves at a time and generally begins thinking about making another batch when there is only one loaf left in the freezer. The family eats one loaf immediately, and then freezes the rest, which can then be pulled out as needed. Over the years, he has expanded his baking repertoire beyond

Rubaud's style of loaf, and he now regularly makes naan, pretzels, rolls, and even hamburger buns. But the long, slowly fermented style of loaf remains his most consistent product.

The efforts toward mastery Mark mentions are also crucial to his commitment to making bread consistently and often. He has to organize the rest of his daily tasks around the many steps and constant nurturing required to make Rubaud's style of bread. He explains that he bakes bread on days when he either does not have to be in the office or has time to go home in the middle of the day. Meanwhile, he has had to adapt the standard of practice, deciding not to stick completely to Rubaud's method. For example, he is unwilling to lose sleep to feed the poolish in the middle of the night. Instead, he makes the poolish the night before he intends to bake. He lets it sit overnight and then begins the process of creating the final dough in the morning. Mike is naturally a tinkerer, and this has transferred to his baking. Yet the repetition of this work, the needing to make six loaves every ten to fourteen days consistently over the past fifteen years or so, has meant that his tinkering has turned into a complex dance between a known, coherent system and a number of adaptations. He adopts the category of cooking as a craft in both senses: he intervenes into a dominant industrial supply chain by making bread himself, and he makes bread often enough to develop tacit knowledge and build a familial tradition.

Mark has journeyed far beyond the initial recipe he learned at the workshop in Gerard's remote bakeshop, but the prescriptions, proportions, and methods remain crucial to his practice. He has made many iterations of his bread over the years. Often, he'll search out new and different recipes. However, he always funnels recipes through the Rubaud method, beginning each batch of bread by making a levain out of some flour and water; his levain is equal parts water and flour, with a small amount of commercial yeast (less than a teaspoon). He also always uses Rubaud's kneading method. When I ask him about the other baking that he now does and whether Rubaud's idiosyncratic definition of craft has influenced him, he pulls out his copy of the Rombauer *The Joy of Cooking*. He talks about the basic pie dough recipe, which he has adapted. He was not comfortable with the volume measurements given in the book, so he changed them all to grams. Now he can use his scale, which he bought after Rubaud told him, "Go out and get a scale, and then I can teach you how to bake." He also showed me three different recipes for ciabatta that he developed from Rubaud's core recipe. The first is a very exact typed version. The second two are on sticky notes, more cryptic and basic in their message.

The steps and the process now reside in Mark's head and hands. Learning to make bread from Rubaud has made Mark a contemporary craftsman. His twenty-first-century apprenticeship in craft baking engages tradition, repetition, technology, and more. An intergenerational transfer of knowledge and skill has also occurred, just not the one we might assume. Far from the alpine bakery with the giant wood-fired oven roaring in the basement that inspired a twenty-first-century version of making bread, has a new version of cooking as a craft emerged?

For Robertson, Rubaud, and others, baking bread involves virtuosity and an intervention into an industrial food system where their identity as "artisan" bakers embraces a moral and aesthetic definition of cooking "from scratch" as well as a type of economic livelihood. Artisan bakers have a primary fidelity to a certain process rather than a particular outcome. These bakers base their businesses on using a wood-fired oven and nurturing wild yeast through a slow fermentation process. These principles could easily become the craft practices that define a certain type of bread baking for generations to come, at home and at work.

Finally, though, what about Anina's burek? Her fidelity to a certain process resembles that of Robertson, Rubaud, and Mark. However, the motivations, reasons, and rationales behind mastering the making of burek could be seen as quite different. Thus, it could be argued that Anina's burek is more authentically a craft dish because Anina does not make it by choice in an attempt to speak against other options, other categories, or other identities. Making burek is constitutive, fundamental, and intrinsic to her identity as Bosnian; in a sense, making burek is being Bosnian. It just happens that the tasks required to make burek from scratch require complex types of tacit knowledge for it to work. Thus, Anina is a craftswoman by default and not by design.

But there is a connection between Anina and Mark. Since we always need to *learn* how to make a dish, we can never think that making either burek or a crusty loaf of bread is a passive process that happens through osmosis. The methods and techniques must first be transmitted, and then the novice must keep working to develop mastery and demonstrate their craft. Their identities, stories, and relationships to their work might be worlds apart, but someone taught Anina to make burek and Mark to make bread. And, through repetition, they have mastered their crafts. Today, with industrial processes involved in every component of producing food, from the harvesting of the wheat to the mixing of the dough, craft defined by a loaf of bread or a family cake made "from scratch" might be a red herring. Instead, we could consider cooking a craft when there is the evidence of the hand, either in the home or in the bakery. This might not be the same care work, with food dominating and defining our social obligations, but this *is* work done with care. And as long as the means and methods of making burek and bread continue to be taught to someone—whether family members, friends, or employees—the transfer of knowledge continues, and the category of cooking as craft does not disappear.

CHAPTER FIVE

Cooking Is for Health

Laura, wife of a farmer and mother of two, thinks of cooking primarily as a chore, but she also sees making meals as a way of providing healthy food for her family. When she goes through the process of deciding the next dinner-time meal, her goal is to make a meal that is nutritious and balanced. She makes many small choices along the way to attain this ideal. When she makes rolls for one meal (she was the only person we filmed making bread), she discusses her "tricks." One is, as she puts it, "adding bits of nutrition" to each and every meal, such as incorporating whole wheat flour to the rolls so "certain parties" (her son) will consume more whole grains. Another is purchasing only a certain brand of flour, because she believes this company is committed to quality and sources its wheat in a responsible manner. Before she turns on her KitchenAid mixer to combine the flour, yeast, water, and other ingredients, she incorporates healthy *knowledge* into the recipe.

Her definition of a healthy meal would please the members of the expert panel who devised the most recent version of the nationally recommended dietary guidelines: "Fresh food from a variety of food groups prepared with the least destruction of nutrients and with the most flavor. Also the family has to eat it." In the Executive Summary of the 2015 version of the USDA Dietary Guidelines, the committee states:

> Analysis of data on food categories, such as burgers, sandwiches, mixed dishes, desserts, and beverages, shows that the composition of many of these items could be improved so as to increase population intake of vegetables, whole grains, and other under consumed food groups and to lower population intake of the nutrients sodium and saturated fat, and the food component refined grains. . . . Thus, the U.S. population should be encouraged and guided to consume dietary patterns that are rich in vegetables, fruit, whole grains, seafood, legumes, and nuts; moderate in low- and non-fat dairy products and alcohol (among adults); lower in red and red meat; and low in sugar sweetened foods and beverages and refined grains.[1]

The blue-ribbon committee charged with creating these guidelines (there were fourteen members representing the fields of nutrition, medicine, and public health) reviewed the latest scientific and medical studies and recommendations for best practices to develop a report for the Secretary of Health and Human Services and the United States Department of Agriculture. The final report, which is over 120 pages long, is intended to shape public policy and inform public opinion. This version of the dietary guidelines is federally mandated (to be revised every five years) under the 1990 National Nutrition Monitoring and Related Research Act. The guidelines have become a fixture in outreach efforts to influence the eating habits of Americans. They are used by policymakers to inform federal policies related to food, nutrition, and health and also act as the basis of numerous nutrition education efforts. For example, the guidelines serve as the parameters for the National School Lunch and School Breakfast programs. In 2011, First Lady Michelle Obama, participating in the launch of MyPlate, a communications initiative based on the guidelines, urged Americans to embrace what Secretary of Agriculture Tom Vilsack described as "not a mandate but a guide." Obama said, "It is a quick simple reminder to all of us about the foods that we are eating. And as a mom, I can already tell you how much this is going to help parents all across the country."[2] In one public service announcement, she exhorts listeners to, "Eat the rainbow."

The first dietary guidelines were published in 1917 (these were initially called Food Guides).[3] They were based on the state of nutrition science at that time and thus primarily focused on the adequate consumption of energy. Over time, the guidelines moved from focusing on "shortfall nutrients" to "constructing foundation diets to supply nutrients in adequate amounts."[4] By the 1950s, nutritionists were more concerned with diseases of affluence than diseases caused by nutritional deficiencies, which led to a focus on nudging Americans toward certain food habits seen as optimal for health. Since that time, there has been an assumption that eating patterns are generally fixed—and usually not in a manner that promotes health—and that the "solution" thus lies in changing such patterns. The earlier versions of the federally mandated guidelines (which have been in place since 1980) focused on educating Americans about individual nutrients and basic food groups. This approach has changed over the years, and the new versions focus more on meals, for as the USDA Center for Nutrition Policy and Promotion points out, "People do not eat food groups and nutrients in isolation but rather in combination, and the totality of the diet forms an overall eating pattern."[5] Healthy meals are now the goal.

Among the cooks observed and interviewed in our study, a sense of obligation toward making "healthy" meals at home—that is, generally translating national dietary recommendations into everyday preparation practices—was always noted. Laura, Carol, Sylvia, Teresa, and Peter—immigrants and native-born men and women with diverse socioeconomic backgrounds—possessed a general understanding that the definition of a healthy meal involved making choices in line with the national dietary recommendations. Laura certainly reinforces the national guidelines in her notion of a healthy meal. So does Claire, who describes a healthy meal as "one that definitely has veggies, . . . and maybe not a lot of protein, and something that is pretty much balanced. You know something with not a lot of fried stuff, . . . something that's really balanced and has some green to it." However, such definitions tend to be aspirational. Although Laura might know a healthy meal when she sees it, the task of making such meals for her family is not easy. Her sense of the burden of cooking for her family combined with her other responsibilities makes fulfilling these recommendations, especially on a consistent basis, problematic. As Teresa points out, there are many ways to bypass or ignore such recommendations: "I probably won't define it as a definition, but I see cooking as a necessity. But some may disagree, especially with places now that have a lot of prepared foods sections, so you don't necessarily need to cook to eat anymore."

The act of *making* the myriad decisions that may or may not fulfill various guidelines for healthy choices might be a crucial moment when the best of intentions go awry. Certain processes involved in meal preparation—from finding the right whole ingredients to knowing ideal types of heat transfer to retain nutrients to determining the appropriate serving size—help create healthy meals, but not everyone knows how or wants to make such decisions.

Meanwhile, given the episodic nature of everyday cooking, the goal of making healthy food might really end up on the back burner. Also, there was another set of processes that Laura, Teresa, and others consistently characterized as fundamental to a healthy meal that was not as clearly reflected in the recommendations found in the USDA Dietary Guidelines. This notion of "healthy" revolved around the material conditions of ingredients. The benefits of choosing fruits, vegetables, and whole grains from the point of individual health and well-being were not perceived to concern just the self but also society at large. And there were environmental factors to consider too. Thus, the prevailing wisdom of these cooks was that it is best to eat a varied diet based on fruits and vegetables, with minimal processed foods, but that one also needs to adopt some vigilance when it comes to how ingredients are grown, harvested, distributed, and so on. In the short introductory surveys we gave all our study participants, we asked what makes a healthy meal, and many home cooks responded with: "Organic food. Vegetarian food." The category of healthy foods is not immutable. What participants considered important was quite diverse: "Unprocessed food (mostly produce w/some bulk–like rices"; "Lots of fruits, vegetables, and whole grains"; "Combination of food groups, low fat, fresh ingredients, and local products." There was a consistent belief that making a healthy meal requires choosing "good" ingredients, and this notion of the products that are considered "good" concerns more than the micronutrients and macronutrients that preoccupied the experts who came up with the dietary guidelines. Many Americans now consider provisioning for meals to be quite difficult—theoretically or practically—because the notion of a healthy meal now starts with where the ingredients were grown and sourced. Our cooks did not find the first step toward making a healthy meal—sourcing and shopping for the appropriate ingredients—straightforward.

Despite Michelle Obama's claim that an initiative like MyPlate makes making the right choices simple, this may not be the case, as the messages competing for attention and seeking to influence daily habits are cacophonous. There are so many potential choices to consider. Today, eating a healthy diet requires habits of vigilance in every decision and for every meal. Although the USDA Dietary Guidelines do not make recommendations on sourcing whole ingredients, our cooks sought out advice that was much more expansive than seeking sources of phytochemicals and shunning sources of saturated fats. The relationship between individual nutrition, culinary skill and knowledge, and social expectations remains fraught for people struggling to put together healthy dinners. There are so many locations for making choices that may or may not lead to making the best meal possible. There are so many voices declaiming the means of attaining such goals. Which choices are right?

The multiplicity and complexity of just what constitutes a healthy meal is also a long-standing issue for experts of all types. Debates about the USDA Dietary Guidelines, especially recent controversy about the inclusion of sustainability as part of the recommendations, reveal the tensions as to where to begin when identifying a healthy meal. When creating the latest round of dietary guidelines, the expert committee decided to explicitly integrate ideas about sustainability into the guidelines. This section of the final report took into account multiple studies and ended up focusing on the high levels of saturated fat found in animals, as well as the associations of animal-based agriculture with climate change. The final recommendations were seemingly straightforward:

> Consistent evidence indicates that, in general, a dietary pattern that is higher in plant-based foods, such as vegetables, fruits, whole grains, legumes, nuts, and seeds, and lower in animal-based foods is more health promoting and is associated with lesser environmental impact (GHG emissions and energy, land, and water use) than is the current average U.S. diet. A diet that is more environmentally sustainable than the average U.S. diet can be achieved without excluding any food groups.[6]

Combining the nutrition science with studies on life-cycle assessments and climate change led to the recommendation that Americans should decrease their consumption of protein from animals. This inclusion of sustainability as a metric for healthy food was not met with universal acclaim. In fact, there was a powerful pushback by members of the livestock industry. This led to a flurry of media coverage and responses from nutrition, health, and environmental experts. Ultimately, Secretary of Agriculture Tom Vilsack and Secretary of Health and Human Services Sylvia Burwell declared that the recommendation to eat more plant-based food and less animal-based food was outside of the mandate for the federally sponsored guidelines: "We do not believe that the 2015 DGAs are the appropriate vehicle for this important policy conversation about sustainability."[7] The dietary guidelines remain focused on consumption patterns, even if Americans now consider *how* they provision to be fundamental to determining if their meals fit into the healthy category, and thus it has become a crucial element of making meals. In nutrition policy, *consuming* healthy meals is considered more crucial than *making* healthy meals, even if multiple decision points are thereby ignored. This bias is unfortunate, since producing such a meal involves numerous decisions and actions that might nudge Americans toward more healthy consumption patterns. Even with the best efforts of a blue-ribbon panel and a First Lady, there remains little integration of nutritional knowledge into everyday culinary practices.

A major barrier to such an integration, something that gets in the way so home cooks cannot easily and consistently make choices that lead to the consumption of healthy meals, is the lack of agreement around what "counts" for good nutrition. Debates and controversies, such as lowering the intake of animal-based foods, have become part of the daily news cycle. No wonder everyone shares real hesitation when attempting to understand the best choices when it comes to making and consuming meals deemed to be healthy. The struggles of both home cooks and food experts reveal that a healthy meal always exists, first and foremost, within a cacophonous social environment, no matter what other expectations we have about food; individual decisions are nested within these larger cultural debates. Over seventy years ago, Audrey Richards began her classic ethnography *Hunger and Work in a Savage Tribe* with these words: "Nutrition as a biological process is more fundamental than sex. In the life of the individual organism it is the more primary and recurrent physical want, while in the wider sphere of human society it determines, more largely than any other physiological function, the nature of social groupings, and the form their activities take. Yet in current sociological theory man's nutritive needs play a very insignificant role."[8]

Richards's point remains apt. There is a robust subfield of nutritional anthropology that has emerged since her initial statement as to the need for more dialogue about nutrition and society. These scholars have traversed the globe to integrate the biological and cultural understandings of food and nutrition, understanding the diversity of human experiences as important and diverse as breastfeeding practices and responses to famine. As David Sutton points out, however, anthropologists (and, it could be argued, sociologists) have not devoted much systematic attention to cooking as an instrumental part of foodwork and food values across cultures. Despite advances in the science of nutrition (the discovery of vitamins, the identification of essential amino acids, new forays into the gut microbiome), there has been very little parallel investigation into the translation of such knowledge, through skilled practices, into the culturally desired goal of a healthy meal. In particular, the translation and transformation of what is known about human physiology in light of the cultural axioms as to what makes food "good for you" remain quite inchoate.

In the preface to Richards's book, Bronislaw Malinowski, arguably one of anthropology's most famous founding fathers asks: "What do we know of nutrition as a creative force in human societies and cultures? In comparative works an accidental, scrappy and unsatisfactory account is given of it; while in the records of field-work we mostly look in vain even for a mention of the manner in which people eat their food, and its influence on social life, or the gradual emergence of economic values out of nutritive appetites."[9] Decades after Malinowski and Richards exhorted anthropologists, sociologists, and psychologists to look more closely at the "manner in which people eat their food," when it comes to the translation of what is known to what actually gets prepared and eaten—the move from understanding to action—we seem no closer to anything more than "scrappy accounts."

In the United States, when considering the intersection of individual nutrition and social expectations, the disjuncture between aspiration and action is particularly puzzling. As Laura and others demonstrate, Americans almost universally accept the common wisdom that "health" should be factored into meal preparations. In 2006, the annual Vermonter Poll, which surveys one thousand Vermont residents on numerous relevant issues of the day, included questions about decisions related to making and eating meals. One of the questions posed was: "When purchasing food for a meal, which of the following factors is the most important, cost, convenience, flavor or health?" The number one factor was health (56.1 percent), the second was cost (22.1 percent), and the third was flavor (13.9 percent), and the forth was convenience (7.9 percent). So, when people are *asked* what they consider important, they say that health is a priority, at least in Vermont. These findings are confirmed by other studies. In a recent study by the International Food Information Council, for example, a similar question was posed: "How much of an impact do the following have on your decision to buy foods and beverages?" The factors were taste, price, healthfulness, convenience, and sustainability. The factors that the survey respondents ranked as having the most impact were taste, health, and price.[10]

Laura, Teresa, and others valiantly attempted to make decisions about their meals based on a general understanding of what nutrition and health experts claim constitutes a healthy meal. But knowing and doing operate more in parallel fashion than in a form of seamless integration. We eat more often than we cook, so translating general recommendations into the right choice for every single meal requires the navigation of a complex food environment. And as Teresa points out, the reason for the gaps might lie in what is possible and available when moving from the task of making to the act of eating a meal. As she goes on to say later in her interview: "Why I make dinner as opposed to [letting] someone else [do it] . . . is [that] I'm controlling what's going into it. Without a doubt, I have control over it." Her commitment to cooking emerges from navigating her environment, as well as from fulfilling obligations: "Cooking for me is part of my everyday life, and it's something that I do to de-stress, to connect with Chris [her husband], to control what's going into my body." In such an environment, the choice to cook can seem to be intrinsically more wholesome than all the other options: "I also probably make not-so-healthy choices sometimes when I cook, and I don't feel bad because it's homemade and I know what's in it, and as long as I don't eat a lot of it, it's okay." Thus, there are two "hidden" realities about the decisions Americans make when preparing healthy meals. First, sourcing the right ingredients is not seen as straightforward or without effort. Second, whenever moving toward good ingredients, appropriate techniques, and accurate serving sizes, the home cook can almost always veer toward alternatives seen as easier (in terms of time, effort, and cost) that ultimately undermine goals for healthy meals. Healthy ingredients, in the proper amounts, for a meal prepared at home are but a small segment of a larger system of easily available foods, and many trade-offs are made between one and the other.

At the same time, the concept of healthy food is imbricated in people's everyday analyses and actions relating to their choices about what to make and eat.[11] One clear theme that emerged from our interviews was the emphasis placed on the main cook of a household taking control of the food their family eats *before* the food reaches the home in order to procure food items that aligned with their definition of "healthy." Numerous perils exist in the greater food environment when it comes to accessing food that represents an ideal of health or healthfulness. The transformation of raw ingredients into a cooked and satisfactory meal was the primary locus of attention paid to "health." When cooking at home, these cooks find health in the choices they make about what counts as an ingredient. The dinner dilemma, it appears, often concerns control versus freedom, where control involves knowing what ingredients are used in a meal and freedom lies in being liberated from the chore of cooking (and planning and even cleaning up). In this duality, the "healthfulness" of a meal is seen sometimes as the main benefit of choosing to cook and at other times as the main means of making the "right" choice when having someone else do the cooking for you. The emergent dilemmas involved in eating a healthy meal, therefore are not based in ignorance; many Americans do possess the knowledge required to make healthy meal choices. Rather, the main struggle is navigating the multiple paths available on any given day, tacking between convenience, taste, and health. Furthermore, these preoccupations are often in conflict with each other, and one type of meal is often chosen *instead* of another.

GATEKEEPING FOR HEALTH

During World War II, soon after Audrey Richards published the first ethnography devoted to food, nutrition, and cultural practices, social psychologist Kurt Lewin developed the channel theory to explain "how food comes to the table and why."[12] Lewin and Margaret Mead, an anthropologist, were lead researchers for the food group of the National Research Council, a research group (including a number of qualitative and quantitative social scientists) aimed at supporting a national effort during the war to ration food by encouraging new cooking and eating behaviors. Each launched research projects that sought to understand everyday food habits with the aim of

Figure 15. Choosing an orange, circa 1950. Box 3, folder 2, Agricultural Extension Service Photographs, Special Collections, University of Vermont Library.

making recommendations to the U.S. government. In his work, Lewin argued that to understand the process of making meals, it was necessary to identify how many "food channels" exist for a household or group. He determined that in any household or group, "entering or not entering a channel and moving from one section of a channel to another is effected by a 'gatekeeper.'" Lewin's theory was prescient. His integration of individual choice, social conditions, and food environments illuminates American habits; decision-making always occurs among and between these elements. He identified the limitations of looking solely at the individual, either physiologically or cognitively, when considering changing how Americans shop, eat, and cook.

Recent studies in food and nutrition have used Lewin's analysis of the social and psychological function of the gatekeeper in a household to bring new insights to nutritional science interpretations of Americans' food behaviors. The goal of these researchers has been to identify means and methods of influencing Americans in order to have more success in the shared goal of optimal nutrition. In a 2003 article, Brian Wansink points out that nutrition education has directed efforts toward encouraging Americans to change their behaviors regarding optimally healthy meals, based on categorizations of all citizens primarily as food consumers. He argues that is time to "move the focus to the cook." He implies that this is what is needed to move beyond the one-size-fits-all prescriptions of much nutrition education: "We examine gatekeepers who are the primary meal planners and cooks, and who are not necessarily female or a stay-at-home parent. . . . There are benefits to focusing on those who are more serious about this role."[13] Wansink modifies Lewin's theory of the gatekeeper to consider the potential of the "nutritional gatekeeper," or the member of a nuclear family who monitors home food consumption. Wansink and others argue that targeting these household members increases the likelihood of successful interventions and policies to encourage new cooking and eating behaviors, particularly an increase in the consumption of nutrient-dense foods and a concomitant decrease in the consumption of energy-dense foods.[14] For example, Wansink claims that identifying the traits of good "nutritional gatekeepers" will allow us to design better nutrition interventions and influence what ends up on Americans' dinner tables; he argues that nutritional gatekeepers "controlled over 72% of the food that was eaten by their children both inside and outside the home."[15]

The focus on a nutritional gatekeeper resonates with our research because we found that one person tended to be the primary cook for their household and each of these cooks attempted to provide healthy meals. More scholarly attention however, should be given to Lewin's ideas about channels and gates, or in the increasingly common parlance of nutrition researchers and advocates, the means of navigating America's "toxic food environment," a landscape of choice that propels people down pathways understood as less than optimal for individual nutritional health.[16] Lewin sought both to identify why people choose to eat in certain ways and to find methods that would help change such habits. His research methods "tried to combine approaches of cultural anthropology with quantitative methods of psychology."[17] His research, which combined projective questionnaires of schoolchildren with interviews of housewives (representing high, medium, and low income levels), led him to come up with what he called a "channel theory," seemingly commonsensical and yet crucial to making sense of everyday meal practices: "Of paramount importance in this theory is the fact that once food is on the table, most of it is eaten by someone in the family. Therefore, one would find the main answer to the question 'why people eat what they eat,' if one could answer the question, 'how food comes to the table and why.'" This insight, that the person who provisions and his or her methods of provisioning are crucial in understanding food habits, still resonates today.

Lewin identified two main channels whereby food reaches the table, the buying channel and the gardening channel, although he also mentioned, but considered secondary, "deliveries, buying food in the country, baking at home, and canning."[18] Seventy years later, many more food channels exist with real impact on the everyday process of gatekeeping for modern American families, making his insights even more relevant. He pointed out that each channel can be perceived as both advantageous and detrimental to the process of making choices: "For example, if food is expensive, two forces of opposite direction operate on the housewife. She is in a conflict. The force away from spending too much money keeps the food from going in that channel. A second force corresponding to the attractiveness of the food tends to bring it in the channel."[19] Now imagine such a process occurring for

Figure 16. Home economics field trip: learning how to kill and pluck a chicken, circa 1960. Record group 24, box 17, publicity photos, Home Economics Department, Special Collections, University of Vermont Library.

multiple meals every day and multiple venues as well. Lewin's navigational notions, the tacking back and forth between options, continues to be relevant, especially when we look closely at the quest to create healthy meals. Laura, Carol, Sylvia, Teresa, and Peter are all willing to be nutritional gatekeepers, but there are so many gates that can possibly be open and shut.

Lewin's extensive look into the full cycle of tasks involved in making meals accentuates the importance of context when it comes to physically getting food, be it raw carrots or a Duncan Hines cake mix. Shopping for food is crucial in the quest to make modern meals. Our physical environments are saturated with choices: we can purchase ingredients at the corner store, the chain grocer, the farmers market, or the big-box store and then prepare food at home, or we can forego those locales and buy a meal at the takeout pizza place or order in from the Chinese restaurant. Today, there are many options for moving food from a raw to a cooked state; supermarket shelves offer an endless array of prepackaged and prepared foods, takeout meals can be purchased and delivered to the car or the front door, and twenty-four-hour-a-day retail sites sell all manner of food. We also increasingly live in urban areas, with less easy access to ways to grow our own food. There is also the constant and remarkably shared perception that time poverty interferes with preparing meals. The organization of contemporary American society, especially the increased number of households with children where both adults work outside the home and of single parent households, has transformed the food environment, and the transformation of the food environment has changed us as well. When the United States Department of Agriculture does an accounting of retail sales in food establishments, grocery stores are only one of a number of possible outlets; others include convenience stores, large multicommodity outlets, and online venues. Every food decision, from large (how many shopping trips every week) to small (a coffee before work), has expanded in number and location. Gatekeeping is a more complex task today because of the increasing options available to people looking to feed themselves and their families. All these choices, which can be cast as freedoms, have created new difficulties.

People still choose to cook, but the decision-making process involved in this act has become infinitely more complex. People's knowledge of what makes a healthy meal has deepened and expanded, but the available choices have multiplied. The reason why we have so many options is linked to the rise in commercial food service and the food industry. The focus by contemporary nutrition researchers and educators on food consumers reflects our changing patterns and our increased reliance on others (both people and machines) to do our work for us. Complexity is in part brought about by increased food choices at the supermarket, more opportunities to purchase food in a retail setting, and new technologies for the kitchen. However, perhaps this reliance is not fully integrated into the cultural consciousness or into our embodied actions; we do not realize how much gatekeeping is needed to create a healthy meal. When it comes to cooking for health, the major challenges for this category "in action" appear to be more navigational than instructional.

Identifying the many available contemporary food channels is crucial to fully comprehending the gatekeeper's tasks. The previous—and seemingly simpler—choice between growing your own ingredients or buying basic ingredients at a single store has expanded to include purchasing partially prepared and fully prepared food options. It is common to hear of an individual who will cook one night, consume leftovers the next night, get takeout the next night, and go out to a restaurant to eat the next night. Making the choice of what to have for dinner now involves navigating a seemingly unlimited combination of possible pathways. The definition of a healthy meal cannot be confined to just what is consumed but now also requires an accounting of how choices are negotiated and decisions made as to sourcing, making, *and* consuming the meal. And such accountability needs to consider these choices and decisions not just on ideal days but on any and all days, weekday or weekend, busy or relaxed, summer or winter.

Therefore, pragmatic knowledge about foods identified as healthy constantly intersects with a food environment that makes it difficult for people to achieve their aspirations for a healthy meal. Partly because deciding what to have for dinner is an everyday activity, people's actions when it comes to this task are often automatic and unreflective. This often leads to a disjuncture between aspirational ideals and daily decisions. For the gatekeepers we interviewed, much of the struggle between an ideal scenario of shopping, cooking, and eating and what actually occurred lay in the difficulty of having to continuously navigate the many possible food channels. People's values about healthy meals were constantly tested because the food environment was consistently perceived as less than ideal. Despite demographic differences, an ideal of obtaining healthy food was always involved in people's processes of navigating a number of pathways when determining what to have for dinner.

The food channels that most often brought pressure to make trade-offs were food-retail stores, takeout establishments, and restaurants. These ready options saturate the landscape of choice, and therefore meals that were not prepared at home always played a part in the calculations toward health. All of our study participants ate meals outside the home on a regular basis, and many articulated it as a "necessary evil" when reflecting on the health benefits of these meals beyond basic sustenance. This was primarily due to the fact that they would no longer be the nutritional gatekeeper for the food that they are eating. As Joan, a woman in her sixties living in a small city, puts it: "I think just [about] the sauces and the things that they use, and I think ignorance is bliss, you know. If I don't know how much butter they put in it, you know, and all that, then I just do things that I just probably wouldn't do here [at home]." By choosing the "food prepared outside the home" channel, Joan recognizes she no longer has control over the ingredients that go into her meal. In these moments, her knowledge does *not* get translated into practice. Context, apparently, matters when following guidelines. In fact, she seems to have a set of rules and regulations that she follows while at home to maintain what she would consider to be a healthy diet, but these rules get broken, or perhaps simply lose relevance, in a restaurant environment.

Another example comes from Teresa: "I find when we cook, it's a balanced meal, [and] when I take out, I'm not paying attention so much to getting a salad and getting a vegetable." She sticks to the nutritional maxim "Eat a balanced meal" when making dinner at home, but just like Joan, a changed environment makes her abandon or reject such guidelines. The challenge of negotiating maxims for healthy meals is doubly compounded when you do not have much money and the channels moving you toward food prepared outside the home are limited. As Sarah, an urban dweller, discusses what is available in her neighborhood, she bemoans: "It's usually crap. I'm always a little frustrated because where I live, I feel like the options aren't real great, and if I do want a little healthier option, it's even that much more expensive, so I get trapped in this 'Do I eat healthy?' or 'Do I spend money?' or 'Where do I go?'" More often than not, she chooses the cheaper food, which she considers to be less healthy overall. She gives a particular example of choosing what she thought was the less healthy burrito for less than five dollars rather than getting the "healthier" sushi. She says that choosing one over the other represents her "healthy versus expense trade-off." In this case, she is someone who eats outside the home very often, and she expresses the frequency as "more than I'd like to both financially and health-wise." Comparing the different meals that she eats outside the home, she recognizes that she often chooses what she feels to be the less healthy option but feels trapped by her sense of time poverty and limited financial means.

Sarah knows what she considers to be a healthy meal, but she only feels able to occasionally make these meals. Ignorance is not the issue. Is the issue a failure of will? A cultural history of blaming people for making unhealthy choices does exist; there is a long-standing American predilection for assuming an association between a healthy person (however this has been understood in any given era) and a morally upright citizen. Melanie DuPuis characterizes the American worldview in this regard as "ingestive subjectivity"; we define ourselves in terms of our "control over choice."[20] She identifies these "moral precepts of the self-controlled citizen" as part of the efforts of the Founding Fathers, and argues that they are still at play today in efforts to create healthy eaters.[21] Charlotte Biltekoff demonstrates that beginning with American dietary reformers of the nineteenth century, ideals for healthful diets were explicitly and implicitly linked with good citizenship.[22] In contemporary America, Megan Carney says that federal efforts to improve the health of impoverished citizens (and noncitizens) by seeking to improve their "food security" can be cast as biopolitics, and so transferring the responsibility of care to individuals.[23] In all these cases, not complying with certain dietary ideals is linked to a failure to address moral obligations.

Sarah, like many Americans facing the multiple available means of provisioning her food, seems to blame herself for not having a healthier diet. She focuses on personal failure rather than her social and economic circumstances and judges herself when it comes to her control over what she cooks and eats: "Actually this past fall I fell into this habit of eating out and getting—this is horribly embarrassing—getting groceries at 7-Eleven. You can imagine what my groceries looked like." She polices her own behavior, casting it as a form of noncompliance to a healthy ideal rather than a problem of her circumstances.

And yet, she does acknowledge the issues of circumstance. She goes on to compare access to fruits and vegetables in the urban area in the United States where she now resides with her past experiences living in Galway, Ireland:

> Everything is a lot more fresh. Meat and eggs have the name of the farmer on them, and it's usually from somebody down the road. The meat's a different color, the eggs are a different color—when you crack them, they're this rich, golden [color], . . . and they taste better. Certain things are cheaper there. . . . The milk tastes fresher. I don't drink a whole lot of milk here necessarily, unless it's in something. They don't have as many chips; they don't have as many candies. My snacks were entirely different. My snacks were whole grain crunchy bread with a little bit of cheese. It was totally different.

In some ways, Sarah understands that the problem might be her urban neighborhood, a locale not catering to her needs. Yet, in order to explain this issue, she identifies it by making a cultural comparison, referring to Ireland, where she had more regular access to ingredients she categorizes as healthy and fresh: "Definitely the freshness is huge. Don't get me wrong, you can eat really unhealthy in Ireland, but I feel like the focus is a little bit different, especially in a place like Galway, where it is a center for a rural area. So they also have farmers market every Saturday [where] my roommates and I would buy most of our produce from local farmers, so you know that's fresh."

Sarah's use of a cultural comparison to move beyond self-blame makes sense. The dilemmas people face in their efforts to align their understandings with their practices do derive from social and cultural conditions. Both the challenges and solutions that appear when putting together a healthy meal are not simply or solely in the hands (literally or figuratively) of individuals. Mary Douglas made this point in regard to assumptions about food and nutrition in a series of essays written over forty years ago about family meals. In this analysis, which is still relevant today, she notes that there was a universal concern for the problems of human nutrition but also a tendency to focus such concerns on individual biology for potential interventions.[24] Thus, "no general principles" had been established on the social aspects of food and nutrition. She succinctly highlighted anthropological assumptions about knowledge and action that were understood to be culturally shared:

> First, it is a prior assumption of cultural anthropology (and one that would underlie all sociological study) that human behavior is a patterned activity. Second, it is assumed that the tendency to fall into patterns is affected by economic and political concerns. Consequently, and thirdly, the patterns that are sufficiently stable to be identified in research are assumed to be adapted to an equally stable distribution of power in the social dimension. As the distribution of power changes so will the cultural patterns affected by it.[25]

The principles she articulates remain relevant to understanding what is involved in putting together a meal defined as healthy. In observing home cooks, both when in conversation and also when watching people cook, the patterns everyone fell into, the constant everyday cycle of aspiring to fulfill the recommendations of the USDA's Dietary Guidelines and then failing to do so, were consistent and relatively stable across age, gender, race, and class. Although cultural patterns are never set in stone, as evidenced by the changes in cooking practices over the past century, the persistence of hyperindividualized guilt and generally passive responses reveals the cultural power of both the ideal and the moral stance toward this ideal.

Douglas subsequently explores the structure of a British meal, which she says always requires "a meat and two veg." What makes this a meal is not just putting the whole chicken in a roasting pan with potatoes and carrots nestled underneath and then placing it in a hot oven. It also involves the general shared principles of mainstream British culture and cuisine (at least in the 1970s). As with Lewin and Mead, Douglas did her research during a period when the choices for not cooking dinner were less pervasive, so her generalizations about what makes a proper British dinner were based solely on household activities. Today, in the United States, any similar sociocultural analysis of the structure of modern meals needs to consider the numerous locales where Americans now eat. Yet her larger claim about stable patterns, at least when considering healthy meals, remains apt. In our subsequent, more recent research on cooking, which included interviewing low-income women from diverse racial backgrounds in Philadelphia about healthy meals, we found that these women shared Sarah's frustrations and concerns. They wanted to make and eat healthy meals and to enact with success this generally accepted category. Like everyone else, their goal was to consume plenty of fresh fruits and vegetables and stay away from saturated fat and refined sugar. They did not want to regularly consume what nutritionists call the Standard American Diet; they wanted to follow the USDA's Dietary Guidelines.[26] But they felt stymied by their financial, locational, and environmental circumstances.[27]

THE DILEMMA OF A HEALTHY MEAL: COMPETING PLACES AND PERCEPTIONS

Again, the preponderance of pathways leading to temptations of all sorts—to alleviate an obligation, save time, or taste a new dish—constantly pits the individual *against* the cultural value of ingestive discipline. Knowledge of a healthy meal in hand, people identify eating out as a "necessary evil" or an inevitable compromise. As Joan reveals when she states that "ignorance is bliss," the tension between shutting out options or acquiescing to such temptations is clear. She values balance in the meals that she prepares at home and often tries to make sure to include a salad and vegetable. When she goes out to eat, however, she does not think about these things nearly as often and thus may not be consuming these foods as often when eating outside the home.

Edna, an older woman living in West Philadelphia, also struggles to navigate between choices that she does not perceive as ideal. She explains her choice to cook as a form of defense against the food environment: "I have to cook, because if I don't cook, I will eat junk food." She also often does not like the way foods are prepared in restaurants and has had bad experiences, not quite getting what she wants or expects: "It always tastes good, but I'm like, come on, you know when you make my salad, you know I like onions, so give me a little bit more onions. I'll pay for it. . . . But it's always a little nice to just go out and have someone make it for you. [But] when I get home, I'm kinda disappointed. So I opt to just cook for myself."

Edna, like Sarah, does not like the provisioning channels available to her in the immediate neighborhood, which has a high proportion of residents living in poverty. She must make special efforts to make the healthy meals she desires:[28]

> I don't like these little neighborhood stores, so I have to travel. The quality is better [elsewhere]. Like, for example, I live in . . . West Philadelphia. We do have several markets. But if I go to another market, like in this area, I'm gonna get great customer service, and the choice of foods are gonna be best. [So] I go to Trader Joe's, Whole Foods, and the Fresh Grocer at the University City. . . . I catch the bus there, or a cab.

The available channels for procuring food, both raw and cooked, are problematic in relation to an ideal of preparing and eating a healthy meal. The temptations of the contemporary American food environment combined with an overall perception of time poverty when it comes to shopping for and cooking meals makes the contemporary gatekeeper's job both easier (you don't always have to cook) and harder (you can't always control what you eat).

The cost of food also factored into the decision-making matrix for many. Ellen, a mother and wife living in a rural area, characterizes a healthy meal as "a variety of foods from different food groups and not a lot of fat." Her definition of a healthy meal helps provide structure for the meals her family eats throughout the week, but other factors are involved as well. Her ability to achieve her goals for healthy meals depends on fairly elaborate provisioning strategies that allow her to create affordable healthy meals:

> Depending what the sales are, I'll make up my menu for the week, and I start with Sunday usually and put the days and decide what I'll make for each

> day. . . . I just pull out recipes, or I'll have recipes in a certain area that I've been wanting to make for a while, and I'll pull them out of there [recipe drawer], and see if it matches up with what's on sale, like if beef or chicken or whatever is on sale. . . . And I will buy some things at . . . the farmers market. . . . I'll get some fresh vegetables and things [there].

And then there are the complexities of trying to purchase healthy food at the grocery store: "When I grocery shop, I pretty much stick to the outer edges of the store, and so it's the fruits, and the vegetables, and . . . the dairy, and down through that aisle. . . . So I shop that way. I also [go to a certain store], and I know there's a lot of stuff that is not good [there], but I also think there are a lot of things that are healthy."

Everyone in our study was concerned about the preponderance of certain options that are deemed inadequate in terms of health but which are often more inexpensive and in other ways attractive. All these choices have also expanded their desires, which are now often in conflict with goals of creating and consuming healthy meals. Sylvia articulates her dilemma as primarily sensorial. Yes, food served at restaurants might not be as healthy as a meal she prepares at home, but she considers this a trade-off rather than a deal-breaker: "I try to use more organic ingredients and less fats [at home], and when everything is fried at restaurants, and the oil has been boiling several times, . . . I try to make some healthy choices, ordering something grilled and a salad, fresh vegetables." When asked if she thinks there is a difference in the degree of healthfulness of what she eats when she is at a restaurant versus when she is at home, she acknowledges the dilemma but does not change her choices: "Certainly. But it is the taste and the variety of food that attracts me to the restaurant." The saturated food environment means that healthy tastes are consistently in conflict with distinctive and unusual tastes, and eating at a restaurant is often identified as providing the latter at the cost of the former. Sylvia understands her actions: "I'm apt to order things that I wouldn't have at home. . . . Every now and then you just get a craving for something [that you really want]." But she goes on to say, "And then I feel guilty."

TRADE-OFFS FOR HEALTH: SOURCING, MAKING, AND TASTING

There is no question that classifying their meals using a "healthy food" matrix influences the perceptions and practices of everyday home cooks. Whether these cooks were urban or rural, rich or poor, black or white, born in the United States or abroad, sourcing and providing healthy meals for themselves and others was a clear and consistent aspiration. In a sense, the decades-long efforts of nutrition and health professionals, the countless empirical studies, the policy efforts to create dietary guidelines, nutrition fact labels, calls for taxes on sugar sweetened beverages, and the outreach efforts of politicians, celebrities, and athletes have been successful. Americans know, accept, and try to enact the category of cooking for health. We believe that healthy meals are what we should be eating, and nutritional gatekeepers like Joan, Teresa, and Sarah do their level best to make that happen. Gatekeeping is a constant, even relentless, task. An African-American woman living in Philadelphia with limited financial resources attains this goal by eating only one meal a day and buying it at Whole Foods to guarantee that it is healthy. In the same neighborhood, a first-generation Filipina American has become dedicated to her urban garden plot in an attempt to source high-quality vegetables cheaply.[29]

However, the aspirations to find "healthy" ingredients and to eat a nourishing dinner are neither universally defined nor universally enacted. The broad recommendations—"lots of fruits and vegetables and not too much sugar and fat"—serve to frame decisions and choices, but other concerns impinge too. These disjunctures reveal that the category of healthy food has something to do with health as defined by a general sense of nutritional competence but there is more to it too. Today, "healthy food" means much more than the lists of micro- and macronutrients, carbohydrates, fats, sugars, and protein that much of the modern discourse on food and health relies on. Sylvia's comments—or perhaps confessions—for example, are telling. In many of her choices, especially when she chooses not to cook and lets someone else do that work on her behalf, aspirations inspired by other cooking categories work as much in conflict as in concert with her interest in making, or at least consuming, a healthy meal.

Another means of making healthy meals, one that has yet to be explicitly addressed by nutrition policy (and given the controversy over the sustainability guidelines, may not be addressed in official policy in the near future), involves knowledge about ingredients that goes above and beyond the generally understood nutritional benefits of consuming more whole grains, fruits, and vegetables. The category of healthy food is thus multilayered and multidimensional; knowing the antioxidant properties of blueberries and the amount of vitamin A and D in sweet potatoes is important but not sufficient to fulfill social ideals for healthy meals. This emerging matrix involves making food that tastes good, is good for you, and is also ultimately good for the planet—it is the integration of aesthetic and moral claims into a category about health. These ingredients, identified with such definitions of "good food," though, could not always fulfill all the requirements. Thus, currently, to make sense of, as Malinowski put it, "this manner in which people eat their food" (at least in the Northeast), requires understanding the powerful intersections of multiple categories of perception and practice to understand how and why social groups make choices about cooking and eating.

Here, the category of healthy food ends up including moral and aesthetic ideals or working in competition with other categories. When asked if the nutrition of a meal is crucial for her, Barbara responds: "Yeah, I'm not one of these people who freaks out about fat or calories, but it has to taste delicious, and it has to be nutritious." For Barbara, fulfilling a healthy goal cannot mean sacrificing other culinary ideals, such as good taste and aesthetic standards:

> I try to make an event out of [getting takeout] too. Like, I try to always try to present it. Like, I would never eat takeout out of the container, no matter what it is. . . . I always make sure it is hot. I want it to feel like I had some sort of [role in] making it or presenting even if I picked it up on the way home. Or I might add some spices or something to it just to tweak it a little bit. . . . It's got to be of a certain quality and not too much quantity.

At home, Barbara makes the takeout meal her own. Today's gatekeepers have an expanded repertoire of conceptual tools that are always in play, even when their primary aspiration is stated to be making a healthy meal.

These days, many feel that tasty food should overlap, at least in some small way, with food categorized to have material qualities that translate into promoting a healthy body.[30] A meal tastes good at multiple levels. Yes, taste is ultimately subjective, and as such, it is a sense that can never truly be physiologically shared. However, that does not mean taste can be understood or explained only at the individual level, as sensory experience is socially and culturally derived. Cultures create evaluative categories for individual taste experiences; these categories frame and explain everyday choices about what to cook and what to eat. A meal might taste good because it is what a meal "should be"—that is, the structure conforms to social expectations and cultural values.

Healthy tastes have a number of meanings, and these meanings are generally positive, even if attaining healthy tastes is also perceived as difficult. Examining why and how these categories shape how Americans interact with food and drink illuminates the obstacle course of trying to interpret how more general cultural ways of knowing get translated into daily life, especially the relationship between aspiration ("I want to eat more healthy food"), value ("Organic food is better"), and practice ("I can't afford that food"; "I don't have time to make healthy food"). As Abby Wilkerson points out, "Protean and highly contested though they may be, public discourses of 'good food' exert a powerful influence, especially demands to make healthy 'goodness' the cornerstone of our food preparation and consumption."[31] Lisa, a single mother living in the Boston area, articulates the dilemma as tasty, quick, and healthy. She needs to track between these aspirations, her culinary knowledge, and her family's expectations. This is apparent when she responds to a question about what is important to her when preparing an everyday meal:

> Taste probably. . . . [When I was growing up,] how [did we] make [food] taste good? The more butter you put in, the more flour you use, the more cream sauces. We do not eat a lot of meat anymore, just by thinking healthy. [Now] we are more of a turkey, chicken [family]. I like [to get] a good piece of meat once every two weeks. I might make this pasta sauce with ground beef once in a while, but even when I make sloppy joes I use turkey. So I am conscious of that. We don't use a lot of cream sauces. If I have company I might. . . . Taste, quick, healthy would probably be my top three.

By acknowledging her culinary heritage (meals with lots of butter and meat, especially red meat) but also incorporating her idea of what makes a healthy meal (one that is close to the recommendations in the USDA's Dietary Guidelines), Lisa affirms the new definition of a good and tasty meal, one choice at a time.

In all our interviews, the definitions given of a healthy meal concerned more than the macro- and micronutrients, fat, salt, and sugar contained in the ingredients. Other factors mattered: Were the carrots organically grown? Was the chicken humanely raised and slaughtered? Were the apples grown within one hundred miles of the store? These questions reflect the success of the local foods movement in the Northeast: as Barbara says, "I'm pretty fussy about what takeout I consider. So, if I get prepared foods, it's only [from shops that source local food]. So, I want local foods, or I want food that's prepared in a way that I would prepare it."

Complex shopping strategies based on a definition of "healthy" founded on moral and aesthetic claims were prevalent among those living in more rural areas of New England; people spent time each week sourcing locally grown foods, and many had gardens. Such complex provisioning strategies were attempts to uphold standards, which were not easily met. Mary lives in a rural area of Vermont and shares such priorities: "I always drink organic milk, and . . . it's Vermont organic milk. I try to buy as much close to home [as possible]. I get everything I'm going to prepare. . . . [The] meat I bought for the dinner is from Niman Ranch, which is Colorado.[32] But it's humanely produced pork, you know, [the] pigs get to roam, . . . and it tastes wonderful!" In the moment of such everyday choices, many people explained their actions using the convenient (if not completely satisfactory) analysis "It could be worse."

This type of trade-off discussion between the goals of a healthy self and a healthy environment was consistent for all the home cooks, which perhaps reveals that a certain "splitting" of the category of healthy meals is now occurring across the United States, depending on community values and demographic characteristics. Robin, a young cook who identifies herself as highly invested in making and eating healthy food, uses a combination of micro and macro definitions to help her choose the ingredients for her meals. She also combines highly individualized definitions of "healthy" and "healthy food" (based on her ongoing struggles with a persistent infection) with broader definitions of these terms that are based on how foods are grown and processed: "I've studied a little bit of nutrition, [so] I know that the amount of time that goes from harvest to eating you lose, it gets to be less and less [nutritious]. So, I have got that in the mind, so I will think, [since rhubarb is in season right now,] can I use that rhubarb tonight or can I incorporate that somehow?"

Lisa explains the complex strategies necessary to source ingredients for healthy meals, and, in doing so, she reflects another barrier in the move from aspiration to action: How do you figure out the best gates for all the available channels? This question is certainly relevant when considering provisioning food; Lisa's access to possibilities is not a concern, but what demands both knowledge and skill is sourcing the "right" ingredients to make her healthy meals. This requires a weekly dance: "I do a massive food shopping once a week. . . . I have the staples in mind that I know I can cook on a regular basis, so I'll make sure I have that, and if, during the week, I want to have fish—I like fresh fish—I don't do the frozen fish thing or anything like that, so I'll stop on the way home, at Whole Foods." Her healthy practices involve *getting* the right ingredients as much as *preparing* the right meal.

In order to commit to making healthy meals, home cooks need to navigate a provisioning system that is bountiful in many ways but perhaps too bountiful in foods not defined as healthy: those that are too energy dense and contain too much salt and too many additives. It is paradoxical, even ironic, that one of the main health messages of nutrition and health professions is to "shop the perimeter" when going to a supermarket. In the health and wellness section of the Mayo Clinic website, readers are told that shopping the perimeter can help control fat and sodium intake.[33] One-stop shopping, which in an earlier era was evoked as a sign of progress and a means of alleviating the home cook's burdens, now interferes with the new indicator, the universal American aspiration of healthy meals for all. To be a healthy cook requires constant vigilance in the market, in the restaurant, and at home.

Although there might be values toward proper provisioning that are shared across New England (due to the long history of small-scale farming in the region and the successful local foods movement) that might explain the number of cooks concerned about sourcing locally grown and organic foods, many responses were broader (such as Lisa's choice to buy fresh rather than frozen fish), reflecting the national conversation about the importance of knowing where your food comes from and how it was made. Multiple channels create numerous choices. This multiplicity can be overwhelming and

Figure 17. "Shopping for Meat," Burlington, Vermont, circa 1950. James Detore Photographs, Special Collections, University of Vermont Library.

difficult to negotiate. A complex calculus occurs with every decision, from where to shop to what to eat: "Last night we had frozen pizza, but it was organic!" And then there is the pressure to cook food at home, given the media discourse on the benefit of home-cooked over store-bought meals, now a constant drumbeat in the background as gatekeepers navigate the plethora of available choices.

EDUCATING FOR HEALTHY MEALS: MARION ROMBAUER AND *THE JOY OF COOKING*

The cultural preoccupation with making healthy meals has had a parallel evolution with the decline in domestic servants and the rise in commercially prepared foods. For a century, explicitly connecting individual health and nutrition with everyday choices became the task of a group of professionals (needless to say, these were primarily women). These experts focused their attention on the domestic sphere. First, it was the domestic scientists; then, home economists. Now the work to transmit health expertise through teaching Americans to cook and eat more healthfully has extended to more fields, particularly nutrition and public health. In these fields, a discourse prevails around the problem of getting Americans to eat healthy food, often revolving around women's recalcitrance or women's ignorance.[34] The domestic science movement was initially concerned with the improved transfer of nutrients (as understood at that time) and the betterment of cooking to that end, which it addressed by creating a paradigm for learning—a pedagogy of sorts. This effort included the development of methods and techniques based on scientific principles (especially uniform measurement), the push toward education in home economics, and the rise of the standard recipe format. Leaders in this movement, such as Fannie Farmer, saw themselves primarily as teachers. Educating and informing housewives and thereby promoting a greater public good drove their agenda. Farmer started out as a student at the Boston Cooking School and then went on to become a teacher and ultimately the institution's principal. Her goal was to create "recipes that work." She was committed to promoting the transfer of proper knowledge through the scientific axioms of precision and replication: "The school had introduced standardized measuring cups and spoons in the mid-1880s. . . . Farmer wanted to make sure that even beginners could measure accurately. 'A cupful is measured level,' she instructed. 'A tablespoon is measured level. A teaspoonful is measured level.'"[35]

The ideas of the early domestic scientists, the transfer of knowledge with the goal of improving American cooking and eating habits and thus bettering the everyday lives of Americans, serve as the historical foundation of the category of cooking for health. In this telling, skills are enhanced with the right forms of knowledge. The watchword here is improvement. From the very first iterations of domestic science pedagogy, the teachers were not primarily committed to open-ended inquiry. Their organization of learning was definitely not to create an exercise in Socratic dialogue: there were no conversations in classrooms or even seminars where different viewpoints were presented and discussed. Nor was learning an exercise in liberation: it was not intended to set women free from their household and familial obligations. Rather, this was learning as an exercise in *betterment*. With better tips, tools, facts, and techniques, the American home cook would be capable of making better meals, which would help create a better and healthier family and society. Each time a home cook decides to use a measuring cup or spoon when making a recipe, builds a meal around an array of vegetables, or substitutes olive oil for butter in a familiar family recipe, they are enacting values toward good, healthy meals with a long genealogy. Or at least they attempt to enact such values. When Laura, the mom and farmer's wife, is making rolls for her family's dinner, she pulls out an oft-used recipe. As she pulls together the ingredients and reads the instructions, she comments on her relationship to this recipe and on prescriptions for exactitude in general: "I follow recipes exactly except for the ingredients and methods." And then she laughs. She goes on to acknowledge that this tyranny of exactitude is relatively recent: "My grandmother's recipes would say things like, 'Take a lump of butter the size of a walnut.' She had very few written recipes." As she very casually measures out the flour for the dough, she starts to chuckle. She then says, "My home ec teacher would be dying several deaths if she saw me measuring flour in this way."[36]

With the expansion of responsibilities of the home cook to include nurturing healthy citizens comes a focus on recipes as a means of effectively changing everyday habits, as seen in changes in editions of *The Joy of Cooking*, revealing an increased preoccupation with recipes that are organized and articulated as a script or blueprint. This reflects a larger trend: over the twen-

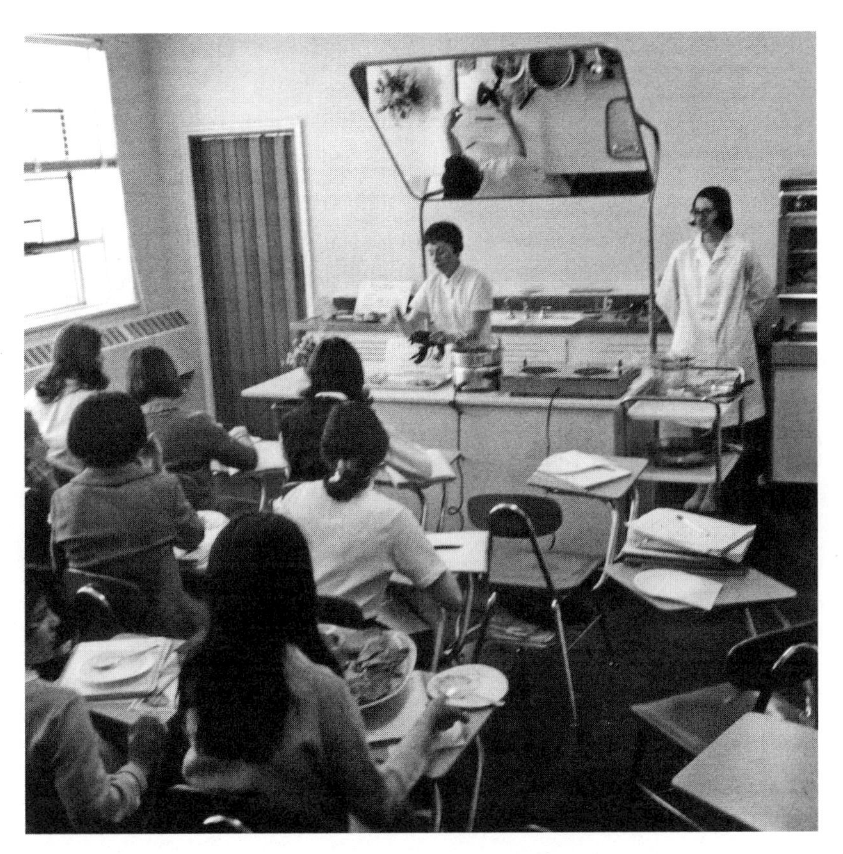

Figure 18. Home economics demonstration: lobster, circa 1965. Record group 24, box 17, publicity photos, Home Economics Department, Special Collections, University of Vermont Library.

tieth century, cookbooks increasingly adopted an instructional tone about the "right" foods to make. The earlier preoccupation with being a "good" housewife, as seen in books such as Catherine Beecher and Harriet Beecher Stowe's *The American Woman's Home or the Principles of Domestic Economy*, became more focused. New editions of *The Joy of Cooking* published from 1936 to 1976 progressively included more instruction about the "right" foods and the "best" ways to entertain. In particular, the tenor and tone of the cookbook changed from the 1943 and 1946 editions, which were solely authored by Irma Rombauer, to subsequent editions, which were revised and edited by her daughter, Marion Rombauer Becker. The breezy and sincere tone of the mother was replaced by the more scholarly and earnest ideas of the daughter. Irma says this in her foreword for the 1940s edition: "This book is the result of a long practical experience, a lively curiosity and a real love for cookery. In it I have made an attempt to meet the needs of the average household, to make palatable dishes with simple means and to lift everyday cooking out of the commonplace." Her version of the cookbook emerged from her social context, and her imagined cook is much like her: a woman who needs to cook but is perhaps a bit bogged down by it all. On the other hand, Marion speaks quite differently in the concluding paragraph of her foreword to the 1975 edition:

> Other features of this book which we ask you to investigate include the chapter on Heat, which gives you many clues to maintaining the nutrients in the food you are cooking. . . . But even more important, we hope that in answering your question, "What shall we have for dinner," you will find in Foods We Eat a stimulus to combine foods wisely. Using this information, you may say with Thomas Jefferson, "No knowledge can be more satisfactory to a man than that of his own frame, its parts, their functions and actions."

Marion's home cook needs more knowledge to perform her obligations better. Certain burdens may have been lifted, literally and figuratively, between the first edition of *The Joy of Cooking* and Marion's 1975 version, but as Marion points out, there are new crosses to bear.

Given the phenomenal success of the cookbook, certain continuities do exist between these editions—why change what worked? According to Marion Rombauer, the form and structure of the recipes, the general format, is consistently unique across all editions. As she explains in her reminiscence-cum-memoir, *Little Acorn:* "[The] most popular asset of the 1936 edition was undoubtedly its revolutionary recipe-form. Bold type carried ingredients, a chronological framework of light-face. You had only to run your eye down the bold items to see if you had suitable ingredients on hand. And you couldn't go wrong in procedure if you followed the sequence of preparation in light-face. This was then called the 'action method.'"[37]

The Joy of Cooking, from its very inception, adopted the dictates of the home economics movement to provide structure and order to American cooking habits through recipes that served up knowledge with precision. Although the recipes always tend to be concise and didactic rather than descriptive, they also have always been organized. The measurements do not call for a "lump of butter" but rather "1 tablespoon butter." And the action method adds another level of organization. The home cook did not have to possess previous experience with the recipe or parse the paragraph to figure out what to do first and second. Following in the footsteps of Fannie Farmer and others, the Rombauers were primarily teachers, as evidenced by their format and tone.

It is not surprising that Marion kept this method when she took over editorial responsibilities for *The Joy of Cooking*. She was a longtime student and practitioner of progressive education; she attended Vassar and then worked as an art teacher at a progressive private school in Saint Louis inspired by the ideas of John Burroughs. The principles outlined in the catalog of the John Burroughs School include "Instead of assigning lessons as daily tasks, teachers seek to make the acquiring of education a great adventure."[38] Among her papers in the archives of the Rombauer and Becker families, there are several manuscripts outlining ideals for progressive education. In one, "The Progressive School Unfettered," a goal of this educational philosophy is to "prepare its pupils now so that they may adapt themselves to new and unforeseen conditions, and may have the ability to find easily and learn quickly those facts which the new and unforeseen conditions demand."[39] Marion translated these ideals into her editorial work on multiple editions of *The Joy of Cooking*. She had long served as an assistant to Irma and as her helpmate in decades-long, contentious dealings with the book's publisher, Bobbs-Merrill.[40] By the mid-1950s, with Irma's health in decline, Marion increasingly took on the major editorial responsibilities. And she had ideas. As Anne Mendelson puts it, "[Irma] had not sought to go beyond this spark of invention [the action format of the recipe]. She was not, like Marion, a knowledge addict burning to take people on written voyages of discovery."[41] Starting with the 1962 edition, Marion changed and enlarged *The Joy of Cooking* by adding sections and extending recipes to make sure the book promoted more general knowledge as well as learning by doing, and a prominent goal was to improve the nation's health.

Marion Rombauer Becker responded to the societal preoccupation with healthy meals, and her influence can be seen in two new chapters that were added to the 1975 edition: "Foods We Eat" and "Know Your Ingredients." This edition had five printings between May 1975 and August 1976, and it was the most successful edition in the history of the book. In the first two printings alone, three hundred thousand books were produced. Mendelson points out that Marion's passions—progressive education, organic gardening, and nutrition—were part of the cultural zeitgeist by that time, and so although this edition was less charming, it had become more relevant.[42] In the 1943 edition of the cookbook, the first section after the table of contents is for cocktails. Irma's first two lines read: "The chief virtue of cocktails is their informal quality. They loosen tongues and unbutton the reserves of the socially diffident." In the 1975 edition, the first section is "Foods We Eat." Marion's more earnest sensibility is immediately apparent:

> Put this puzzle together and you will find milk, cheese and eggs, meat, fish, beans and cereals, greens, fruits and root vegetables—foods that contain our essential daily needs. Exactly how they interlock and in what quantities for the most advantageous results for everyone is another puzzle we must try to solve for ourselves, keeping in mind our age, body type, activities, the climate in which we live, and the food sources available to us.

She effectively combines the narrative of betterment adopted by nutritionists and home economists with an understanding of the myriad channels a conscientious home cook needed to navigate in the 1970s. Unfortunately, some of the "joy" had been erased along the way. This section goes on to integrate the main messages that are still fundamental to the field of nutrition today: "We as well as the experts are inclined to agree that many Americans are privileged to enjoy superabundance and that our nutritional difficulties have to do generally not with under- but overeating."[43] To further the contemporary home cook's understanding of nutrition, she provides a review of nutritional terms (calories, proteins, fats, carbohydrates, etc.) and then gives a list of common foods, standard portion sizes, total calories, and protein content. Apparently, this is to help cooks make judicious choices when perusing the recipes in the cookbook, since she begins this section with a quotation from Jane Austen: "Personal size and mental sorrow have certainly no necessary proportions," but a "large, bulky figure" will more easily be ridiculed.[44] This is quite a change from the simple one-page "Calorie Chart" in the 1946 edition, penned by Irma and buried in the back, which begins thusly: "A malediction on the first calorie counter (must have been a man) and a malediction on Helen Hokinson who shows those whose glamour has begun to glimmer that calories count! Joy killers, both."[45]

Marion Rombauer Becker weaves another narrative throughout the 1975 edition, one related to knowledge about the function and quality of ingredients. In the second paragraph of "Foods We Eat," she informs the reader that all ingredients are not created equal, and so it is important to seek out "the widest variety of the best grown unsprayed foods we can find in their freshest condition." This advice anticipated the now commonplace query of how produce is grown. Or perhaps she helped inspire this groundswell. She continues in a related vein in the chapter "Know Your Ingredients." Here, she combines Fannie Farmer's legacy with her own environmental conscience. She instructs about such diverse topics as public health standards for water, different forms of milk and their various uses in cooking, the nutritional problems with highly bleached flours, and more. The chapter is eighty pages long, and it is almost entirely new text written by Marion. She even includes a section on culinary herbs, and following a long genealogy of literary references in this seemingly banal instructional manual, she invokes Confucius, "a wise man, [who] refused to eat anything not in season. Everyone who has tasted the difference between foods served with fresh rather than dried herbs knows how wise he was."[46] Knowledge, according to Marion, is power. By 1975, this power was focused on helping American home cooks, and this continues today—consider the USDA's Dietary Guidelines and Michelle Obama's Let's Move campaign. Expertise is considered a means of helping Americans obtain healthy dinner meals. However, the effectiveness of all these initiatives—how they are received, absorbed, and enacted—remains to be seen.

NUTRITIONAL GATEKEEPING AND THE TIES THAT BIND

Trisha, a mother of four young children, devotes much of her time, energy, and family budget to creating meals that she feels are healthy for both her family and society. As with Lisa, Trisha understands her quest to be contrary to the culinary practices she learned from her own family; in many ways, her pursuit of healthy food is a small contrarian gesture, a way of breaking free of certain social obligations, the traditional sources of culinary knowledge and skill. Her mother cooked, but according to Trisha, she did not make healthy meals:

> The stuff my mom could really cook when I was growing up was meat oriented: fried chicken, steak, pot roast, meatloaf, tuna noodle casserole. . . . None of it's appropriate for what we cook. . . . We [Trisha and her husband] have a very different style of cooking because we're not really out-of-the-can cookers, and that's been a little bit beyond my family, kind of like, why would you spend the extra money to do all organic, which is what we do.

Her family (who lives in the Midwest) has very different values in relation to food, and this has been a long-term issue, starting when she became a vegetarian in high school. Trisha's first job as a gatekeeper, it seems, is to prevent most intergenerational transfer of knowledge and skill:

> And that's an adjustment for me going to my mom's house. Skippy peanut butter? My son said it looked like a slug when we wiped it on his plate 'cause it was so mushy compared to the peanut butter we have with only peanuts. They think it tastes like candy. They don't want to eat their sandwich because it's too sweet. So my mom . . . she lives in [a Midwestern city], and so we go out there and visit my whole family about once a year, and she's gotten good finally. I give her a list, and she'll go to Whole Foods and get a bunch of food for us before we come, because otherwise I have to grocery shop the day I arrive because my kids won't eat her food. We try to make some dishes, but my family is pretty set in its ways.

By feeding her children these "natural" products, Trisha implies that she has shaped their tastes, making this generation of her family into healthy citizens. Ultimately, her definition of healthy food has influenced even her parents' everyday habits (at least when she visits them).

Trisha aspires to have all her family's food be organic, local, or ideally both. This goal seems consistently linked to notions of caregiving, of making good food choices to be a good mother:

> We did natural food, and we did mostly produce, but we weren't focused on organic, and then our oldest daughter [was born]. She didn't breastfeed, she took formula, and so I had the hardest time finding organic formula, and that was suddenly when I got really focused on that, and we ordered only organic baby food and only organic formula, and when she started eating the food we were eating, that's when we switched over.

This family's commitment to meeting their goals for healthy food involves constant gatekeeping. It also involves an economic commitment: "We started buying all organic and natural food and then watched our grocery bill triple—an unintended consequence. But once we started down that path, we felt like we didn't really want to go back." Trisha's moral stance is absolute—more stringent than most—which allows her to more easily navigate larger social and economic structures that might make others moderate or mediate their integration of an aspiration and an action. Yet her navigation of many channels, while shutting down others, provides an example of the new category of a healthy meal for many Americans in its more ideal, almost Platonic form:

> We almost never eat out. . . . There's not really anywhere great to go as a family, so we don't eat out very often, and when we do, we go to [an artisan pizza restaurant] or something which is almost all local, organic. We know all the farmers—they're friends of ours. It's their cheese or their garlic on the pizza we're eating. And it's our friends who are the chefs, so they can tell us exactly how they made everything on there. Our kids don't know what MacDonald's is. We got them French fries one time when we were driving through somewhere. We doled it out, we gave them each a little, tiny bag, and they each had four or five in the car, and they said, "This is yucky, I don't like it! Can I have an apple?" And we laughed so hard because we hadn't had MacDonald's in years. It is gross! . . . We never do fast food. Even when we travel, we bring food with us.

For Trisha, even the act of choosing local, organic pizza brings the "right" version of the natural world into her family life, and doing so allows her to provide healthy meals whether inside or outside the home. Trisha's perception of her gatekeeping role affirms Kurt Lewin's insights into food gatekeepers, that they often make decisions based on a notion of "food for us . . . [and] even the food that is recognized as that for [other] human beings still may not be accepted as food for one's family."[47] Lewin relies primarily on the classification of cultural acceptance and availability to explain this behavior, but today, moral acceptance seems crucial too.

Trisha's daughter is the little girl described in the introduction, trying to help make dinner by squeezing the lemon to make lemon juice. That night, the family meal is fajitas. All four children are running around the kitchen, often clamoring for attention, and in Isabel's case, always looking for a chance to help. The making of this meal and the conversation that ensues does revolve around learning (and teaching) to make healthy meals, understood first as vegetarian and then as "fresh and unprocessed vegetables, a minimum amount of fat." This conversation begins when Josh, Trisha's husband, returns from the local food cooperative with the ingredients needed for dinner. Immediately, he and Trisha start discussing the tomatoes (this meal is made in the winter). Josh says, "All I could get were the hydroponic types"; Trisha replies, "Oh, the ones that look like they are on steroids." He starts making the dinner by cutting up the red and green peppers, onions, and tomatoes he just purchased while Trisha unloads the rest of the items. In planning meals, Trisha is very concerned about the ingredients and making sure there is always a green vegetable on the plate. Josh is also mindful: "In general, I try to do the 'food groups,' although I know we are supposed to think of something different now, the food pyramid, but I don't know what that is. I try to have something from the grain group, the vegetable group, obviously we don't do meat, but we do try proteins, often from beans, pasta, peas, something like that." At one point, Trisha asks, "Why aren't you saying organic?" John replies, "I don't think that is crucial." Clearly, they agree on some aspects of the category but not on others. So, some meal components might depend on just who is doing the provisioning on any given day.

Making vegetarian meals is a priority, and both Trisha and John rely on cookbooks, if not as blueprints, at least as guides. The fajita recipe comes from a family favorite, *Claire's Corner Copia Cookbook*. They have made it many times, so John does not directly refer to the recipe while he is cooking. "I freestyle a bit," he says. He does admit that he still has to rely on *The Joy of Cooking* when he makes waffles because "the proportions have to be exact." They both agree that Josh is the more naturally confident cook, which they mostly attribute to his mother, who they both identify as an enthusiastic cook. However, John also credits his experiences at sleep-away camp, where he was assigned to be the quartermaster and thus required to prepare and plan the meals. They both see that focusing on vegetarian food and the quality of ingredients is influencing their children's understanding of food. Isabel, the daughter who always wants to help cook, had recently said to her mother while eating at a restaurant, "Mom, is that an artichoke in your sandwich?" Josh laughs and says, "[When I was young,] I [only] knew what fish sticks were." This family creates an understanding of food that extends from the microscale (lots of vitamins, no pesticides) to macroscale (lots of vegetables, no McDonald's) through the transmission of knowledge and skills based in healthy ingredients and meals.

To understand healthy eating today, we must acknowledge that there is no simple cause and effect when it comes to everyday decisions about what to eat. Tremendous complexity is involved in putting even a single dinner on the table. The reality is that even though such chores and tasks might be perceived as banal, they ultimately have tremendous significance. Unfortunately, most guidelines and recommendations focus on conveying messages about the ease of making healthy choices, but that is not most people's lived experience. Looking more closely at the complex dynamic between gatekeeper, channels, and gates reveals the impact the *array* of choices in the modern food environment has on everyday decisions about what to have for dinner. Gatekeepers are always sailing in choppy waters, working in less than ideal conditions, and seeking a safe harbor that is increasingly difficult to find. Today, the process of choosing and then transforming raw ingredients into the final product—meals for self and others—is constantly being refined and reimagined. The gatekeepers attempt to control their food environment by limiting the kinds of food items they purchase, the amount of each ingredient they use in a recipe, and the size of portions the family consumes in or outside the home. Despite the various, complex, and often contradictory gates and channels that must be navigated, the main goal for all gatekeepers is putting a nutritious meal on the table for their family or friends. But achieving such a goal is no simple task, for making a modern meal requires navigating chaotic and saturated food environments. Kurt Lewin's articulation of gardening and shopping channels seems comfortingly simple. Where have all our choices, our many gates and channels, really led us?

What Next?

So, here we are: a nation with many cooks, where we have the privilege to not be burdened every single day by having to cook for either ourselves or for others. There really is little distinction between public and private spheres in our everyday relationship to food. Home cooks matter when it comes to making modern meals, but so do professional chefs, artisan bakers, commissary cooks, and manufacturing lines. Sourcing, provisioning, cooking, serving, cleaning—we can do any one of these tasks without doing any other. We can demand, cajole, expect, or request someone else to do any or all of these tasks. The only food-related act we still must do on our own (at least for most of our lives) is eat. Perhaps that accounts for our national preoccupation with our status as food consumers. All our other relationships with food are now primarily external, which means that we must rely on others every step of the way to the dinner table.

We have gained certain choices, but have we sacrificed others? This constant scenario of possibility—should dinner be organic pizza, takeout Thai, frozen fried chicken, Mom's tuna noodle casserole?—is both a privilege and a burden. The complex intersections of these possibilities with larger and insistent structures of modern life—gender roles, income inequality, time poverty, industrial and global supply chains (to name a few)—mean that American home cooks have more choice but not necessarily more freedom. As mentioned in the introduction, Peg Bracken, author of the *I Hate to Cook Book*, penned these honest lines in 1960 as she tried to liberate women from the obligations of that era of American history: "This book is for those of us who hate to [cook], who have learned through hard experience that some activities become no less powerful through repetition: childbearing, paying taxes, cooking." Fifty years later, the work of food still generates such ambivalence.

Meanwhile, we continue to rely on others to handle the contradictions intrinsic to such constant and necessary obligations, thereby solving some problems but inevitably creating others. These tensions will not disappear, either immediately or in the long run, unless the many oracles of food and technology who are always predicting the end of all this nonsense (i.e., cooking traditional meals for nourishment) have their way. The ideas of dialing up our food or eating it via tubes, as Warren Belasco points out, may have seemed logical and reasonable in their day, but here we are a century later, still heating up the pan, putting in the bacon, and frying it up.[1] Not that such technofixes don't get proffered to us. For example, now we have Soylent, a line of meal alternatives billed as "engineered foods to fit your full life," created by a Silicon Valley entrepreneur with a background in chemistry. The main product, a drink designed to provide "all the protein, carbohydrates, micronutrients and lipids a body needs to thrive," provides 20 percent of required daily intake of calories per serving.[2] The earnest inventor, Rob Rhinehart, said in an interview that his goal is to get to "the point where we don't have to worry about hunger, or nutrition. Where people make food just because it's beautiful—like gardening, or painting. I'm looking forward to the point where food can just be art." He believes that this will allow people to focus on making food only when it is enjoyable; he, too, envisions a future where food is not associated with obligation.[3]

If we want to avoid a future full of Soylent (which has been described as tasting like chalky cake batter), we need to pay more attention to making meals. And this needs to incorporate all the steps involved, moving beyond the components that seem more appealing, either analytically or sensorially. Cooking remains too central to human culture to be put into the pile of lost cultural practices; not only are we the sole animals who cook, but we are also social animals, and as such we need and want to nurture others. We are not required to assume a future where we have completely abandoned the work of moving food from the raw to the cooked and handed it over to robots and machines. In the future, however, the knowledge and practices paramount to making meals might reside chiefly in the hands and heads of a small group of experts, or what we know and do in regard to preparing food might become ever more finite, ending up as a limited repertoire. Meanwhile, our ambivalence about the *necessity* of cooking means that we try to share this burden whenever possible, although not always equitably or in a fair manner. Due to our social as well as biological needs, the acts and aspirations around cooking will not disappear, although cooking will surely not look the same as when Catherine Beecher and Harriet Beecher Stowe, Auguste Escoffier, or Irma Rombauer and Marion Rombauer Becker were having their say. In light of our considerations, let's acknowledge all the tasks involved in cooking as profoundly social, crucial to our identities as members of families and communities and as upholders of traditions, while also realizing that such realities might propel ever broader meditations on who we are and how we live that go far beyond any decision to buy pizza or make casserole. As Tim Ingold points out, "The tasks you do depend on who you are, and in a sense the performance of certain tasks makes you the person who you are."[4]

The transformation toward purchasing and consuming food outside of the home has changed identities and practices. Americans can now easily exist primarily as food *consumers*, but does that make us a nation of ignorant cooks?[5] Do we really want to make such an assumption, perpetuating the didactic and moralizing discourses about the world of American home cooks that have been in place for generations? Instead, given our public health concerns, why not focus on all the knowledgeable cooks (in commissary kitchens, school cafeterias, fine-dining establishments, etc.) and find out what they know and what they can do to influence Americans?

Making Modern Meals has investigated the processes, meanings, and skills that are part and parcel of everyday American cooking and has conceived meals, primarily dinner, as a site of complexity and contradiction, a constantly morphing hybrid that is at times a domestic duty, at times an act of creative expression, and at times a paid occupation. There is so much more we need to understand. The list is possibly endless, but for now, here are some questions that might move us forward: How do we understand the problem of provisioning in the life of the modern cook? Who are destined to be the teachers of the next generation of American cooks? When should we learn how to cook? What do we need to learn in order to cook across all categories—one day with burden, another day with pleasure, another with health in mind, and finally, hopefully, most of the time with multisensory artfulness? How do we make sure that all cooks are treated with respect—social, economic, and political? Why don't we have time to cook, and does that matter?

Our complex and contradictory culinary landscape will continue to exist, in some way, in the future. We can make certain moves that will allow for a future in which Americans are knowledgeable and engaged in the various tasks required to make a meal but not overwhelmed by the tasks required to do so. The next questions we need to address are: What are such moves, and how do we make them?

+ + + +

A nineteenth-century physician and art collector, Giovanni Morelli, used his scientific training to develop a new technique for authenticating artwork. He argued that very close examination of details in a painting, looking for idiosyncrasies or repetitions, would reveal whether a work was authentic or a copy. This technique is often compared to detective work, where fingerprints are used to link the criminal to the crime. In both cases, the evidence of the hand solves the mystery. The notion of the evidence of the hand has become a means of explaining the technique of artists more broadly. Morelli himself explains his point: "Almost all painters have certain peculiarities that escape their control, since they do not act consciously in those instances."[6] Looking for the evidence of the hand in cooking, however, reveals more than a particularly technical capacity. The "certain peculiarities that escape [our] control" involve social, aesthetic, and ethical gestures as well. Examining many small gestures can solve the mystery of contemporary cooking; compiling a lot of evidence creates a compelling case. Such an inquiry, looking very closely at the equivalent of individual brush strokes and gradients of color, both across the background and for certain telling details, reveals our culinary lifeworld. With the evidence of the hand, we can address what moves us forward and holds us back.

+ + + +

As I absorbed the extent that American cooking is a fluid practice while also realizing that our modes of categorizing our actions and aspirations involve, in equal measure, both public and private spheres of American life, I noticed a new way to get help when figuring out what to make for dinner: meal delivery services. I could not pass up the opportunity for a quick investigation: Was ordering a box of ingredients for a dinner, with a recipe, tips, and online videos included, a glimpse into our culinary futures?

In collaboration with an undergraduate working on her senior thesis, we devised a project.[7] First, we recruited five people (with roughly the same demographics as the participants in our original study) who had never used meal delivery services before but were interested in doing so. We provided them with a week of meals from the largest service and then interviewed them about it. Along the way, a number of friends and family joined in, albeit more informally, so I ended up talking to nine people.

Meal delivery services theoretically address most of the dilemmas articulated by everyone we spoke to in our initial study—Carol in her small urban apartment, Laura in her sprawling farmhouse kitchen, Claire getting back into cooking after years of eating out with an expense account, Josh and Trisha seeking to make healthy meals for their growing family—removing much of the chore of making meals (no shopping is necessary, ingredients are already measured out, a clear recipe is provided, etc.). However, meal delivery services are not easily categorized as either domestic or commercial varieties of culinary practice. You make the meals in your home, but to order them, you go to a website where the meals of the week are presented, much like a restaurant or takeout menu. You don't know the people who source the ingredients and do the initial prep work, such as pouring just the right amount of soy sauce into a tiny plastic jar so that you have just the right amount for a dish. If you watch one of the supplementary videos, you are instructed by an expert, as if you were watching a chef on a cooking show. It could be argued that what we have here is the best of both worlds (or spheres). In our small and quick study, everyone identified something about using the service that was helpful or pleasurable. One participant noted: "I think having it all prepped out, the portion size and all of that, takes some of the—"stress" isn't the word—but some thinking out of it, and there are no less dishes, but it is like a restaurant because you get to choose, 'What dishes do I want?' [And] if you don't mind cooking, it is a great experience. And our food was excellent."

The affective function of the service was universally positive: it removed the worry, the obligation, and the sense of "What now?" As one young woman living in urban Philadelphia put it: "I like it because it makes it easier for me, considering I don't cook often and the fact that I don't have to worry about not having enough of something when I make something because they pretty much give you everything you need." In a sense, the service fulfills a similar role as Avis DeVoto's maid Mary: it alleviates some of the burden of cooking without removing completely the identity of the home cook or the action of making a meal. As another person said, "It is like having a prep cook in the kitchen with you."

However, there were a number of concerns and dissatisfactions, primarily related to flexibility and autonomy. A meal delivery service offers a narrower range of meal choices than a restaurant or takeout menu. This is probably due to the national reach of these companies, which means that complex sourcing, storing, and shipping arrangements are required to make sure all the perishable items remain fresh and safe. Thus, the system creates constraints over choice. Many people chafed at the limited options, perhaps because Americans are so accustomed to a food environment saturated with choices: you can chose to have Thai, Italian, or Mexican food on any given night. One participant made the following comment, and her sentiment was reinforced by many: "I think when I do order takeout, I would just prefer to do that, because it is sort of an indulgence, and it means that I don't have to cook for myself." The sense of autonomy in relation to this everyday necessity seemed hard to relinquish. Although the benefits of the service were clear, they did not trump people's *expectation* of cooking as a fluid practice. The question became: Why would I choose to cook one of three meal options when I can just as easily go to the new ramen restaurant nearby, explore any number of meal choices, and not have to do any dishes?

There is an irony to our present circumstances: by removing constraints (gender obligations, limited access to ingredients, an inconsistent and expensive food supply, etc.), we don't seem to be able to envision a culinary future that asks us to narrow our options. Thus, although many cooks seem overwhelmed by the many choices that need to be made every day to decide what to eat for dinner, Americans don't want them taken away. As my mother says, "Who wants to go back to the farm once you have seen Paris?" So, it seems, our culinary future must engage with all cooks. We should not harangue home cooks to change their ways, but we could create new collaborations between all sorts of cooks, making sure to teach everyone about making meals that are good for ourselves, our social relations, and our society. We could also decide what types of knowledge and skill are worth being transferred from generation to generation and then work to create environments for such culinary transmissions—not only in homes but also in social settings, schools, and restaurants.

+ + + +

In her book *Dangerous Digestion: The Politics of American Dietary Advice*, Melanie DePuis argues that the tendency of Americans to moralize about food is an impulse toward purity and safety, a means of bounding a dangerous and complex world. She argues, instead, for an acceptance of what she calls "ferment." As she puts it, "If purity is a narrative about the safety of who we are and the perils we have avoided, ferment tells us about how to live with the choices we have made, the perils we have chosen, our alliances with those not like us, and the uncertainty of that process."[8] To her, ferment is "the

Figure 19. "Preston Street Cooking Class, Louisville, K.Y.," 1910. Art and Picture Collection, New York Public Library Digital Collections.

more realist approach to social change." The cooks in this book are clearly in the middle of such ferment. Cooking is a chore, cooking is an occupation, cooking is an art, cooking is a craft, cooking is for health, but these categories in action are never completely controllable. And this is good. They do not exist in a Platonic form, as ideals to be met, dictates to be followed, or romantic fantasies; rather, they can benefit American cooks. The possibilities for change—if we believe in such a possibility in the face of all the structural constraints of our day—lie in our ability to identify how and why we cook (or do not cook) and then to keep (or start) cooking in spite of those reasons. It is not simply knowledge that will set us free or skill that will make us competent. It is knowledge in the service of skill and skills in the process of making us confident that will make us a nation of cooks. It is also important to identify all the everyday cooks, both in the domestic and commercial domains, to look at them with more attention and move beyond old and perhaps tired assumptions and decide just what they need in order to combine knowing and doing with consistency and confidence, be it in the home, a restaurant, or a commissary kitchen.

So, to conclude, let's consider the dreams of a home cook. In an interview, Edna, the cook from Philadelphia who struggles to make ends meet and still make the meals she desires, was asked what she would change about making meals if she had all the money in the world. This was her response:

> Do you really want to hear this? . . . I would not cook. Someone would actually cook for me. [And we would do it] together. We would work this together. It would be a great—we would do this collectively, together. . . . And then I would incorporate what I know, to others. I wouldn't just keep this to myself. . . . For real, that's what I would do. If I was financially comfortable, yes, I would set the example of how to eat, and then I would share this to others, because we're losing too many Americans.

Cooking together to help build a better world, and all of us knowing how to make a meal but not always feeling obligated to do so. These are dreams that should come true.

Appendix

Overview of Qualitative Research Methods

Two qualitative research projects, carried out in collaboration with graduate students in the University of Vermont's Department of Nutrition and Food Sciences and the Food Systems graduate program, helped define the themes of the book and also provided the descriptions and perceptions of home cooks. Both were funded by United States Department of Agriculture Hatch grants (project VT-H01218 and VT-H02109).

Other research—participant-observation at bakeries, archival and manuscript review at the Schlesinger Library on the History of Women at the Radcliffe Institute of Advanced Study at Harvard University and the Special Collections at the University of Vermont, and close textual analysis of cookbooks and other related documents—was done solely by the author and was organized in relation to the themes that emerged from the videotapes, interviews, and surveys collected by the research projects.

A QUALITATIVE AND LONGITUDINAL STUDY OF COOKING SKILL AND COOKING KNOWLEDGE

The inclusion criteria required that participants were eighteen years or older; acted as the primary meal preparer in the household; could set aside four to six hours to complete all three parts of the study; and lived in the desired geographic region. There were three groups of people recruited. One set (thirteen participants) was made up of people who lived in the largest metropolitan area in Vermont (160,000 residents) or in a nearby shire town (with a population of 8,200). Another set (six participants) focused on rural residents, and participants were excluded if any member of the household commuted to the city of Burlington, Vermont, for work or school; to qualify for this set, participants had to live forty-five to sixty minutes north-northeast of Burlington, resulting in participant recruitment from Franklin and Lamoille Counties in Vermont, or in the most rural counties in the state. Another set (six participants) comprised people who lived within the city limits of Boston, Massachusetts.

Participants were selected through a combination of network and snowball sampling. Network sampling was accomplished by finding local contacts in the area of interest to help recruit subjects. Once a handful of participants were enrolled in the study, the strategy transformed to snowball sampling. Initial data were collected from January 2007 to August 2009. Follow-up research was done from 2009 to 2011. The age of participants ranged from late twenties to early seventies. There were six men and nineteen women. There were three recent immigrants, from Russia, Bosnia, and Trinidad. Fifteen of these participants were married, six were single, and four were divorced. Ten had young children or recent postgraduates living at home; three no longer had children living at home; the rest had no children. The participants' annual income ranged from $15,000 to over $75,000. As part of a later study (see below), five more individuals were interviewed and videotaped.

At the conclusion of all the research projects, thirty home cooks had participated, having generated thirty open-ended interviews and over fifty hours of ethnographic video footage of home meal preparation activities. The interviewing and videotaping were done by the author as well as by Alyssa Nathanson, Anthony Epter, Shauna Henley, and Maria Carabello.

Researchers would visit each participant's home on two separate days. During the initial visit, researchers administered the semistructured interview, gave the participant a questionnaire to fill out, and conducted the first video recording of the preparation of a typical dinnertime meal. On the second visit, the researcher collected the questionnaire, often videotaped the participant preparing a second meal (that did not have to be the same meal as the first visit), and gave the participant their compensation for their time and hospitality. The researchers recorded participants preparing a dinnertime meal, starting with raw ingredients and ending up with a final meal. The practice of recording participants prepare two meals was implemented after the first eleven interviews and videotapes were already completed. The decision to videotape two meal preparation cycles was to ascertain if participants were picking everyday meals or if they were choosing "special" meals to impress the researchers; it was not found to be the case that the meals were out of the ordinary. Videotaping allowed us to capture for posterity the skills and knowledge of the participants. These video sessions were also useful because they gave the researchers a chance to follow up on questions from the interviews or ask additional questions that did not fit into the timeframe of the interview. These multiple forms of engagement allowed for the creation of a richer, more ethnographic data set.

LEARNING TO COOK AND DEVELOPING FOOD AGENCY

Another research project, associated with the ethnographic research project that led to *Making Modern Meals*, was launched in 2014. This is an ongoing interdisciplinary, mixed-method, and multi-institution collaborative project looking at the connection between learning how to cook using a certain pedagogy and the development of long-term food agency. Much of this project involved taking the results of the first study and figuring out the best way to, one, define cooking in a manner that more accurately reflects lived reality and, two, develop a culinary pedagogy that teaches cooking in a relevant manner. The research began in July 2014 and was completed in May 2017. Two components of the food agency project provided data and analysis that were used in *Making Modern Meals*. One was the work done by Maria Carabello that involved observing and videotaping "inexperienced" and "experienced" home cooks. We decided that these types of cooks were not well represented in the earlier ethnographic videotapes and interviews. We determined that the participants in the earlier project exhibited modest to advanced cooking abilities. Thus, between August and October 2014, we recruited and filmed five additional home cooks, who self-identified as "inexperienced" or "experienced." This helped to ensure that the spectrum of experience levels captured in our final collection of videos would range from novice to professional; "inexperienced" and "experienced" home cooks were recruited through a posting on the web-based Front Porch Forum, a free community-building service that is available in and around Burlington, Vermont.

In a subsequent study conducted in Philadelphia between June and December 2015, Caitlin Morgan interviewed and observed community members and students at Drexel University taking a healthy cooking class. Our research group worked with the instructor on the course pedagogy. The community members in this study resided in the Mantua or Powelton neighborhoods of Philadelphia. Mantua is part of an area that was deemed a Promise Zone under President Obama. It includes 35,315 residents and has an overall poverty rate of 50.78 percent, nearly double the city's rate, which is 26.9 percent. Out of sixteen students who enrolled in the class, fourteen (nine community members and six Drexel students) participated in open-ended interviews while they were enrolled, six (community members) participated in follow-up interviews, and three (students) were in a focus group. All the community members interviewed were African American, Asian, or Pacific Islander. Eighty-five percent of the participants in the study had an annual income of $50,000 a year or below; 30 percent made less than $25,000 a year.

NOTES

INTRODUCTION

1. *Oxford Dictionary (US)*, s.v. "cook," accessed August 5, 2016, www.oxforddictionaries.com/us/definition/american_english/cook.

2. *Oxford Dictionary (US)*, s.v. "cooking," accessed August 5, 2016, www.oxforddictionaries.com/us/definition/american_english/cooking.

3. Katherine Snell, "Interview with Kyla Wazana Tompkins," *Columbia Journal of Literary Criticism* 13, no. 1 (2015): 53.

4. Catharine E. Beecher and Harriet Beecher Stowe, *The American Woman's Home, or The Principles of Domestic Science* (New York: J. B. Ford, 1869), 276.

5. Amy Trubek, *Haute Cuisine: How the French Invented the Culinary Profession* (Philadelphia: University of Pennsylvania Press, 2000), 125.

6. Ibid.

7. George Orwell, *Down and Out in Paris and London* (Orlando: Harcourt Brace, 1961), 57.

8. Peg Bracken, *The I Hate to Cook Book* (New York: Harcourt Brace, 1960), ix.

9. The practice of cooking and eating outside the home began with institutions such as restaurants, taverns, and inns. Antonin Carême, one of France's early culinary authors (he published a number of books including the 1828 *Le cuisinier parisien, ou L'art de la cuisine française au dix-neuvième siècle*) and widely

considered one of the country's great chefs, worked exclusively in the homes of European aristocracy, including the French diplomat Lord Talleyrand, the Rothschild banking family, and the prince regent of England, later George IV. In the early nineteenth century, increased urbanization led to increased possibilities for purchasing food and thus to new job opportunities for paid cooks. By the late nineteenth century, with the rising importance of commercial food production and the emergence of new elite social classes, many cooks and chefs had moved out of domestic service and ultimately sought employment in restaurants and other fine dining establishments in Paris, London, New York, and other cities.

10. David Sutton, *Secrets from the Greek Kitchen: Cooking, Skill, and Everyday Life on an Aegean Island* (Oakland: University of California Press, 2014), 15–20.

11. Ibid., 19.

12. Michael Pollan, *Cooked: A Natural History of Transformation* (New York: Penguin, 2013), 8.

13. This section is a slight alteration of text from an earlier published essay: Amy Trubek, "Looking at Cooking," *Anthropology Now* 4, no. 3 (December 2012): 24–32.

14. United States Department of Agriculture Economic Research Service, "Data Products: Table 8—Food Expenditures by Families and Individuals as a Share of Disposable Personal Money Income." Last updated January 26, 2016, www.ers.usda.gov/data-products/food-expenditures.aspx#26634.

15. Elizabeth E. Sloan, "What, When, and Where America Eats: A State-of-the-Industry Report," *Food Technology* 60, no. 1 (2006): 19–27.

16. Ibid.

17. Abigail M. Okrent and Aylin Kumcu, "U.S. Households' Demand for Convenience Foods," United States Department of Agriculture, Economic Research Service, Economic Research Report 211, July 2016, www.ers.usda.gov/publications/pub-details/?pubid=80653.

18. The idea of *Lebenswelt* was initially articulated by philosopher Edmund Husserl and has been taken up by many anthropologists interested in going beyond the concept of "worldview," which is seen to not be focused enough on embodied understandings of cultural values and actions. For an example of phenomenologically oriented anthropology, see the works of Michael Jackson, such as *Minima Ethnographica* (1998).

19. There is a robust strain of food scholarship and food advocacy arguing that Americans have lost forms of power over their choices and their abilities due to the increasing dominance of industries and corporations, which make access to commercially prepared foods so easy that they have created a cultural belief that these mixes, cans, pouches, and meals are a natural part of living life and feeding ourselves. The implications this has for home cooking will be addressed in several of the chapters in this book.

20. Roland Barthes, "Science vs. Literature," *Times Literary Supplement* (London), September 28, 1967, pp. 897–98.

21. Glenn Branch, "Whence Lumpers and Splitters?" *NCSE Blog*, December 2, 2014, www.ncse.com/blog/2014/11/whence-lumpers-splitters-0016004.

22. Sociologist Sarah Bowen and her colleagues have initiated such work among low-income African American women in North Carolina. See Bowen, Sarah, Sinikka Elliott, and Joslyn Brenton, "The Joy of Cooking?" *Contexts* 13, no. 3 (2014): 20–25.

23. The overall goal was to incorporate individuals that reproduced the geographic and demographic variety representative of the region. For more detailed information, see the appendix.

24. David Sutton introduced me to this idea, and for that (among other gifts) I am forever grateful.

25. It could be argued, and it is worth investigating, that the location of a type of decline might more accurately occur in what and when we cook in relation to our standard meal times: What exactly has happened to the home-cooked lunch? Why is snacking now considered permissible at all times?

26. For more information on this research, see Maria Carabello, "Defining Food Agency: An Ethnographic Exploration of Home and Student Cooks in the Northeast," master's thesis, University of Vermont, 2015; Jacob Lahne, Julia Wolfson, and Amy Trubek, "Development of the Cooking and Food Preparation Action Scale (CAFPAS): A New Framework for Measuring the Complexity of Cooking," *Food Quality and Preference* (forthcoming); Caitlin Morgan, "Expanding Food Agency: Exploring the Theory and Its Scale," master's thesis, University of Vermont, 2016; Amy Trubek, Maria Carabello, Caitlin Morgan, and Jacob Lahne, "Empowered to Cook: The Crucial Role of Food Agency in Making Meals," *Appetite* 116 (September 2017): 297–305; Julia Wolfson, Stephanie Bostic, Jacob Lahne,

Caitlin Morgan, Shauna Henley, Jean Harvey, and Amy Trubek, "Moving to a Comprehensive Understanding and Assessment of Cooking," *British Food Journal* 119, no. 5 (2017): 1147–58.

27. Tim Ingold, *Perception of the Environment: Essays on Livelihood, Dwelling, Skill* (London: Routledge, 2000), xx.

28. Ibid., 4.

29. Sutton, *Secrets from the Greek Kitchen*, 9.

30. Richard Sennett, *The Craftsman* (New Haven: Yale University Press, 2009).

31. Ibid., 7.

32. This final paragraph is a slightly revised version of the conclusion of an article published in *Anthropology Now:* Trubek, "Looking at Cooking," 32.

CHAPTER 1. COOKING IS A CHORE

1. There is a robust body of scholarship about women, domesticity, and social relations. See, for example, Marjorie DeVault, *Feeding the Family: The Social Organization of Caring as Gendered Work* (Chicago: University of Chicago Press, 1991); and Susan Strasser, *Never Done: A History of American Housework* (New York: Macmillan, 1982).

2. Alice P. Julier, *Eating Together: Food, Friendship, and Inequality* (Urbana: University of Illinois Press, 2013), 26.

3. Megan A. Carney, *The Unending Hunger: Tracing Women and Food Insecurity across Borders* (Oakland: University of California Press, 2015), 69.

4. *Merriam-Webster's Collegiate Dictionary*, 10th ed., s.v. "chore."

5. Carole Counihan, *A Tortilla Is Like Life: Food and Culture in the San Luis Valley of Colorado* (Austin: University of Texas Press, 2010), 136.

6. Ibid., 136

7. Amy Trubek, "Professional Cooking and Kitchens," in *Cultural History of Food*, vol. 6, ed. Amy Bentley (London: Bloomsbury, 2012), 127–144.

8. Richard Wrangham, *Catching Fire: How Cooking Made Us Human* (New York: Basic, 2009).

9. E. Barrie Kavasch, "My Grandmother's Hands" in *Through the Kitchen Window: Women Explore the Intimate Meanings of Food and Cooking*, ed. Arlene Voski Avakian, 2nd ed. (Oxford: Berg, 2005), 104.

10. E. Barrie Kavasch, "Song of My Mother," in Avakian, *Through the Kitchen Window*, 42–43.

11. Caroline Urvater, "Thoughts for Food," in Avakian, *Through the Kitchen Window*, 213.

12. Some notable examples of these analyses by anthropologists are Counihan, *A Tortilla Is Like Life;* Joy Adapon, *Culinary Art and Anthropology* (Oxford: Bloomsbury Academic, 2008); and Sutton, *Secrets from the Greek Kitchen*.

13. In a sense, the impulse among early feminist anthropologists to ignore or bracket cooking was an honest attempt to move beyond ubiquitous connections between gender roles and foodwork that limited the ability to see all the other ways women contributed to cultural life.

14. Counihan, *A Tortilla Is Like Life*, 120.

15. Charlotte Biltekoff's *Eating Right in America: The Cultural Politics of Food and Health* (Durham, NC: Duke University Press, 2013) convincingly links such moralizing impulses not only to domestic reformers attempting to improve American home cooking but also to the dietary health movement and the scientific discipline of nutrition.

16. Nicole Tonkovich, introduction to *The American Woman's Home*, by Catherine E. Beecher and Harriet Beecher Stowe (New Brunswick, NJ: Rutgers University Press, 2002), x.

17. Megan Elias, *Stir It Up: Home Economics in American Culture* (Philadelphia: University of Pennsylvania Press, 2008), 6.

18. Beecher and Beecher, *American Woman's Home*, 13.

19. Ibid., 167.

20. Ibid., xi.

21. Mary J. Lincoln, *Boston Cook Book: What to Do and What Not to Do in Cooking* (Boston: Roberts Brothers, 1884), v–vi.

22. Ibid., vii–viii.

23. Ibid., xx.

24. Biltekoff, *Eating Right in America*, 14.

25. Ingold, *Perception of the Environment*, 5.

26. Beecher and Beecher, *American Woman's Home*, 14.

27. Rebecca Sharpless, *Cooking in Other Women's Kitchens: Domestic Workers in the South, 1865–1960* (Chapel Hill: University of North Carolina Press, 2010), 21.

28. Ibid., 21–22.

29. Laura Shapiro, *Perfection Salad: Women and Cooking at the Turn of the Century* (New York: Farrar, Straus, and Giroux, 1986), 53–55.

30. Ibid., 112.

31. Elias, *Stir It Up*, 12.

32. Ibid., 176.

33. Marion Talbot, quoted in Elias, *Stir It Up*, 15.

34. Biltekoff, *Eating Right in America*, 28.

35. Laura Shapiro, *Something from the Oven: Reinventing Dinner in 1950s America*, (New York: Viking, 2004), xxv.

36. Ibid.

37. See Arlie Russell Hochschild, *The Second Shift: Working Parents and the Revolution at Home*, with Anne Manchung (New York: Penguin, 2003).

38. Brenda Beagan, Gwen E. Chapman, Andrea D'Sylva, and B. Raewyn Bassett, "'It's Just Easier for Me to Do It': Rationalizing the Family Division of Foodwork," *Sociology* 42, no. 4 (2008): 653–71, doi:10.1177/0038038508091621.

39. Ibid., 660.

40. Ibid., 662.

41. Ibid., 663.

42. The author's son, Edgar Rombauer, makes this claim in the foreword to the 75th anniversary edition of *The Joy of Cooking* (New York: Scribner, 1998). Anne Mendelson has calculated the number as a more modest 10 million; see Mendelson, *Stand Facing the Stove: The Story of the Women Who Gave America the* Joy of Cooking (New York: Simon and Schuster, 1996), 413.

43. Mendelson's engaging and encyclopedic biography of Irma S. Rombauer and Marion Rombauer Beck, *Stand Facing the Stove: The Story of the Women Who Gave America* The Joy of Cooking, is a fantastic resource for learning about the two women and the success of *The Joy of Cooking*.

44. Mendelson, *Stand Facing the Stove*, 86–90.

45. Ibid., 104.

46. Ibid., 106.

47. Rombauer, *The Joy of Cooking* (1998), 19–21.

48. Irma Rombauer, *The Joy of Cooking*, 2nd ed. (Indianapolis: Bobbs Merrill, 1946), 10.

49. Julia Child, "How Good Is the New 'Joy of Cooking'?" *McCall's Magazine*, October 1975: 63–68, MC 449 box 36, folder 500, Papers of the Rombauer-Becker Family, Schlesinger Library, Cambridge, MA.

50. Mendelson, *Stand Facing the Stove*, 2.

51. Ibid.

52. Ibid.

53. Lynn Campbell to Irma Rombauer, September 29, 1954, MC 449, box 36, folder 520, Papers of the Rombauer-Becker Family, Schlesinger Library, Cambridge, MA.

54. Irma Rombauer and Marion Rombauer Becker, *The Joy of Cooking* (Indianapolis: Bobbs Merrill, 1975), foreword.

55. Rombauer, *The Joy of Cooking* (1998), 25.

56. Report by Nancy Pastor, MC 449, box 39, folder 444, Papers of the Rombauer-Becker Family, Schlesinger Library, Cambridge, MA.

57. Report by Anne Ross, MC 449, box 39 folder 444, Papers of the Rombauer-Becker Family, Schlesinger Library, Cambridge, MA.

58. Marguerite Martyn, "A Talented Hostess Writes a Cookbook," *Saint Louis Post-Dispatch Daily Magazine*, Box MC 449, box 39, folder 561, Papers of the Rombauer-Becker Family, Schlesinger Library, Cambridge, MA.

59. Adapon, *Culinary Art and Anthropology*.

60. Ingold, *Perception of the Environment*, 325.

CHAPTER 2. COOKING IS AN OCCUPATION

1. Sharpless, *Cooking in Other Women's Kitchens*.

2. United States Department of Agriculture Economic Research Service, "Data Products: Table 8."

3. Okrent and Kumcu, "Convenience Foods."

4. Ibid., 7.

5. Ibid.

6. United States Bureau of Labor Statistics, "American Time Use Survey: Household Activities," last modified December 20, 2016, www.bls.gov/tus/charts/household.htm.

7. Ibid.

8. Leslie Cunningham-Sabo and Amanda Simons. "Home Economics: An Old-Fashioned Answer to a Modern-Day Dilemma?" *Nutrition Today* 47, no. 3 (2012): 128–32, doi:10.1097/NT.0b013e3182574 4a5; Daniel Celnik, Laura Gillespie, and Michael E. J. Lean, "Time-Scarcity, Ready-Meals, Ill-Health and the Obesity Epidemic," *Trends in Food Science and Technology* 27, no. 1 (2012): 4–11, doi:10.1016/j.tifs.2012.06.001.

9. Irma Rombauer, *The Joy of Cooking*, facsimile of the first edition (New York: Scribners, 1998), 60.

10. Ibid., 296.

11. Catharine E. Beecher and Harriet Beecher Stowe, *Principles of Domestic Science as Applied to the Duties and Pleasures of Home* (New York: J. B. Ford, 1870), 290.

12. Ibid., 277.

13. Ibid.

14. See also Psyche Williams-Forson, *Building Houses of Chicken Legs: Black Women, Food and Power* (Raleigh: University of North Carolina Press, 2006); and Kyla Wazana-Tompkins, *Racial Indigestion: Eating Bodies in the 19th Century* (New York: New York University Press, 2012).

15. John Egerton, foreword to *The Jemima Code: Two Centuries of African American Cookbooks*, by Toni Tipton-Martin (Austin: University of Texas Press, 2015), ix.

16. Ibid., 2.

17. Ibid., 7.

18. Donna Gabaccia, *We Are What We Eat: Ethnic Food and the Making of Americans* (Cambridge, MA: Harvard University Press, 1998).

19. Sharpless, *Cooking in Other Women's Kitchens*, 7.

20. Ibid., 8.

21. Ibid., 15.

22. Ibid., 184–87. Sharpless includes an appendix with the weekly wages of a number of women from throughout the South. Wages remained between $2.00 and $15.00 a week through 1950.

23. Joan Reardon, ed., *As Always, Julia: The Letters of Julia Child and Avis DeVoto* (New York: Mariner, 2011), 29.

24. Ibid., 35.

25. Tonkovich, introduction, xvi.

26. Ibid. Quotation originally from Joan Hedrick, *Harriet Beecher Stowe, A Life* (New York: Oxford University Press, 1994), 119.

27. Rachel Laudan, "Servants in the Kitchen: They Have a History Too," *Rachel Laudan*, April 26, 2016, www.rachellaudan.com/2016/04/servants-have-a-history-too.html.

28. Rachel Laudan, "Servants in the Kitchen: Now You See Them, Now You Don't," *Rachel Laudan*, April 11, 2016, www.rachellaudan.com/2016/04/servants-in-the-kitchen-now-you-see-them-now-you-dont.html.

29. Hewlett was one of a group of black female cooks at the University of Mississippi who were interviewed as part of an oral history project carried out by the Southern Foodways Alliance.

30. Fairy Bell Hewlett, "Fairy Bell Hewlett, Retired Cook," interview by John T. Edge, May 7, 2004, transcript, Oral History, Southern Foodways Alliance, www.southernfoodways.org/app/uploads/Fairy_Bell_Hewlett_full.pdf, 1–26.

31. Ibid., 9.

32. Matthew Sobek, contributor, "Occupations," in *Historical Statistics of the United States: Millennial Edition Online*, ed. Susan B. Carter, Scott Sigmund Gartner, Michael R. Haines, Alan M. Olmstead, Richard Sutch, and Gavin Wright (Cambridge: Cambridge University Press, 2006), http://hsus.cambridge.org/HSUSWeb/HSUSEntryServlet, "Part B: Work and Welfare."

33. Ibid., table Ba1117–1130.

34. Harvey Levenstein, *Revolution at the Table: The Transformation of the American Diet* (New York: Oxford University Press, 1988), 18.

35. Ibid., 64.

36. Sobek, "Occupations," "Part B: Work and Welfare," table Ba-X.

37. Irma Rombauer, *The Joy of Cooking*, 3rd ed. (Indianapolis: Bobbs Merrill, 1946), foreword.

38. Amy Bentley, *Inventing Baby Food: Taste, Health, and the Industrialization of the American Diet* (Berkeley: University of California Press, 2014).

39. See Amy Trubek, *Haute Cuisine: How the French Invented the Culinary Profession* (Philadelphia: University of Pennsylvania Press, 2000); Rebecca Sharpless, *Cooking in Other Women's Kitchens;* and Gary Alan Fine, *Kitchens: The Culture of Restaurant Work*, 2nd ed. (Berkeley: University of California Press, 2009).

40. Michael Symons, *A History of Cooks and Cooking*, The Food Series (Champaign: University of Illinois Press, 2000), 35.

41. Krishnendu Ray, *The Ethnic Restaurateur* (New York: Bloomsbury Academic, 2016), 66.

42. Ibid., 67

43. Symons, *A History of Cooks and Cooking*, 292.

44. Trubek, *Haute Cuisine*, 31.

45. Ibid., 33.

46. Paul Freedman, "American Restaurants and Cuisine in the Mid-Nineteenth Century," *New England Quarterly* 84, no. 1 (March 2011): 5–55.

47. Ibid., 40.

48. Ibid., 41.

49. Ray, *Ethnic Restaurateur*, 10–12.

50. Ibid., 13.

51. Ibid., 14.

52. Ibid., 63.

53. Susan B. Carter et al., eds., *Historical Statistics of the United States: Millennial Edition* (New York: Cambridge University Press, 2006).

54. Sobek, " Occupations." This section contains the following subheadings: "Labor," "Labor Force," "Occupations," "Wage and Wage Inequality," "Hours and Working Conditions," "Labor Unions," and "Household Production."

55. Ibid., 2–35.

56. Ibid., 2–150.

57. Levenstein, *Revolution at the Table*.

58. Reardon, *As Always, Julia*, 29–30.

59. Ibid., 52.

60. The modern discourse on both why Americans do not cook and why they should cook relies on an us-versus-them narrative; the underlying assumption is that a monolithic food industry uses mass-manufacturing methods to make our food and coercive advertising to get us to purchase it while individual cooks are unable or insufficiently educated to protest. In an interview, *New York Times* journalist Mark Bittman gets into a conversation with Michael Pollan that returns to a domestic ideal when considering cooking practice: "You're going to use higher-quality ingredients than whoever's making your home-meal replacement would

ever use. You're not going to use additives. So the quality of the food will automatically be better. . . . So there's something in the very nature of home cooking that keeps us from getting into trouble" (Mark Bittman, "Opinionator Column: Pollan Cooks!" *New York Times*, April 17, 2013, http://opinionator.blogs.nytimes.com/2013/04/17/pollan-cooks). Here, home cooking serves primarily as a proxy for "food not prepared by the food industry." In this sense, Pollan, Bittman, and others discussing the fate of cooking skill and knowledge are advocating for a certain *style* of cooking as a means of fighting against structural changes in the larger food system. This may be an excellent argument for protesting the shift in identity that has occurred for many Americans now that we are primarily food consumers rather than food producers of any kind, but along the way, a tremendous amount of implicit and explicit cooking activity gets ignored.

61. Nicole I. Larson et al., "Food Preparation by Young Adults Is Associated with Better Diet Quality," *Journal of the American Dietetic Association* 106, no. 7 (2006): 2001–7.

62. In another study, it was found that full-time workers spent 38–46 minutes preparing a meal whereas part-time workers spent 53–56 minutes preparing a meal. See Lisa Mancino and Constance Newman, "Who Has Time to Cook? How Family Resources Influence Food Preparation," USDA Economic Research Service, 2007.

63. Frances Short, "Domestic Cooking Skills: What Are They?" *Journal of the HEIA* 10, no. 3 (2003): 13–22.

64. Tim Lang and Martin Caraher, "Is There a Culinary Skills Transition? Data and Debate from the UK about Changes in Cooking Culture," *Journal of the HEIA* 8, no. 2 (2001): 2–14.

65. Mancino and Newman, "Who Has Time to Cook?"

66. Angela Meah and Matt Watson, "Saints and Slackers: Challenging Discourses about the Decline of Domestic Cooking," *Sociological Research Online* 16, no. 2 (2011): 6, doi:dx.doi.org/10.5153/sro.2341.

CHAPTER 3. COOKING IS AN ART

1. Robert Valgenti, "Cucinare come interpretazione," in *Cibo, estetica e arte: Convergenze tra filosofia, semiotica e storia*, ed. Nicola Perullo (Pisa: ETS, 2014).

2. Sennett, *Craftsman*, 37.

3. Tim Ingold, *Making: Anthropology, Archaeology, Art and Architecture* (London: Routledge, 2013), 1.

4. Valgenti, "Cucinare come interpretazione," 57.

5. Sennett, *Craftsman*, 38, 65.

6. Priscilla Parkhurst Ferguson, *Word of Mouth: What We Talk About When We Talk About Food* (Oakland: University of California Press, 2014), 80.

7. Short, "Domestic Cooking Skills," xx.

8. Ibid., xi.

9. Ibid., xxii.

10. Ibid.

11. Ibid., 81. It can be argued that cooking a certain way, or cooking using a certain standard or identity or philosophy, allows both the action and the result to transcend the quotidian. This is a contested claim, as investigations of professional cooks, or those paid to cook for others in public and commercial settings, have been haunted by the question as to whether "art" can ever emerge from an everyday task performed by everyday people. For more on this issue, see Trubek, *Haute Cuisine;* Ferguson, *Accounting for Taste;* Ray, *Ethnic Restaurateur.*

12. Gary Alan Fine, *Kitchens: The Culture of Restaurant Work* (Berkeley: University of California Press, 1996), 10.

13. Ibid., 14.

14. Ibid., 178.

15. Trubek, *Haute Cuisine*, 3.

16. Ibid., 13.

17. Julia Child, Louise Bertholle, and Simone Beck, *Mastering the Art of French Cooking*, vol. 1, rev. ed. (New York: Alfred A. Knopf, 1983), vii–viii.

18. Marcus Samuelsson, *Yes, Chef: A Memoir,* with Veronica Chambers (New York: Random House, 2013), 62.

19. Ibid., 153.

20. Ibid., 160.

21. Ibid.

22. Fine, *Kitchens*, 25.

23. Sennett, *Craftsman*, 80.

24. Fine, *Kitchens*, 25.

25. Ibid.

26. Maryann McCabe and Timothy de Waal Maleyft, "Creativity and Cooking: Motherhood, Agency and Social Change in Everyday Life," *Journal of Consumer Culture* 15, no. 1 (2015): 48–65.

27. Ibid., 55.

28. Ibid., 58.

29. Emily Brady, "Smells, Tastes, and Aesthetics," in *Philosophy of Food*, ed. David Kaplan (Berkeley: University of California Press, 2012), 53–54.

30. Ibid., 56.

31. Ibid., 69.

32. Ibid., 72

33. Ibid., 75.

34. Carolyn Korsmeyer, *Making Sense of Taste: Food and Philosophy* (Ithaca: Cornell University Press, 1999), 4. For further discussion by philosophers of food, aesthetics, and philosophy, see Raymond Boisvert and Lisa Heldke, *Philosophers at Table: On Food and Being Human* (New York: Reaktion, 2016).

35. Dana Polan, *Julia Child's* The French Chef (Durham, NC: Duke University Press, 2011), 53

36. Ibid., 85.

37. See Barbara Ketcham Wheaton, *Savoring the Past* (Philadelphia: University of Pennsylvania Press, 1983); Ferguson, *Accounting for Taste;* and Janet Theophano, *Eat My Words: Reading Women's Lives through the Cookbooks They Wrote* (New York: Palgrave MacMillan, 2002).

38. Signe Rousseau, *Food Media: Celebrity Chefs and the Politics of Everyday Interference* (London: Berg, 2012), 53.

39. Sutton, *Secrets of the Greek Kitchen*, 12.

40. Ibid., 38.

CHAPTER 4. COOKING IS A CRAFT

1. See Sutton, *Secrets from the Greek Kitchen*, chapters 3–6.

2. Sennett, *Craftsman*, 81. Anthropologists looking at cooking (see Sutton, *Secrets from the Greek Kitchen*) and the emergence of new forms of artisan food practice in the United States (see Heather Paxson, *The Life of Cheese* [Berkeley: University of California Press, 2012]; and Brad Weiss, *Real Pigs: Shifting Values in the Field of Local Pork* [Durham, NC: Duke University Press, 2016]) have brought new insights into Ingold's notion of "enskilment" with their nuanced considerations

of what such practices mean in relation to ideals of tradition and authenticity. In modern commercial craft practice, these forms of enskilment are understood as a form of protest, a move against the highly technological industrialized modes of production (from making artisan cheese to raising heirloom pigs) now dominant in the American food system.

3. Shannon Watts, *Radical Homemakers: Reclaiming Domesticity from a Consumer Culture* (Richmondville, NY: Left to Right, 2010), 120–25.

4. Julia Wolfson et al. "What Does Cooking Mean to You? Perceptions of Cooking and Factors Related to Cooking Behavior," *Appetite* 97 (2016): 146.

5. Ibid., 150.

6. In *Inventing Baby Food: Taste, Health and the Industrialization of the American Diet*, Amy Bentley charts the complex matrix of natural, industrial, and homemade categories for a fundamental form of nourishment: food for babies. The creation and acceptance of commercial baby food, she points out, was partly because it was promoted as both a symbol of modernity and a type of convenience (17).

7. Shapiro, *Something from the Oven*, xix.

8. Ibid., xxiv.

9. Michael Polanyi, *The Tacit Dimension* (Garden City, NY: Anchor, 1967), xx.

10. Sennett, *Craftsman*, 39–44.

11. Regional specialties can also fall into this category: a friend from the South's biscuits, or another friend's Texas barbecue.

12. James F. Scott, *Domination and the Arts of Resistance: Hidden Transcripts* (New Haven: Yale University Press, 1990), xiii.

13. Mike Sheridan pointed out this important connection, and our discussion about the links between craft baking and forms of resistance proved crucial to the final structure and argument of this chapter.

14. William G. Panschar and Charles C. Slater, *Baking in America*, Northwestern University Studies in Business History (Evanston, IL: Northwestern University Press, 1956), 24.

15. Cathy Kaufman, "Bread," in *The Oxford Companion to American Food and Drink*, ed. Andrew F. Smith (Oxford: Oxford University Press, 2007), 61.

16. Ibid.

17. Katherine Leonard Turner, "Tools and Spaces: Food and Cooking in Working-Class Neighborhoods, 1880–1930," in *Food Chains: From Farmyard to*

Shopping Cart, ed. Warren Belasco and Roger Horowitz (Philadelphia: University of Pennsylvania Press, 2009), 229.

18. Katherine Leonard Turner, *How the Other Half Ate* (Berkeley: University of California Press, 2014), 59–60.

19. Ibid., 60.

20. Ibid., 65.

21. Panschar and Slater, *Baking in America*, 49.

22. Kaufman, "Bread," 62.

23. Ibid., 12.

24. Panschar and Slater, *Baking in America*, 5.

25. Josh Sosland, "Bread Market Remains Challenging," *Food Business News*, September 17, 2013, www.foodbusinessnews.net/articles/news_home/Business_News/2013/09/Bread_market_remains_challengi.aspx?ID=%7BDF39136B-7B1E-4C35-831E-558A8E92BAAF%7D&cck=1.

26. United States Bureau of the Census, *Historical Statistics of the United States: Colonial Times to 1970*, bicentennial ed. (Washington, DC: U.S. Department of Commerce, Bureau of the Census, 1975).

27. Data for 1980–2000 classifies labor in "bakery products," which is distinct from "grain mill products" and "sugar and confectionary products." Data for 2010 is classified as "bakeries and tortilla making."

28. Panshar and Slater, *Baking in America*, 35.

29. Ibid., 55.

30. Ibid., 113.

31. Ibid., 69.

32. Ibid., 70.

33. Ibid, 227.

34. MarketLine, "Industry Profile Bread & Rolls in the United States," October 2015, www.reportlinker.com/p0171586-summary/Bread-Rolls-in-the-United-States.html.

35. Roy Blount, *Alphabet Juice* (New York: Sarah Crichton, 2009).

36. In 2012, a New York bagel bakery sued Dunkin Donuts for false advertising. See Nadia Arumugam, "Taste Test: Dunkin' Donuts' Fake 'Artisan' Bagels vs Real Artisan Bagels," *Forbes*, April 26, 2012, www.forbes.com/sites/nadiaarumugam/2012/04/26/taste-test-dunkin-donuts-fake-artisan-bagels-vs-real-artisan-bagels.

37. The process for creating active dry yeast was developed in the 1860s by Charles and Maximillian Fleischmann.

38. Michael Pollan, *Cooked: A Natural History of Tranfsormation* (New York: Penguin, 2013), 219.

39. Once the craft category emerged as central to the perceptions, if not practices, of home cooks, I went on to do participant-observation and interviews with home and commercial bakers committed to definitions of "scratch" and "by hand baking."

40. In the process of figuring out the role of the artisan baker in the contemporary iteration of the craft category, I also did participant-observation and ethnographic interviewing at three bakeries relying on wild yeast fermentation to make their breads: Rubaud's (Westford, VT), Vergennes Laundry (Vergennes, VT), and Tartine (San Francisco, CA). I also did participant-observation and ethnographic interviewing of Mark, a home baker who learned how to bake bread from Gerard Rubaud.

41. Although I did record exact proportions for all aspects of his recipe, Rubaud, following his combination of pursuing tradition with contemporary business acumen, considers it proprietary, and does not wish it to be made available to the public.

42. Since the leavening process when using levain usually occurs at a lower temperature, the breads taste tangy but not sour.

43. Panschar and Slater, *Baking in America*, 59.

44. As part of my investigation of craft bakers, I carried out participant-observation at a bakery near my home. The owner had apprenticed with Gerard Rubaud. As I observed her work, I realized that she represents a new generation of food workers who are invested in the aesthetics of craft. In this sense, she is committed to a set of ideas about quality (e.g., she invests in Vermont Butter and Cheese butter, which costs $5.80 a pound, compared to Cabot butter, which is also locally produced but at a much higher volume and costs $2.20 a pound) and also beauty (her background is in architectural studies), and the look and feel of the bakery is important to her. She mentioned that she knows some customers don't "get" the aesthetic and ask her questions like "When will you be hanging pictures?" and "When are you going to put paint over the primer?" She is also committed to making Rubaud's style of wild yeast levain. She uses plenty of

technology in the service of this laborious process, including a machine to grind the grains, an electronic thermometer to check the temperature of the water, a digital weight scale, a Hobart mixer, a KitchenAid mixer, and a Kemper dough machine. This is somewhat of a contrast with Rubaud, although he has fewer production pressures and does not have a retail shop. The work has been arduous, but she has developed a loyal and consistent following. However, the intense physical and temporal demands of this craft aesthetic have been difficult to maintain. She and her husband and business partner recently changed the operation from a morning bakery to an afternoon and evening café.

CHAPTER 5. COOKING IS FOR HEALTH

1. "Scientific Report of the 2015 Dietary Guidelines Advisory Committee: Part A. Executive Summary," Office of Disease Prevention and Health Promotion, Health.gov, accessed August 15, 2016, https://health.gov/dietaryguidelines/2015-scientific-report/02-executive-summary.asp.

2. "New My Plate Food Guidelines Unveiled at USDA," YouTube video, 1:52, posted by "USDA," June 7, 2011, www.youtube.com/watch?v=ZgeS6VcdIVI.

3. B. Haughton, J. D. Gussow, and J. M. Dodds, "An Historical Study of the Underlying Assumptions for United States Food Guides from 1917 through the Basic Four Food Group Guide," *Journal of Nutrition Education* 19, no. 4 (1987): 169–76, http://agris.fao.org/agris-search/search.do?recordID=US8845880.

4. Ibid.

5. "Dietary Guidelines," United States Department of Agriculture, Center for Nutrition Policy and Promotion, accessed August 5, 2016, www.cnpp.usda.gov/dietary-guidelines.

6. "Scientific Report of the 2015 Dietary Guidelines Advisory Committee: Part D. Chapter 5: Food Sustainability and Safety—Continued," Office of Disease Prevention and Health Promotion, Health.gov, accessed August 15, 2016, https://health.gov/dietaryguidelines/2015-scientific-report/10-chapter-5/d5-3.asp.

7. Tom Vilsack and Sylvia Burwell, "2015 Dietary Guidelines: Giving You the Tools You Need to Make Healthy Choices," blog, United States Department of Agriculture, October 6, 2015, www.usda.gov/media/blog/2015/10/6/2015-dietary-guidelines-giving-you-tools-you-need-make-healthy-choices.

8. Audrey Isabel Richards, *Hunger and Work in a Savage Tribe: A Functional Study of Nutrition among the Southern Bantu* (Glencoe, IL: Free Press, 1948), 1.

9. Ibid., 11.

10. These results are from an online survey of over one thousand Americans between the ages of eighteen and eighty. See "2016 Food and Health Survey: 'Food Decision 2016: The Impact of a Growing National Food Dialogue,'" International Food Information Council Foundation, May 11 2016, www.foodinsight.org/articles/2016-food-and-health-survey-food-decision-2016-impact-growing-national-food-dialogue.

11. A definition of a healthy meal was solicited from all participants in the introductory survey, but ideas about healthy meals also emerged during home visits. As they cooked and talked, many participants mentioned health, eating a healthy diet, or being mindful of incorporating healthy foods into their diet.

12. Kurt Lewin, "Forces behind Food Habits and Methods of Change," in *The Problem of Changing Food Habits*, National Research Council Bulletin, ed. by National Research Council Committee on Food Habits (Washington, DC: National Research Council and National Academy of Sciences, 1943), 37.

13. Brian Wansink, "Profiling Nutritional Gatekeepers: Three Methods for Differentiating Influential Cooks," *Food Quality and Preference* 14, no. 4 (2003): 289.

14. Brian Wansink, "Empowering Nutrition Gatekeepers: The Parents," *Journal of Nutrition Education and Behavior* 43, no. 5 (2011): 307; Maartje P. Poelmana et al., "The Home Food Environment of Overweight Gatekeepers in the Netherlands," *Public Health Nutrition* 18, no. 10 (2015): 1815–23.

15. Brian Wansink, "Nutritional Gatekeepers and the 72% Solution," *Journal of the American Dietetic Association* 106, no. 9 (2006): 1324–27.

16. For an influential example, see Marion Nestle's writings, including her books *Food Politics* (2002) and *Soda Politics* (2015) and her blog, *Food Politics* (www.foodpolitics.com).

17. Lewin, "Forces behind Food Habits," 35.

18. Ibid., 37.

19. Ibid.

20. E. Melanie DuPuis, *Dangerous Digestion* (Oakland: University of California Press, 2015), 6.

21. Ibid., 55.

22. Biltekoff, *Eating Right in America.*

23. Carney, *Unending Hunger.*

24. Mary Douglas, "Food as a System of Communication," in *In the Active Voice* (London: Routledge and Kegan Paul, 1982), 83–87.

25. Ibid., 85.

26. David Grotto and Elisa Zied, "The Standard American Diet and Its Relationship to the Health Status of Americans," *Nutrition in Clinical Practice* 25, no. 6 (December 2010): 603–12.

27. These women participated in a course called Healthy Cooking, sponsored by Drexel University. Our research group worked with the instructor on the course pedagogy, and Caitlin Morgan and Maria Carabello observed and interviewed the participants.

28. The women in this study resided in the Mantua neighborhood of Philadelphia. This neighborhood is part of an area that was deemed a Promise Zone under President Obama. It has 35,315 residents and an overall poverty rate of 50.78 percent, nearly double the city's rate of 26.9 percent. Sarah Bowen and her colleagues have been doing similar research among low-income women of color in the American South. Her research reports similar findings regarding the frustrations and difficulties of procuring adequate and healthy foods, although the provisioning strategies were quite different in the two areas. See Bowen, Elliott, and Brenton, "The Joy of Cooking?"

29. This research was done as part of a subsequent project on food agency and was carried out by Caitlin Morgan.

30. In a recent article discussing their qualitative study that looked at the link between food choices and healthy food, Sara E. Shaefer and her colleagues point out a series of ambiguities in people's understanding of health, both as an objective construct and an internal perception. They concluded that taste often plays a role in either confirming or refuting definitions of healthy food. See Sara E. Shaefer, Charlotte Biltekoff, Carolyn Thomas, and Roxanne N. Rashedi, "Healthy, Vague: Exploring Health as a Priority in Food Choice," *Food Culture and Society* 19, no. 2 (2016): 227–50.

31. Abby Wilkerson, "Judging, Tasting, Knowing 'Good' Food," *Food, Culture and Society* 19, no. 2 (2016): 223–26.

32. Niman Ranch is actually headquartered in California.

33. Mayo Clinic Staff, "Grocery Store Secret: Shop the Perimeter," Healthy Lifestyle, Nutrition and Healthy Eating, Mayo Clinic, August 6, 2014, www.mayoclinic.org/healthy-lifestyle/nutrition-and-healthy-eating/in-depth/health-tip/art-20048842.

34. See Shapiro, *Perfection Salad;* Levenstein, *Revolution at the Table;* and Biltekoff, *Eating Right in America.*

35. Laura Shapiro, "Fanny Farmer," in *Oxford Companion to American Food and Drink*, ed. Andrew Smith (Oxford: Oxford University Press, 2007), 451.

36. Linda's understanding that recipes used to be, to use Nahum Waxman's words, "inspiration and guidance" but have now become increasingly didactic and prescriptive is reflected in many cookbooks published from 1930 to today. The recipe as a type of aide-memoire has started to disappear.

37. Marion Rombauer Becker, *Little Acorn* (Indianapolis: Bobbs-Merrill, 1982). This book does not have page numbers.

38. John Burroughs School Catalogue (no date), box 449, folder 281, Papers of the Rombauer-Becker Family, Schlesinger Library, Cambridge, MA.

39. The Progressive School Unfettered (typed manuscript, no date), box 441, folder 281, Papers of the Rombauer Becker Family, Schlesinger Library, Cambridge, MA.

40. In her magisterial work *Stand Facing the Stove: The Story of the Women Who Gave Us* The Joy of Cooking (New York: Simon and Schuster, 1996), Anne Mendelson outlines, in great detail, the agreements, disagreements, lawsuits, and conciliations that took up much of the Rombauer and Becker family's time and energy for decades.

41. Mendelson, *Stand Facing the Stove*, 37.

42. Ibid., 392–95.

43. Irma Rombauer and Marion Rombauer Becker, *The Joy of Cooking* (Indianapolis: Bobbs Merrill, 1975), 1.

44. Ibid., 8.

45. Irma Rombauer, *The Joy of Cooking*, 3rd ed. (Indianapolis: Bobbs Merrill, 1946), 781. Helen Hokinson was a cartoonist and a frequent contributor to the *New Yorker.*

46. Rombauer and Becker, *Joy of Cooking* (1975), 577.

47. Lewin, *Forces behind Food Habits*, 41.

CONCLUSION

1. Warren Belasco, *Meals to Come: A History of the Future of Food* (Berkeley: University of California Press, 2006).

2. Soylent, accessed September 11, 2016, www.soylent.com.

3. Roc Morin, "The Man Who Would Make Food Obsolete," *Atlantic*, April 28, 2014, www.theatlantic.com/health/archive/2014/04/the-man-who-would-make-eating-obsolete/361058.

4. Ingold, *Perception of the Environment*, 325.

5. See Brian Wansink, *Mindless Eating: Why We Eat More Than We Think* (New York: Random House, 2006); and Marion Nestle, *Food Politics* (Berkeley: University of California, 2002).

6. Glauco P. Tocchini-Valentini and Marta A. Tocchini-Valentini, "Comparative Anatomy: Giorgione's Venus, Connoisseur Morelli, and the Reverend Bayes," *FASEB Journal* 26, no. 1 (2012): 5–8.

7. Adelaide Cummings, a senior environmental studies major at the University of Vermont, approached me about doing research on meal-delivery services, and we worked together to devise a two-phase study: first, five home cooks were given a complementary subscription for one week's worth of meals and then interviewed about their experiences within one week of completing the service; second, regular users of meal-delivery services were surveyed about their usage.

8. E. Melanie DuPuis, *Dangerous Digestion: The Politics of American Dietary Advice* (Oakland: University of California Press, 2015), 14.

BIBLIOGRAPHY

ARCHIVE AND INTERVIEW SOURCES

Papers of Julia Child, 1925–1993. Schlesinger Library, Cambridge, MA.

Papers of the Rombauer-Becker Family, 1795–1992. Schlesinger Library, Cambridge, MA.

Focus group results and interview transcripts. "Learning to Cook and Developing Food Agency," USDA Hatch Grant VT-H02109.

Interview transcripts, surveys, and ethnographic videos. "A Qualitative and Longitudinal Study of Cooking Skill and Knowledge," USDA Hatch Grant VT-H01218.

BOOKS AND ARTICLES

Adapon, Joy. *Culinary Art and Anthropology*. Oxford: Bloomsbury Academic, 2008.

Ahlgren, Mia, Inga-Britt Gustafsson, and Gunnar Hall. "Attitudes and Beliefs Directed towards Ready-Meal Consumption." *Food Service Technology* 4, no. 4 (2004): 159–69. doi:10.1111/j.1471-5740.2004.00102.x.

Asp, Elaine H. "Factors Affecting Food Decisions Made by Individual Consumers." *Food Policy* 24, nos. 2–3 (1999): 287–94. doi:10.1016/S0306-9192(99)00024-X.

Avakian, Arlene Voski, ed. *Through the Kitchen Window: Women Writers Explore the Intimate Meanings of Food and Cooking*. 2nd ed. Oxford: Berg, 2005.

Barbas, Samantha. "'I'll Take Chop Suey': Restaurants as Agents of Culinary and Cultural Change." *Journal of Popular Culture* 36, no. 4 (2003): 669–86. doi:10.1111/1540-5931.00040.

Barthes, Roland. "Science vs. Literature." *Times Literary Supplement* (London), September 28, 1967.

Beagan, Brenda, Gwen Chapman, Josée Johnston, Deborah McPhail, Elaine Power, and Helen Vallianatos. *Acquired Tastes: Why Families Eat the Way They Do*. Vancouver: University of British Columbia Press, 2015.

Beagan, Brenda, Gwen E. Chapman, Andrea D'Sylva, and B. Raewyn Bassett. "'It's Just Easier for Me to Do It': Rationalizing the Family Division of Foodwork." *Sociology* 42, no. 4 (2008): 653–71. doi:10.1177/0038038508091621.

Beck, Margaret E. "Dinner Preparation in the Modern United States." *British Food Journal* 109, no. 7 (2007): 531–47. doi:10.1108/00070700710761527.

Becker, Marion Rombauer. *Little Acorn*. Indianapolis: Bobbs-Merrill, 1982.

Beecher, Catharine E., and Harriet Beecher Stowe. *The American Woman's Home*. Edited by Nicole Tronovich. New Brunswick, NJ: Rutgers University Press, 2002

———. *The American Woman's Home, or Principles of Domestic Science*. New York: J. B. Ford, 1869.

———. *Principles of Domestic Science as Applied to the Duties and Pleasures of Home*. New York: J. B. Ford, 1870.

Belasco, Warren. *Meals to Come: A History of the Future of Food*. Berkeley: University of California Press, 2006.

Bentley, Amy. *Inventing Baby Food: Taste, Health, and the Industrialization of the American Diet*. Berkeley: University of California Press, 2014.

Berry, Leonard L. "Market to the Perception (Marketers Who Target Consumers Who Feel Rushed for Time)." *American Demographics* 12, no. 2 (1990): 32.

Biltekoff, Charlotte. *Eating Right in America: The Cultural Politics of Food and Health*. Durham , NC: Duke University Press, 2013.

Bittman, Mark. *Cooking Solves Everything: How Time in the Kitchen Can Save Your Health, Your Budget, and Even the Planet*. San Francisco: Byliner, 2011.

———. "Is Junk Food Really Cheaper?" *New York Times*, September 24, 2011. www.nytimes.com/2011/09/25/opinion/sunday/is-junk-food-really-cheaper.html.

———. "A No-Frills Kitchen Still Cooks." *New York Times*, May 9, 2007. www.nytimes.com/2007/05/09/dining/09mini.html.
———. "Opinionator Column: Pollan Cooks!" *New York Times*, April 17, 2013. http://opinionator.blogs.nytimes.com/2013/04/17/pollan-cooks.
———. "So Your Kitchen Is Tiny. So What?" *New York Times*, December 13, 2008. www.nytimes.com/2008/12/14/weekinreview/14bittman.html.
———. "The Truth about Home Cooking." *Time*, October 9, 2014. www.time.com/3483888/thetruth-about-home-cooking.
———. "When Cooking, Invest Time. Or Work. Not Both." *New York Times*, September 22, 2014. www.nytimes.com/2014/09/24/dining/when-cooking-invest-time-or-work-not-both.html.
Blisard, Noel, Jayachandran N. Variyam, and John Cromartie. "Food Expenditures by US Households: Looking Ahead to 2020." USDA Economic Research Service, 2017. www.ers.usda.gov/webdocs/publications/41537/31005_aer821fm_002.pdf?v=41452.
Blount, Roy. *Alphabet Juice*. New York: Sarah Crichton, 2009.
Boisvert, Raymond, and Lisa Heldke. *Philosophers at Table: On Food and Being Human*. New York: Reaktion, 2016.
Boone-Heinonen, Janne, Penny Gordon-Larsen, Catarina I. Kiefe, James M. Shikany, Cora E. Lewis, and Barry M. Popkin. "Fast Food Restaurants and Food Stores: Longitudinal Associations with Diet in Young to Middle-Aged Adults; The CARDIA Study." *Archives of Internal Medicine* 171, no. 13 (2011): 1162–70. doi:10.1001/archinternmed.2011.283.
Bowen, Sarah, Sinikka Elliott, and Joslyn Brenton. "The Joy of Cooking?" *Contexts* 13, no. 3 (2014): 20–25.
Bracken, Peg. *The I Hate to Cook Book*. New York: Harcourt Brace, 1960.
Brady, Emily. "Smells, Tastes, and Aesthetics." In *Philosophy of Food*, edited by David Kaplan, 69–86. Berkeley: University of California Press, 2012.
Branch, Glenn. "Whence Lumpers and Splitters?" *NCSE Blog*. December 2, 2014. www.ncse.com/blog/2014/11/whence-lumpers-splitters-0016004.
Brembeck, Helene. "Home to McDonald's." *Food, Culture, and Society* 8, no. 2 (2005): 215–26. doi:10.2752/155280105778055308.
Brown, Dona. *Inventing New England: Regional Tourism in the Nineteenth Century*. Hanover: University of New England Press, 1997.

Burnett, John. "Eating in the Open Air in England." In Jacobs and Scholliers, *Eating Out in Europe*, 21–38.

Capps, Oral, John R. Tedford, and Joseph Havlicek. "Household Demand for Convenience and Nonconvenience Foods." *American Journal of Agricultural Economics* 67, no. 4 (1985): 862–69. doi:10.2307/1241827.

Carabello, Maria. "Defining Food Agency: An Ethnographic Exploration of Home and Student Cooks in the Northeast." Master's thesis, University of Vermont, 2015.

Carney, Megan A. *The Unending Hunger: Tracing Women and Food Insecurity across Borders*. Oakland: University of California Press, 2015.

Carter, Susan B., Scott Sigmund Gartner, Michael R. Haines, Alan L. Olmstead, Richard Sutch, and Gavin Wright, eds. *The Historical Statistics of the United States: Millennial Edition*. New York: Cambridge University Press, 2006.

Celnik, Daniel, Laura Gillespie, and Michael E. J. Lean. "Time-Scarcity, Ready-Meals, Ill-Health and the Obesity Epidemic." *Trends in Food Science, and Technology* 27, no. 1 (2012): 4–11. doi:10.1016/j.tifs.2012.06.001.

Child, Julia. "How Good Is the New 'Joy of Cooking'?" *McCall's Magazine*, October 1975: 63–68.

Child, Julia, Louise Bertholle, and Simone Beck. *Mastering the Art of French Cooking*. Vol. 1. Rev. ed. New York: Alfred A. Knopf, 1983.

Child, Lydia Maria Francis. *The Frugal Housewife, Dedicated to Those Who Are Not Ashamed of Economy*. 6th ed., Boston: Carter, Hendee and Babcock, 1831.

Costa, Ana Isabel de Almeida, Mathijs Dekker, Rijkelt R. Beumer, Frank M. Rombouts, and Wim M. F. Jongen. "A Consumer-Oriented Classification System for Home Meal Replacements." *Food Quality and Preference* 12, no. 4 (2001): 229–42.

Costa, Ana Isabel de Almeida, Diane Schoolmeester, Mathijs Dekker, and Wim M. F. Jongen. "To Cook or Not to Cook: A Means-End Study of Motives for Choice of Meal Solutions." *Food Quality and Preference* 18, no. 1 (2007): 77–88. doi:10.1016/j.foodqual.2005.08.003.

Counihan, Carole. *A Tortilla Is Like Life: Food and Culture in the San Luis Valley of Colorado*. Austin: University of Texas Press, 2010.

Cunningham-Sabo, Leslie, and Amanda Simons. "Home Economics: An Old-Fashioned Answer to a Modern-Day Dilemma?" *Nutrition Today* 47, no. 3 (2012): 128–32. doi:10.1097/NT.0b013e3182574 4a5.

Darian, Jean C. and Steven W. Klein. "Food Expenditure Patterns of Working-Wife Families: Meals P." *Journal of Consumer Policy* 12, no. 2 (1989): 139–64.

DeVault, Marjorie. *Feeding the Family: The Social Organization of Caring as Gendered Work*. Chicago: University of Chicago Press, 1991.

Devine, Carol M., Margaret Jastran, Jennifer A. Jabs, Elaine Wethington, Tracy J. Farrell, and Carole A. Bisogni. "'A Lot of Sacrifices': Work-Family Spillover and the Food Choice Coping Strategies of Low Wage Employed Parents." *Social Science and Medicine* 63, no. 10 (2006): 2591–2603. doi:10.1016/j.socscimed.2006.06.029.

Douglas, Mary. "Food as a System of Communication." In *In the Active Voice*, 83–87. London: Routledge and Kegan Paul, 1982.

DuPuis, E. Melanie. *Dangerous Digestion: The Politics of American Dietary Advice*. Oakland: University of California Press, 2015.

Egerton, John. Foreword to *The Jemima Code: Two Centuries of African American Cookbooks*, by Toni Tipton-Martin, ix–xx. Austin: University of Texas Press, 2015.

Eikenberry, Nicole, and Chery Smith. "Healthful Eating: Perceptions, Motivations, Barriers, and Promoters in Low-Income Minnesota Communities." *Journal of the American Dietetic Association* 104, no. 7 (2004): 1158–61. doi:10.1016/j.jada.2004.04.023.

Elias, Megan. *Stir It Up: Home Economics in American Culture*. Philadelphia: University of Pennsylvania Press, 2008.

Ferguson, Priscilla Parkhurst. *Accounting for Taste*. Chicago: University of Chicago Press, 2004.

———. *Word of Mouth:What We Talk About When We Talk About Food*. Oakland: University of California Press, 2014.

Fine, Gary Alan. *Kitchens: The Culture of Restaurant Work*. 2nd ed. Berkeley: University of California Press, 2009.

Finkelstein, Joanne. *Dining Out: A Sociology of Modern Manners*. New York: New York University Press, 1989.

Flammang, Janet. *The Taste for Civilization: Food, Politics, and Civil Society*. Urbana: University of Illinois Press, 2009.

Flandrin, Jean-Paul, and Massimo Montanari. *Food: A Culinary History*. New York: Penguin, 2000.

Freedman, Paul. "American Restaurants and Cuisine in the Mid-Nineteenth Century." *New England Quarterly* 84, no. 1 (March 2011): 5–55.

French, Simone A., Mary Story, and Robert W. Jeffery. "Environmental Influences on Eating and Physical Activity." *Annual Review of Public Health* 22, no. 1 (2001): 309–35.

Fogel, Robert W. Preface to *America's Eating Habits: Changes and Consequences*, edited by Elizabeth Frazão, ii–iii. Washington, DC: Economic Research Service, 1999.

Furst, Tanis, Margaret Connors, Carole A. Bisogni, Jeffery Sobal, and Laura Winter Falk. "Food Choice: A Conceptual Model of the Process." *Appetite* 26, no. 3 (1996): 247–66. doi:10.1006/appe.1996.0019.

Gabaccia, Donna. *We Are What We Eat: Ethnic Food and the Making of Americans*. Cambridge, MA: Harvard University Press, 1998.

Gibbs, Nancy. "Why the Family Meal Is Cooking Again." *Time*, June 3, 2006.

Glanz, Karen, Michael Basil, Edward Maibach, Jeanne Goldberg, and Dan Snyder. "Why Americans Eat What They Do: Taste, Nutrition, Cost, Convenience, and Weight Control Concerns as Influences on Food Consumption." *Journal of the American Dietetic Association* 98, no. 10 (1998): 1118–26.

Grotto, David, and Zied, Elisa. "The Standard American Diet and Its Relationship to the Health Status of Americans." *Nutrition in Clinical Practice* 25, no. 6 (2010): 603–12.

Hales, D. "What (and Who) Is Really Cooking at Your House?" *Parade Magazine*, November 16, 2003.

Harnack, Lisa, Mary Story, Brian Martinson, Dianne Neumark-Sztainer, and Jamie Stang. "Guess Who's Cooking? The Role of Men in Meal Planning, Shopping, and Preparation in US Families." *Journal of the American Dietetic Association* 98, no. 9 (1998): 995–1000.

Haughton, B., J. D. Gussow, and J. M. Dodds. "An Historical Study of the Underlying Assumptions for United States Food Guides from 1917 through the Basic Four Food Group Guide." *Journal of Nutrition Education* 19, no. 4 (1987): 169–76. http://agris.fao.org/agris-search/search.do?recordID=US8845880.

Hedrick, Joan D. *Harriet Beecher Stowe: A Life*. New York: Oxford University Press, 1994.

Hertzler, A. A., and F. A. Bruce. "Cooking, Recipe Use and Food Habits of College Students and Nutrition Educators." *International Journal of Consumer Studies* 26, no. 4 (2002): 340–45.

Hewlett, Fairy Bell. "Fairy Bell Hewlett, Retired Cook." Interview by John T. Edge, May 7, 2004. Transcript, Oral History, Southern Foodways Alliance. www.southernfoodways.org/app/uploads/Fairy_Bell_Hewlett_full.pdf.

Hines, Mary Anne, Gordon Marshall, and William Woys Weaver. *The Larder Invaded: Reflections on Three Centuries of Philadelphia Food and Drink*. Philadelphia: Library Company of Philadelphia, 1987.

Hochschild, Arlie. *The Second Shift: Working Parents and the Revolution at Home*. With Anne Manchung. New York: Penguin, 2003.

Hurley A. "From Hash House to Family Restaurant: The Transformation of the Diner and Post-World War II Consumer Culture." *Journal of American History* 83, no. 4 (1997): 1282–1308.

Hyland, Rob, Rosie Stacy, Ashley Adamson, and Paula Moynihan. "Nutrition-Related Health Promotion through an After-School Project: The Responses of Children and Their Families." *Social Science and Medicine* 62, no. 3 (2005): 758–68.

Ingold, Tim. *Making: Anthropology, Archaeology, Art and Architecture*. London: Routledge, 2013.

———. *Perception of the Environment: Essays on Livelihood, Dwelling, Skill*. London: Routledge, 2000.

Inness, Sherrie. *Kitchen Culture in America: Popular Representations of Food, Gender, and Race*. Philadelphia: University of Pennsylvania Press, 2001.

Jabs, Jennifer, Carol M. Devine, Carole A. Bisogni, Tracy J. Farrell, Margaret Jastran, and Elaine Wethington. "Trying to Find the Quickest Way: Employed Mothers' Constructions of Time for Food. *Journal of Nutrition Education and Behavior* 39, no. 1 (2007): 18–25.

Jackson, Michael. *Minima Ethnographica: Intersubjectivity and the Anthropological Project*. Chicago: University of Chicago Press, 1998.

Jacobs, Marc, and Peter Scholliers, eds. *Eating Out in Europe: Picnics, Gourmet Dining and Snacks since the Late 18th Century*. London: Berg, 2003.

Julier, Alice P. *Eating Together: Food, Friendship, and Inequality*. Urbana: University of Illinois Press, 2013.

Kaufman, Cathy. "Bread." In *The Oxford Encyclopedia of Food and Drink in America*. Edited by Andrew F. Smith. Oxford: Oxford University Press, 2007.

Kavasch, E. Barrie. "My Grandmother's Hands." In Avakian, *Through the Kitchen Window*, 104–10.

———. "Song of My Mother." In Avakian, *Through the Kitchen Window*, 42–46.

Kearney, J. M., and S. McElhone. "Perceived Barriers in Trying to Eat Healthier: Results of a Pan-EU Consumer Attitudinal Survey." *British Journal of Nutrition* 81, no. S2 (1999): S133–37.

Kim, C. "Working Wives' Time-Saving Tendencies: Durable Ownership, Convenience Food Consumption, and Meal Purchases." *Journal of Economic Psychology* 10 (1989): 391–409.

Korsmeyer, Carolyn. *Making Sense of Taste: Food and Philosophy*. Ithaca: Cornell University Press, 1999.

Lahne, Jacob, Julia Wolfson, and Amy Trubek. "Development of the Cooking and Food Preparation Action Scale (CAFPAS): A New Framework for Measuring the Complexity of Cooking." *Food Quality and Preference* (forthcoming).

Lang, Tim, and Martin Caraher. "Is There a Culinary Skills Transition? Data and Debate from the UK about Changes in Cooking Culture." *Journal of the HEIA* 8, no. 2 (2001): 2–14.

Larson, Nicole I., Cheryl L. Perry, Mary Story, and Dianne Neumark-Sztainer. "Food Preparation by Young Adults Is Associated with Better Diet Quality." *Journal of the American Dietetic Association* 106, no. 7 (2006): 2001–7.

Laudan, Rachel. "Servants in the Kitchen: Now You See Them, Now You Don't." *Rachel Laudan* (blog). April 11, 2016. www.rachellaudan.com/2016/04/servants-in-the-kitchen-now-you-see-them-now-you-dont.html.

———. "Servants in the Kitchen: They Have a History Too." *Rachel Laudan*. April 26, 2016. www.rachellaudan.com/2016/04/servants-have-a-history-too.html.

Levenstein, Harvey. *Paradox of Plenty: A Social History of Eating in Modern America*. Berkeley: University of California Press, 2003.

———. *Revolution at the Table: The Transformation of the American Diet*. New York: Oxford University Press, 1988.

Lewin, Kurt. "Forces behind Food Habits and Methods of Change." In *The Problem of Changing Food Habits*, National Research Council Bulletin, edited by National Research Council Committee on Food Habits, 35–65. Washington, DC: National Research Council and National Academy of Sciences, 1943.

———. *Resolving Social Conflicts: Selected Papers on Group Dynamics [1935–1946]*. Edited by Gertrud Weiss Lewin. New York: Harper, 1948.

Lhuissier, Anne. "Eating out During the Workday: Consumption and Working Habits among Urban Labourers in France in the 2nd Half of the 19th Century." In Jacobs and Scholliers, *Eating Out in Europe*, 337–49.

Lincoln, Mary J. *Boston Cook Book: What to Do and What Not to Do in Cooking*. Boston: Roberts Brothers, 1884.

Lowry, Richard, Deborah A. Galuska, Janet E. Fulton, Howell Wechsler, Laura Kann, and Janet L. Collins. "Physical Activity, Food Choice, and Weight Management Goals and Practices among US College Students." *American Journal of Preventive Medicine* 18, no. 1 (2000): 18–27.

Lyon, Phil, Anne Colquhoun, and Emily Alexander. "Deskilling the Domestic Kitchen: A National Tragedy or the Making of a Modern Myth?" *Food Service Technology* 3, nos. 3–4 (2003): 167–75.

Mancino, Lisa, and Constance Newman. "Who Has Time to Cook? How Family Resources Influence Food Preparation." USDA Economic Research Service, 2007.

MarketLine. "Industry Profile Bread & Rolls in the United States." October 2015. www.reportlinker.com/p0171586-summary/Bread-Rolls-in-the-United-States.html.

McCabe, Maryann, and Timothy de Waal Maleyft. "Creativity and Cooking: Motherhood, Agency and Social Change in Everyday Life." *Journal of Consumer Culture* 15, no. 1 (2015): 48–65.

McLaughlin, C., V. Tarasuk, and N. Kreiger. "An Examination of At-Home Food Preparation Activity among Low-Income, Food-Insecure Women." *Journal of the American Dietetic Association* 103 (2003): 1506–12.

Meah, Angela, and Matt Watson. "Saints and Slackers: Challenging Discourses about the Decline of Domestic Cooking." *Sociological Research Online* 16, no. 2 (2011): 1–23. doi:dx.doi.org/10.5153/sro.2341.

Mendelson, Anne. *Stand Facing the Stove: The Story of the Women Who Gave America the* Joy of Cooking. New York: Simon and Schuster, 1996.

Morgan, Caitlin. "Expanding Food Agency: Exploring the Theory and Its Scale." Master's thesis, University of Vermont, 2016.

Mothersbaugh, David L., Robert O. Herrmann, and Rex H. Warland. "Perceived Time Pressure and Recommended Dietary Practices: The Moderating Effect of Knowledge of Nutrition." *The Journal of Consumer Affairs* 27, no. 1 (1993): 106–26.

Nestle, Marion. *Food Politics*. Berkeley: University of California Press, 2002.

———. *Soda Politics*. Berkeley: University of California Press, 2015.

Nickols, Sharon Y., and Karen D. Fox. "Buying Time and Saving Time: Strategies for Managing Household Production." *Journal of Consumer Research* 10, no. 2 (1983): 197–208.

Okrent, Abigail M., and Aylin Kumcu. "U.S. Households' Demand for Convenience Foods." United States Department of Agriculture, Economic Research Service. Economic Research Report 211, July 2016. www.ers.usda.gov/publications/pub-details/?pubid=80653.

Orwell, George. *Down and Out in Paris and London*. New York: Harcourt Brace, 1961.

Palojoki, Päivi, and Terttu Tuomi-Gröhn. "Food Choice: The Importance of Everyday Context." *Journal of the HEIA* 9, no. 3 (2002): 12–18.

Panschar, William G., and Charles C. Slater. *Baking in America*. Northwestern University Studies in Business History. Evanston, IL: Northwestern University Press, 1956.

Paxson, Heather. *The Life of Cheese*. Berkeley: University of California Press, 2012.

Pilcher, Jeffrey. "Many Chefs in the National Kitchen: Cookbooks and Identity in Nineteenth Century Mexico." In *Latin American Popular Culture: An Introduction*, edited by William Beezley and Linda Curcia-Nagy, 123–41. Oxford: Rowan-Littlefield, 2000.

Poelmana, Maartje P., Emely de Veta, Elizabeth Velema, Jacob C. Seidella, and Ingrid H. M. Steenhuisa. "The Home Food Environment of Overweight Gatekeepers in the Netherlands." *Public Health Nutrition* 18, no. 10 (2015): 1815–23.

Polan, Dana. *Julia Child's* The French Chef. Durham, NC: Duke University Press, 2011.

Polanyi, Michael. *The Tacit Dimension*. The Terry Lectures. Garden City, NY: Anchor, 1967.

Pollan, Michael. *Cooked: A Natural History of Transformation*. New York: Penguin, 2013.

Ray, Krishnendu. *The Ethnic Restaurateur*. New York: Bloomsbury Academic, 2016.

Reardon, Joan, ed. *As Always, Julia: The Letters of Julia Child and Avis DeVoto*. New York: Mariner, 2011.

Richards, Audrey Isabel. *Hunger and Work in a Savage Tribe: A Functional Study of Nutrition among the Southern Bantu*. Glencoe, IL: Free Press, 1948.

Rombauer, Irma. *The Joy of Cooking*. 1st ed. Indianapolis: Bobbs-Merrill, 1931.

———. *The Joy of Cooking*. 3rd ed. Indianapolis: Bobbs-Merrill, 1946.

———. *The Joy of Cooking*. Facsimile of the first edition. New York: Scribners, 1998.

Rombauer, Irma, and Marion Rombauer Becker. *The Joy of Cooking*. Indianapolis: Bobbs-Merrill, 1964.

———. *The Joy of Cooking*. Indianapolis: Bobbs-Merrill, 1975.

Rombauer, Irma, Marion Rombauer Becker, and Ethan Becker. *The Joy of Cooking*. 75th anniversary edition. New York: Scribner, 1998.

Rousseau, Signe. *Food Media: Celebrity Chefs and the Politics of Everyday Interference*. London: Berg, 2012.

Sahlins, Marshall David. *Islands of History*. Chicago: University of Chicago Press, 1985.

Samuelsson, Marcus. *Yes, Chef: A Memoir*. With Veronica Chambers. New York: Random House, 2013.

Scott, James. *Domination and the Arts of Resistance: Hidden Transcripts*. New Haven: Yale University Press, 1990.

Sennett, Richard. *The Craftsman*. New Haven: Yale University Press, 2009.

Shaefer, Sara, Charlotte Biltekoff, Carolyn Thomas, and Roxanne N. Rashedi. "Healthy, Vague: Exploring Health as a Priority in Food Choice." *Food Culture and Society* 19, no. 2 (2016): 227–50.

Shapiro, Laura. "Fanny Farmer." In *Oxford Companion to American Food and Drink*, edited by Andrew Smith, 215. Oxford: Oxford University Press, 2007.

———. *Perfection Salad: Women and Cooking at the Turn of the Century*. New York: Farrar, Straus, and Giroux, 1986.

———. *Something from the Oven: Reinventing Dinner in 1950s America*. New York: Viking, 2004.

Sharpless, Rebecca. *Cooking in Other Women's Kitchens: Domestic Workers in the South, 1865–1960*. Chapel Hill: University of North Carolina Press, 2010.

Short, Frances. "Domestic Cooking Practices and Cooking Skills: Findings from an English Study." *Food Service Technology* 3, nos. 3–4 (2003): 177–85.

———. "Domestic Cooking Skills: What Are They?" *Journal of the HEIA* 10, no. 3 (2003): 13–22.

———. *Kitchen Secrets: The Meaning of Cooking in Everyday Life*. London: Bloomsbury Academic, 2006.

Simmons, Amelia. *American Cookery, or The Art of Dressing Viands. . . .* Hartford, CT: Hudson and Goodwin, 1796.

Simmons, Dean, and Gwen E. Chapman. "The Significance of Home Cooking within Families." *British Food Journal* 114, no. 8 (2012): 1184–95.

Sloan, Elizabeth A. "What, When, and Where America Eats: A State-of-the-Industry Report." *Food Technology* 60, no. 1 (2006): 19–27.

Smith, Andrew. *The Oxford Encyclopedia of Food and Drink in America*. Oxford: Oxford University Press, 2007.

Snell, Katherine. "Interview with Kyla Wazana Tompkins." *Columbia Journal of Literary Criticism* 13, no. 1 (2015): 50–58.

Sobek, Matthew. "Occupations." In *Historical Statistics of the United States: Millennial Edition Online*, edited by Susan B. Carter, Scott Sigmund Gartner, Michael R. Haines, Alan M. Olmstead, Richard Sutch, and Gavin Wright. Cambridge: Cambridge University Press, 2006. http://hsus.cambridge.org/HSUSWeb/HSUSEntryServlet.

Strasser, Susan. *Never Done: A History of American Housework*. New York: Macmillan, 1982.

Sutton, David E. *Secrets from the Greek Kitchen: Cooking, Skill, and Everyday Life on an Aegean Island*. Oakland: University of California Press, 2014.

Symons, Michael. *A History of Cooks and Cooking*. The Food Series. Champaign: University of Illinois Press, 2000.

Theophano, Janet. *Eat My Words: Reading Women's Lives through the Cookbooks They Wrote*. New York: Palgrave MacMillan, 2002.

Tocchini-Valentini, Glauco P. and Marta A. Tocchini-Valentini. "Comparative Anatomy: Giorgione's Venus, Connoisseur Morelli, and the Reverend Bayes." *FASEB Journal* 26, no. 1 (2012): 5–8.

Tonkovich, Nicole. Introduction to *The American Woman's Home*, by Catharine E. Beecher and Harriet Beecher Stowe, xix–xxxii. New Brunswick, NJ: Rutgers University Press, 2002.

Trubek, Amy. *Haute Cuisine: How the French Invented the Culinary Profession*. Philadelphia: University of Pennsylvania Press, 2000.

———. "A Knack for Cooking: What Are the Required Tools?" In *Food and Material Culture: Proceedings of the Oxford Symposium on Food and Cooking*, edited by Mark McWilliams, 336–43. Devon: Prospect Books, 2013.

———. "Looking at Cooking." *Anthropology Now* 4, no. 3 (December 2012): 24–32.

———. "Professional Cooking and Kitchens." In *Cultural History of Food*, vol. 6, edited by Amy Bentley, 127–44. London: Bloomsbury, 2012.

Trubek, Amy, Maria Carabello, Caitlin Morgan, and Jacob Lahne. "Empowered to Cook: The Crucial Role of Food Agency in Making Meals." *Appetite* 116 (September 2017): 297–305.

Turner, Katherine Leonard. *How the Other Half Ate*. Berkeley: University of California Press, 2014.

———. "Tools and Spaces: Food and Cooking in Working-Class Neighborhoods, 1880–1930." In *Food Chains: From Farmyard to Shopping Cart*, edited by Warren Belasco and Roger Horowitz, 217–32. Philadelphia: University of Pennsylvania Press, 2009.

United States Bureau of Labor Statistics. "American Time Use Survey: Household Activities." Last modified December 20, 2016. www.bls.gov/tus/charts/household.htm.

———. "Food for Thought: BLS Spotlight on Statistics." November 2010. www.bls.gov/spotlight/2010/food/pdf/food.pdf.

United States Bureau of the Census. *Historical Statistics of the United States: Colonial Times to 1970*. Bicentennial ed. Washington, DC: U.S. Department of Commerce, Bureau of the Census, 1975.

United States Department of Agriculture Economic Research Service. "Data Products: Table 8—Food Expenditures by Families and Individuals as a Share of Disposable Personal Money Income." Last updated January 26, 2016. www.ers.usda.gov/data-products/food-expenditures.aspx#26634.

United States Department of Labor. "Employment Characteristics of Families Summary." Last modified April 20, 2017. www.bls.gov/news.release/famee.nr0.htm.

Urvater, Caroline. "Thoughts for Food." In Avakian, *Through the Kitchen Window*, 213–16.

Valgenti, Robert. "Cucinare come interpretazione." In *Cibo, estetica e arte: Convergenze tra filosofia, semiotica e storia*, edited by Nicola Perullo, 57–67. Pisa: ETS, 2014.

van Asselt, Esther, Arnout Fischer, Aarieke E. I. de Jong, Maarten J. Nauta, and Rob de Jonge. "Cooking Practices in the Kitchen: Observed versus Predicted Behavior." *Risk Analysis* 29 (2009): 533–40.

Wansink, Brian. "Changing Eating Habits on the Home Front: Lost Lessons from World War II Research." *Journal of Public Policy and Marketing* 21 (2002): 90–99.

———. "Empowering Nutrition Gatekeepers: The Parents." *Journal of Nutrition Education and Behavior* 43, no. 5 (2011): 307.

———. *Mindless Eating: Why We Eat More Than We Think*, New York: Random House, 2006.

———. "Nutritional Gatekeepers and the 72% Solution." *Journal of the American Dietetic Association* 106, no. 9 (2006): 1324–27.

———. "Profiling Nutritional Gatekeepers: Three Methods for Differentiating Influential Cooks." *Food Quality and Preference* 14, no. 4 (2003): 289–97.

Warde, Alan, and Lydia Martens. *Eating Out*. New York: Cambridge University Press, 2000.

Warde, Alan, Lydia Martens, and Wendy Olsen. "Consumption and the Problem of Variety: Cultural Omnivorousness, Social Distinction and Dining Out." *Sociology* 33 (2001): 105–27.

Watts, Shannon. *Radical Homemakers: Reclaiming Domesticity from a Consumer Culture*. Richmondville, NY: Left to Right, 2010.

Wazana-Tompkins, Kyla. *Racial Indigestion: Eating Bodies in the 19th Century*. New York: New York University Press, 2012.

Weiss, Brad. *Real Pigs: Shifting Values in the Field of Local Pork*. Durham, NC: Duke University Press, 2016.

Wheaton, Barbara Ketcham. *Savoring the Past*. Philadelphia: University of Pennsylvania Press, 1983.

Wilkerson, Abby. "Judging, Tasting, Knowing 'Good' Food." *Food, Culture and Society* 19, no. 2 (2016): 223–26.

Williams-Forson, Psyche. *Building Houses of Chicken Legs: Black Women, Food and Power*. Raleigh: University of North Carolina Press, 2006.
Wolfson, Julia A., Sara N. Bleich, Katherine Clegg Smith, and Shannon Frattaroli. "What Does Cooking Mean to You? Perceptions of Cooking and Factors Related to Cooking Behavior." *Appetite* 97 (2016): 146.
Wolfson, Julia, Stephanie Bostic, Jacob Lahne, Caitlin Morgan, Shauna Henley, Jean Harvey, and Amy Trubek. "Moving to a Comprehensive Understanding and Assessment of Cooking." *British Food Journal* 119, no. 5 (2017): 1147–58.
Wrangham, Richard. *Catching Fire: How Cooking Made Us Human*. New York: Basic, 2009.

ACKNOWLEDGMENTS

The process of researching and writing this book has been a truly collaborative experience. Although I alone wrote this manuscript, typing on various keyboards, generating page after page of descriptions, stories, and analyses of American cooks, and then printing out drafts, revising with pen, and working on it all again, wonderful graduate students at the University of Vermont helped me with the research, which involved going into the homes of generous participants. I must thank them first. Alyssa Nathanson, Anthony Epter, and Shauna Henley were the first graduate students of my professional career at a university. They put up with my lateral thinking style, my many competing responsibilities, and my commitment to a fine-grained, ethnographic approach to research. Each one of them recruited participants, went into their homes, and videotaped, interviewed, and surveyed them. They all also identified crucial emergent themes in the research using a grounded theory approach; these themes became woven into this book. It is the truth when I say that none of this book's accomplishments would have been possible without these three. And then there are the dozens of people who welcomed all of us into their homes, showing us how they made their dinners, reflecting on cooking, and sharing their stories, past and present. Thank you all. Over the following few years, more graduate students became involved in analyzing the amazing video ethnographies and interview database that we had collected. These folks helped carry out another round of reviewing the videotapes, with me, alone, and in small groups. We continued to work together and built a robust understanding of the rich and complex material. I am so grateful for Jacob Lahne, Maria Carabello, and Alison Burns. Each provided crucial insights. Over the past two years, Caitlin Morgan has joined the conversation as well; she is an astute observer and editor, and her assistance was invaluable as I put together the manuscript, the images, and the bibliography. I only hope I can be equally helpful with her future writing endeavors.

Also at the University of Vermont, Cynthia Belliveau, Jean Harvey, and Teresa Mares have been exemplary compatriots in this now decade-long engagement with cooking practice and cooking knowledge. Cynthia and I started talking about cooking twenty years ago, and we started teaching courses using a cooking lab almost a decade ago, based on many of our realizations about the importance of learning how to cook, wherever you are and whatever age you are. Her insights helped shape my understanding as I worked on this project. Jean always understood the importance of engaging with this topic and was supportive in ways big and small. Teresa has watched me give talks, reviewed chapters, and come into the kitchen many times; she has always provided insightful comments. Tyler Doggett and Luis Vivanco were excellent readers of individual chapters of the manuscript; I am lucky to have them as colleagues.

Further afield, this book would be so much less without the creative engagement and collegial support of David Sutton. His idea to videotape people cooking and his generosity in sharing that idea planted the seeds for the project. Our countless conversations, in person and on Skype, have made all the difference in my cooking inquiries—but he is not responsible for any of my failures! Lisa Heldke, a fellow food studies scholar, has been an inspiring colleague. Jonathan Deutsch, a food studies scholar who is also committed to looking closely at cooking, read my entire manuscript and provided many helpful suggestions. Michael Sheridan contributed many crucial insights, both as a baker and an anthropologist; what's better than two anthropologists sitting around talking about poolish? Thanks also to Darra Goldstein, Sarah Bowen, Nathalie Cooke, Priscilla Parkhurst Ferguson, and Ellen Oxfeld for their timely comments. A reviewer who chose to remain anonymous also provided important queries that helped make this book better. I have presented talks on aspects of my investigation into home cooking in a number of places over the years and always came away with a fresh perspective and a renewed commitment to finish this book. For inviting me to present aspects of this project, my gratitude goes to the Department of Anthropology at the University of Vermont, the Department of Sociology and Anthropology at Middlebury College, the Program in American Studies at Princeton University, the Oxford Symposium on Food and Cooking, the School of Culinary Arts at the Dublin Institute for Technology, the Department of Nutrition and Food Studies at New York University, and the annual conference of the Association for the Study of Food and Society.

It has been my good fortune to have received crucial grants that have allowed me to pursue this project. The research in the kitchens of home cooks was funded by a United States Department of Agriculture Hatch Grant. The research on *The Joy of Cooking* and *Mastering the Art of French Cooking* and my review of the archives of Irma Rombauer, Marion Rombauer Becker, and Julia Child was underwritten by a crucial grant from the Schlesinger Library on the History of Women at the Radcliffe Institute for Advanced Study at Harvard University. The historical research was also facilitated by the online collections of the Southern Foodways Alliance and the HEARTH collection at Cornell University, as well as University of Vermont's Special Collections and the library's bound and online collection of historical labor statistics. For all their assistance and inspiration during that phase of research, I would like to thank Marylene Altieri, Prudence Doherty, and Rachel DiStefano. More recent research on learning to cook and the concept of food agency also made its way into the book and was funded by a second United States Department of Agriculture Hatch Grant. For their collaboration on that project, I would like to thank my collaborators at Drexel University: Jonathan Deutsch, James Feustel, and Jake Lahne. For her own work and her insights into mine, I want to thank Julia Wolfson at the University of Michigan. Kate Marshall and Bradley Depew at UC Press provided thoughtful counsel as I meandered to the finish line of this project. Genevieve Thurston's queries and edits made the book better. Thanks also to Caroline Knapp. Kelly Finan has been a marvelous collaborator, fluently translating my concepts into graphs and illustrations, allowing this book to tell a story beyond words. Violet Loveys, a talented University of Vermont undergraduate, graciously gave me permission to print her fantastic drawing of her food lab's mise-en-place. A big thank you to Lizzy Pope and Josh Taylor for being willing hand models, and to Serena Parnau for the great pictures. Kitty Cowles helped me think through ideas and set up contacts with her usual panache. Lee Brouillard was always supportive while making me countless lattes at the Middlebury College Library café; thanks too to the library for its fantastic study carrels, where most of this book was written.

Vanessa Wolff's engagement has been crucial. Over the years, we have had many conversations about cooking and what it means to us, and this book is better because of her thoughtful engagement with my obsession. She was the first one to read the full manuscript; is there a greater gift from a friend? Angela Landis, Tracy Himmel Isham, Jon Isham, Alex Wolff, Chris and Beth Keathley, Kristina Simmons, Matt Landis, Bing Broderick, Ellen Brodsky, Karen Jurina, Ted Rybeck, Gen Drutchas, and Bob Sanches were always up for an engaged conversation, often over a great meal. Beth Stanway and Amy Beaupre participated in my final experiment, and I thank them for being such thoughtful lab rats. Many members of my family were happy to share their own stories, relevant links and clippings, and, of course, plenty of meals. Thanks to Louise, Dave, Jessica, and Anne Trubek, Margie Rubins, and Alice and George Wislocki. Last, but certainly not least, thank you to Brad and Katherine; you have my gratitude forever. You have been my companions (in the kitchen and at the table) throughout this long process, and what a pleasure that has been. Here's to all the meals to come.

ILLUSTRATION CREDITS

The following are original illustrations by Kelly Finan:

Trying to Juice a Lemon, page 1

Taking a Recipe out of the Recipe Box, page 27

Chopping an Onion, page 112

Rolling the Burek Dough, page 153

Taking Vegetables out of the Bag, page 187

The following is an original illustration by Violet Loveys:

Tabbouleh Mise-en-Place, page 233

The following is an original woodcut produced by an artist in the Works Progress Administration between 1935 and 1943:

"Woman in the Kitchen," Schomburg Center for Research in Black Culture, Art, and Artifacts Division, New York Public Library, New York Public Library Digital Collections, page 65

INDEX